A Land without a People

Acclaim for *Expulsion of the Palestinians: The Concept of 'Transfer' in Zionist Political Thought, 1882–1948*

'A recent book by the Israeli-Palestinian scholar Nur Masalha documents the concept of "transfer" in Zionist thinking from Herzl, Weizmann, Ben-Gurion to their heirs, Shamir and Rabin. Going over mountains of Hebrew-language documents Masalha shows that every Zionist leader of the Left, Right or Centre, with no significant exceptions, was in favour of ridding Palestine of Palestinians, by all means necessary, force and bribery included.'
Edward Said, *London Review of Books*

'Dr Masalha shows, using documents from Israeli archives, that the flight of the Arab population from what became Israel in 1948 – which Israel's first president, Chaim Weizmann, hailed as "a miraculous clearing of the land" – was in fact "less of a miracle than the culmination of over a half century of effort, plans, and (in the end) brute force".'
Edward Mortimer, *Financial Times*

'Nur Masalha helps to contextualize the debate with an articulate, well-researched analysis of the concept of "transfer" in Zionist thought . . . Relying almost exclusively on Israeli sources, Masalha demonstrates that the notion of transfer was held by both Labour Zionists and revisionist Zionists.'
Lawrence Tal, *Times Literary Supplement*

'Dr Masalha's book will excite controversy, not because his conclusions can be challenged – the sources leave no doubt about the facts – but because the book exposes in detail the nature of the Zionist design and the means by which it was achieved . . . an important and scrupulous piece of revisionist history.'
Michael Adams, *Middle East International*

Nur Masalha was born in Galilee in 1957. He has taught at the Hebrew University, Jerusalem, at the Universities of London, Bristol and Bir Zeit, Palestine, and is an honorary fellow of the Centre for Middle Eastern and Islamic Studies, University of Durham. He is the author of *Expulsion of the Palestinians: The Concept of 'Transfer' in Zionist Political Thought, 1882–1948*. He lives in London.

by the same author
Expulsion of the Palestinians: The Concept of 'Transfer'
in Zionist Political Thought, 1882–1948

A Land without a People

Israel, Transfer and
the Palestinians 1949–96

Nur Masalha

faber and faber

First published in 1997
by Faber and Faber Limited
3 Queen Square London WCIN 3AU

Photoset by RefineCatch Limited, Bungay, Suffolk
Printed in England by Clays Ltd, St Ives plc

A CIP record for this book
is available from the British Library

ISBN 0–571–19100–2

10 9 8 7 6 5 4 3 2 1

Contents

Contents

Acknowledgements

The support of the Palestine Studies Trust, UK, and the Institute for Palestine Studies (IPS), Washington, DC, is gratefully acknowledged. At IPS, I am particularly grateful to Professor Walid Khalidi and Dr Philip Mattar, both of whom encouraged me to undertake this project. I thank them and the IPS for granting me the Institute's Constantine Zurayk Fellowship sponsored by Mr 'Abdul-Muhsin al-Qattan. Among the institutions that made this work possible by helping with source material were the Israel State Archives, the Central Zionist Archives in Jerusalem, the Hebrew University of Jerusalem Library, the School of Oriental and African Studies Library in London. Many friends and colleagues have helped me greatly with logistics, ideas, criticism, material, and discussions. Among them I would like to thank Elias 'Edey, Mark Mechler, Linda Butler, Ahmad Khalidi, Ahmad Khalifa, Eric Hooglund (for his editorial assistance), David McDowall, Peter Colvin, 'Abbas Shiblak, Israel Shahak, Ghada Karmi, Tim Niblock, Uri Davis, Anoushiravan Ehteshami, Leila Mantura, Michael Adams, Ian Gilmour, Sharif Kana'ane, Anis al-Kassim, Lawrence Tal, Muhsin Yusif, and the late Saliba Khamis. Needless to say that I alone am responsible for the book and its shortcomings. Finally, I owe an invaluable debt to my wife, Stephanie, for her insightful comments while this work was being written.

Introduction

After 1948, the idea of 'transferring' the Palestinians – a euphemism denoting the organized removal of the Arab population to neighbouring or distant countries – remained widely held in Israel. Delicately described by its proponents as 'population exchange', the idea of Arabs returning to Arabia, emigrating, or being resettled and rehabilitated in Arab countries, is deeply rooted in Zionism. As demonstrated in my earlier book *Expulsion of the Palestinians: The Concept of 'Transfer' in Zionist Political Thought 1882–1948* (1992), the transfer notion was embedded in the Zionist perception that the Land of Israel or Palestine is a Jewish birthright and belongs exclusively to the Jewish people as a whole, and, consequently, Palestinian Arabs are 'strangers' who either should accept Jewish sovereignty over the land or depart. My previous volume also showed that the concept had occupied a central position in the strategic thinking of the Zionist movement and the *Yishuv* (the Jewish community in Palestine until 1948) as a solution to the Zionist land and 'Arab demographic' and political problems. Although the desire among the Zionist leaders to 'solve' the 'Arab question' through transfer remained constant until 1948, the envisaged modalities of transfer changed over the years according to the circumstances. From the mid-1930s onwards a series of specific plans, generally involving Transjordan, Syria, and Iraq, were produced by the Yishuv's transfer committees and senior officials.[1] I also have shown that the idea was advocated by the most important Zionist leaders, including David Ben-Gurion, Avraham Granovsky, Theodor Herzl, Zeev Jabotinsky, Berl Katznelson, Leo Motzkin, Arthur Ruppin, Moshe Sharett, Nahman Syrkin, Menahem Ussishkin, Yosef Weitz, Chaim Weizmann, and Israel Zangwill.

The justifications used in defence of the transfer plans in the 1930s and 1940s formed the cornerstone of the subsequent arguments for transfer, particularly in the proposals and plans put forward after 1948 and in the wake of the 1967 conquest of the West Bank and Gaza. After 1967, proponents of transfer continued to assert, often publicly, that there was nothing 'immoral' about these proposals; that the earlier twentieth-century transfer of Greeks and Turks, Indians and Pakistanis, Germans and other Europeans provided a 'precedent' for similar measures vis-à-vis the Palestinian Arabs; that the uprooting and transfer of the Palestinians to Arab countries would constitute a mere relocation from one district to another; that the Palestinians would have no difficulty in accepting Jordan, Syria, or Iraq as their homeland; that the Palestinian Arabs had little emotional attachment and few real ties to the particular soil in Palestine and would be just as content outside the 'Land of Israel'; that the Palestinian Arabs were marginal to the Arab nation and their problems might be facilitated by a 'benevolent' and 'humanitarian' policy of 'helping people to leave'. Such assertions were crucial to legitimize Zionism's denial of the Palestinian Arabs' right to self-determination in Palestine before 1948 or even in part of Palestine (the West Bank and Gaza) after 1967. Proponents of transfer asserted that the Palestinians were not a distinct people but merely 'Arabs', an Arab population, or 'Arab community' that happened to reside in the land of Israel.

Closely linked to this idea of the non-existence of the Palestinians as a nation and their non-attachment to the particular soil of Palestine was the idea of their belonging to an Arab nation with vast territories and many countries. After all, if the Palestinians did not constitute a distinct separate nation and were not an integral part of the country and were without historical ties to it, then they could be transferred to other Arab countries without undue prejudice. Similarly, if the Palestinians were merely a marginal local part of a larger population of Arabs, then they were not a major party to the conflicts with Israel; therefore, Israeli efforts to deal over their heads were justified. It is thus that Israeli pronouncements were full of references to the vast Arab territories and to the notion that the Palestinians were bound to other centres in Syria, Iraq, and the Arabian Peninsula, the homeland of the Arab people.

This book discusses the major transfer schemes that Israeli

ministers and senior officials promoted after 1948. In 1948, the Zionist concept of transfer had not been applied universally, and the Israeli army's expulsion policy failed to rid the new Jewish state of a small Arab minority that remained in situ. However, having expelled 750,000 Palestinian Arabs from the greatly enlarged boundaries of the state and having reduced the Arab population from a large majority to a small minority, the pragmatic Labour leadership believed that it largely, although not entirely, had solved its land/settlement and political/'demographic' problems, and was prepared reluctantly to tolerate the presence of a small, politically subordinate and economically dependent Arab minority – some 150,000 Palestinians of the over 900,000 who used to reside in the areas that became the state of Israel in the aftermath of the 1948 war.

In search of international recognition for the newly proclaimed state, the Israeli Provisional State Council, the forerunner of the Knesset, included in the Independence Charter a promise that the Jewish state would 'uphold the full social and political equality of all its citizens, without distinction of religion, race, and sex'. What, in fact, took place was exactly the opposite. After its establishment, Israel treated the Palestinians still remaining within its frontiers almost as foreigners. It swiftly imposed a military government in the areas inhabited by the Arab minority, expropriated over half of the lands of this 'non-Jewish' population, and pursued various policies of demographic containment, political control, exclusionary domination, and systematic discrimination in all spheres of life. The military government was imposed by Prime Minister and Defence Minister David Ben-Gurion, and it became associated closely with his hostile attitude toward the Arab minority, his authoritarian style, and his almost unchallenged leadership of the ruling Labour Party. The daily *Haaretz* reported in 1958 that Ben-Gurion had refused the identity card issued to him because it was printed in Arabic as well as Hebrew.[2] Remarking on this report, Uri Avnery, then chief editor of *Ha'olam Hazeh* magazine and later a member of the Israeli Knesset, wrote:

Ben-Gurion has always been utterly reactionary in his opposition to anything Arab. The prime minister has never visited an Arab town or village since the establishment of the state. When he visited the Jewish town of Upper Nazareth, he refused to visit Arab Nazareth, only a few hundred metres away from the Jewish town. In the first ten years after the establishment of the state, Ben-Gurion did not receive a single delegation of Arab citizens.[3]

Ben-Gurion's view of the Arab citizens echoed deep-seated sentiments within the Labour establishment, sentiments that found their most crude embodiment in the establishment of military rule in the Arab areas. Generally speaking, the supporters of Ben-Gurion's militarist approach deemed that the 'security' aspect must take precedence over any other considerations in dealing with the Arab minority.

Officially the purpose of imposing martial law and military government on Israel's Arab minority was security. However, its establishment, which lasted until 1966, was intended to serve a number of both stated and concealed objectives. The first objective was to prevent the return of the Palestinian refugees, or 'infiltrators' in Israeli terminology, to their homes. 'In the process other Arabs who had not infiltrated the country were sometimes driven out as well.'[4] A second goal was:

> to evacuate semi-abandoned [Arab] neighbourhoods and villages as well as some which had not been abandoned – and to transfer their inhabitants to other parts of the country. Some were evacuated from a 'security cordon' along the borders, and others were removed in order to make room for Jews.[5]

The third purpose of the military government was to maintain control of and supervision over the Israeli Arabs, who were separated and isolated from the Jewish population.[6]

On 24 March 1949, Ben-Gurion appointed a committee that was directed to submit to him recommendations on whether the military government should be abolished, or, alternatively, whether any changes in its policies toward the Arab minority ought to be carried out. By determining the composition of the committee, Ben-Gurion seemed to have ensured the outcome of its investigations.

The committee was headed by General Elimelech Avner, who was the head of the military government, and its two other members were Major Michael Hanegbi, the military governor of the Negev, and Yehoshu'a Palmon of the Foreign Ministry. In its report, submitted to the Prime Minister on 3 May 1949, the committee stressed that the continuation of a forceful military government was essential for security, demographic, and land settlement reasons. The committee maintained, *inter alia*, that comprehensive and effective supervision of the Arab population was needed to: a) prevent it from becoming a fifth column; b) prevent 'infiltration' of Palestinian refugees back to their homes and villages; c) find 'a solution to the problem of the Arab refugees who are present within the boundaries of the state [because the problem of internal refugees] requires the transfer [of Arab communities] from one place to another, the concentration of land for their resettlement, the transfer of [Arab] workers to employment centres, [and] directed [Jewish] settlement policies . . . The implementation of all these requires a regime with military character, which is not subject to the rules of normal procedure'; and d) '[facilitate] greatly the implementation of the desired demographic and land policies, and the process of populating [with Jews] the abandoned Arab villages and towns.'[7]

The use of force and coercion formed an important element in Israel's policy toward its Arab citizens in the post-1948 period. The institution of the military government, together with the imposition of the Defence Emergency Regulations promulgated by the British Mandatory authorities in 1945, empowered the military governors to close off the Arab localities and to restrict entry or exit to those who had been issued with permits by the military authorities. These regulations also enabled the Israeli authorities to evict and deport people from their villages and towns; to place individuals under administrative detention for indefinite periods without trial; and to impose fines and penalties without due process.[8] The military governors were also authorized to close Arab areas in order to prevent internal Arab refugees (the so-called 'present absentees' were estimated at 30,000, or one-fifth of those remaining) from returning to homes and lands that had been confiscated by the state and taken over by new and old Jewish settlements.[9] Yehoshu'a

Palmon of the Foreign Ministry suggested in a letter to the Custodian of the Absentees' Property, Zalman Lifschitz of the Prime Minister's Office, and the attorney general that 'in the cases in which [internal] refugees want to sell their property in their former place of residence and leave the country, we should encourage them to do that'.[10] Copies of the letter were sent to the foreign minister, the military government, and Yosef Weitz. A year later, Palmon, then adviser on Arab affairs in the Prime Minister's Office, wrote a letter to Foreign Minister Moshe Sharett in which he expounded his views on the prickly issue of the property of the 'present absentees':

> Arab residents of Israel, who, from a social, religious, or cultural viewpoint, are not inclined to remain in Israel, after they would receive all or a respectable part of the compensation for their property, and their hope for what they had not received [their actual property] was lost, they would look for and find a way to leave the country.[11]

The Israeli State Archives in Jerusalem contain tens of official files with extensive information pertaining to Israel's policies toward the Arab minority, including what is usually described in Israel as 'population transfers'. Although a substantial part of these files are open to researchers and have been used for this book, many official files remain classified. However, some idea about the contents of these closed files may be gathered from the Archives' index listing those files of the Ministry of Minorities: Expulsion of Inhabitants; Transfer of Inhabitants; Concentration of Arab Residents; Complaints about Police Treatment; Demolition of Arab Houses; and Acts against Civilians.[12]

One of the first incidents of eviction of Israeli Arabs was the forced evacuation of the villages of Iqrit and Bir'im in November 1948. In his book, *Israel's Border Wars, 1949–1956*, Israeli historian Benny Morris discusses the issue of 'Expelling Border Communities [Israeli Arabs] and Nudging Back the Borders':

> At the end of 1948 . . . Israel decided to clear its border areas of [Israeli] Arab villages, to a depth of five or ten kilometres. The motive of the

policy – initially implemented at the beginning of November along the Lebanese border – was military: Arab villages along the border, just behind IDF positions and patrol roads, constituted a threat. They could receive and assist Arab troops and irregulars should the Arabs renew the war; harbour saboteurs and spies; and serve as way stations for infilt-rating [Palestinian refugees] returnees, thieves, and smugglers. Partly depopulated villages, such as Tarshiha in the Galilee, beckoned infiltra-tors [returning refugees] bent on resettlement. And some semi-abandoned border villages, such as Zakariya, in the Jerusalem Corridor, were a socio-economic burden on the state since the young adult males were mostly dead, incarcerated, or had fled to Jordan, while the old, the women, and the children of the village lived off government hand-outs. Lastly, the authorities wanted as small an Arab minority as possible in the new Jewish state.

In part, these border-area transfers were designed to hamper infiltra-tion [of Palestinian refugees] into Israel.[13]

A combination of military-strategic, demographic-settlement, and Zionist ideological considerations governed Israeli transfer activ-ities in the post-1948 period. Some expulsions continued to be carried out throughout the 1950s, mostly in the early and middle years.

In October 1952, Ben-Gurion asked the then Minister-without-portfolio Pinhas Lavon (later Defence Minister) to look into the functioning of the military government. Lavon's report, which was presented a few weeks later, criticized the military government as inefficient and harbouring much corruption. Lavon also attempted to deal with claims he heard from army General Staff representatives, that the reason for the difficulties and ineffi-ciency of the military government was the lack of a consistent policy toward the Arab minority. This inconsistency, according to the army, was the result of the activities of civilian ministries among the Arab population, in parallel with army activities. The army, Lavon wrote, wanted exclusive and total authority in deal-ing with the Arab minority. However, he recommended not to accept the army's demand although he opposed abolition of the military government and the Defence Emergency Regulations promulgated by the British Mandatory authorities in 1945. Lavon's report was most telling:

> The claim about the 'lack of a consistent policy' [made by representatives of the General Staff] is based on the demand to [adopt] a policy which would lead to the emigration of the Arab residents from the territory of the State of Israel . . . Such emigration is undoubtedly desirable, but it is doubtful whether it would be possible to achieve that – the emigration of tens of thousands of Arabs – with the means available to a military government in time of peace, in a democratic state, which is open to criticism, supervision, and is in need of [the] world's sympathy. The harm [resulting] from half measures is clear, and their benefit is doubtful. Absolutely effective means [which would bring about the total departure of the Arab minority] cannot be pursued by the state of Israel, without the shaking of its international position.

While describing the idea of a wholesale mass exodus of the Arab minority as 'desirable' but not practicable for international as well as domestic reasons, Lavon, like most Israeli ministers and senior officials, was still in favour of an active policy of encouraging 'voluntary' transfer:

> The above explanation does not come [however] to weaken or belittle the efforts being made in order to obtain the consent of Arab residents [Israeli citizens] to emigrate to foreign countries. Such plans deserve encouragement and full support from the [official] institutions concerned. The required financial investment is certainly worthwhile, and it is desirable that the treasury [Finance Ministry] ought actively to enter into details [of these plans].[14]

'More Land and Less Arabs'

Demography, land, and water were always at the heart of the conflict between the Zionist immigrants/settlers and the native Palestinians. The quest for land and demography also underpinned the Zionist concept of transfer in the pre-1948 period. In a sense, Zionism's long lasting battle against the native Palestinians was a battle for 'more land and less Arabs'. This battle essentially was dictated by Zionism's premises and fundamentals: the 'ingathering' of the world's Jews in Palestine, the acquisition and conquest of land ('Kibbush Haadamah'), and the establishment of a state for the Jews – who mostly had yet to arrive in Palestine – at the expense of the displaced and 'transferred' Palestinians. The creation of Israel did not alter Zionism's premises and fundamentals with regard to the Palestinian minority remaining under Israeli control. Indeed, the principal objectives of the Israeli state, as defined in terms of its Zionist ideology, is the fulfilment of the Jewish majority's aspirations, and those of would-be Jewish immigrants, frequently at the expense of the aspirations of the Palestinian minority.

Although, in the 1950s, most Labour leaders did not view the existence of a small, politically controlled and economically dependent, Arab minority in the Jewish state as seriously endangering the Zionist programme, the most influential leaders, including Ben-Gurion and Sharett, supported various proposals and schemes aimed at further reducing that Arab minority. For example, 'Operation Yohanan' was an attempt to transfer Arab citizens to Brazil and Argentina, while the 'Libyan Operation' envisioned their resettlement in Libya. The available evidence shows that during the early years of the state, the Arab question in Israel was considered temporary. In fact, many Israeli Jews expected the Arab minority to disappear so that they would not have to establish permanent relations with it.[15] In *The Arabs in Israel*, Sabri Jiryis writes:

> Apparently there were many who hoped to be rid of the Arabs, if not by 'sending' them after their brothers beyond the borders, then at least by 'exchanging' them for Jews from the Arab nations. International events stifled such hopes, however, and it finally became clear that an Arab minority was definitely staying on.[16]

Over the years, Israeli Jews became more realistic in their attitudes toward the existence of an Arab minority in Israel. In his book *1949: The First Israelis*, Israeli historian Tom Segev shows that the Israeli leadership was worried about the presence of an Arab minority who had already been allowed to vote and be elected to the

Knesset.[17] 'There are too many Arabs in the country,' declared
Yitzhak Ben-Tzvi (president of Israel from 1952 to 1963) at a meeting of the Labour Secretariat on 8 January 1949. Ben-Tzvi, a close
associate of Ben-Gurion and one of Labour's most influential and
popular leaders, voiced the sentiments of many leaders of the ruling
party.[18] Several months later, at another meeting of the Labour
Secretariat, Knesset member Shlomo Lavi said:

> The large number of Arabs in the country worries me. The time may
> come when we will be the minority in the State of Israel. There are
> now 170,000 Arabs in the country, including 22,000 school-age chil-
> dren. The natural increase among Arabs is high and keeps growing,
> especially if we give them all the economic advantages which we are
> intending to give: health, education and big profits. There is no such
> rate of natural increase anywhere in the world, and we have to give
> careful thought to this imminent danger. Such an increase could match
> our immigration . . . We may reach the point when the interests of the
> Arabs rather than of the Jews will determine the character of the
> country . . .[19]

Another Labour MK, Eliahu Hacarmeli, who since the mid-1930s
had supported the concept of *total* transfer, insisted on a *total* transfer
of Israel's Arab minority at the same meeting:

> I'm not willing to accept a single Arab, and not only an Arab but any
> gentile. I want the State of Israel to be entirely Jewish, the descendants of
> Abraham, Isaac and Jacob . . .[20]

Similar thoughts were expressed by MK Yehiel Duvdevany, of
Kibbutz Giv'at Hashloshah: 'If there was any way of solving the
problem by way of a transfer of the remaining 170,000 Arabs we
would do so . . .'[21] Zeev Onn, the Labour Secretary and a prominent leader of the Histadrut added: 'The landscape is also more beau-
tiful – I enjoy it, especially when travelling between Haifa and Tel
Aviv, and there is not a single Arab to be seen.'[22] Equally revealing is
the reaction of Ben-Gurion while touring the Galilee in the 1950s.
Seeing many Arab villages in the distance, he became angry and

declared: 'Whoever tours the Galilee gets the feeling that it is not part of Israel.'[23]

This study concentrates on the evolution of the transfer concept from 1948 to 1967 and discusses various official and unofficial transfer proposals put forward after June 1967. The work will also show how leading figures from the Israeli politico-military establishment have spoken out publicly in support of Palestinian removal from the occupied territories. The transfer notion is not the exclusive property of the extreme right – the Moledet and Tehiya parties and the Kach and the Gush Emunim settlers. Exponents and practitioners of population transfer permeate the Israeli establishment, the Labour party as well as the Likud. Of course, Israeli views have been affected by the 1993 Declaration of Principles between Israel and the Palestine Liberation Organization. Nevertheless, one can still observe a division between those who support annexation and eventual transfer and those who prefer territorial compromise and complete or partial withdrawal from the occupied territories. Yet, even those figures of Labour Zionism regarded as doves have reiterated their support for retaining maximum land and minimum Arabs from the West Bank and Gaza, views that demonstrate how deep-rooted is the transfer idea in Labour Zionism. One also cannot but notice the obvious parallels that exist between Zionist procedure in the pre-1948 period, which was dominated by the Labour Mapai Party, and in the territories conquered in June 1967. This similarity of procedure is the result of similar circumstances – a land predominantly (in 1967 entirely) owned and populated by non-Jews that has to be 'redeemed', settled and eventually turned into land of the Israeli/Jewish state. The 'conquest of land' (Kibbush Haadamah) always has been Zionism's major task. This also explains the view that is heard increasingly loudly in contemporary Israel: there is no room for two peoples in the Land of Israel.

It is hardly necessary to mention that the various transfer proposals and plans discussed in this study do not carry the same weight. Certainly those put forward or supported by mainstream Labour or Likud leaders are far more important than those advocated by the Kach movement or the Moledet Party. A clear distinction must be made between those 'voluntary' schemes attempted by the Labour ministers in the 1950s and in the period between June 1967 and 1970 and the compulsory plans advocated by the extreme right today. Furthermore, the criticism voiced by a significant minority of Israelis against these transfer proposals forms an important part of the discussion on the transfer debate in Israel.

Methodologically this work is divided into two major parts that correspond to two different periods with different sets of circumstances: A) from 1949 to 1967; B) since the 1967 conquests. In the 1950s the Israeli government had to deal with a small Arab minority which was granted Israeli citizenship; after June 1967 the Israeli government had to deal with a territory entirely populated by non-Jews and a perceived major 'demographic problem'. Hence, the modalities of transfer changed after 1967 and the revival of the transfer concept since then points to the parallels that exist between the Zionist transfer schemes in the pre-1948 era and in the era since June 1967.

This work is based, in part, on recently declassified archival material in the Israeli State Archives and the Central Zionist Archives in Jerusalem, as well as private papers in the Institute for Settlement Studies in Rehovot. The Israeli Hebrew press has also been a very important source for the period since 1967. These primary sources were supplemented by secondary works in Hebrew, English, and Arabic. However, definitive conclusions on the issue in question, particularly the period after June 1967, will have to wait until Israel declassifies more official documents.

Notes to Introduction

1. Nur Masalha, *Expulsion of the Palestinians: The Concept of 'Transfer' in Zionist Political Thought, 1882–1948* (Washington, DC: Institute for Palestine Studies, 1992), pp. 93–141.
2. *Haaretz*, 30 April 1958.
3. Quoted in David Gilmour, *Dispossessed: The Ordeal of the Palestinians* (London: Sphere Books, 1982), pp. 93–94.
4. Tom Segev, *1949: The First Israelis* (New York: The Free Press, 1986), p. 52.
5. Ibid.
6. Ibid.
7. See Israeli State Archives (ISA), Foreign Ministry, 2401/19a.
8. Segev, *1949*, p. 51.
9. See Penny Maddrell, *The Beduin of the Negev* (London: The Minority Rights Group, Report No. 81, 1990), p. 7.
10. ISA, Foreign Ministry, 2401/21.
11. ISA, Foreign Ministry, 2401/21b.
12. See Segev, *1949*, p. 64.
13. Benny Morris, *Israel's Border Wars, 1949–1956* (Oxford: Clarendon Press, 1993), p. 138.
14. For Lavon's report, see ISA, Foreign Ministry, 2401/19a.
15. Sammy Smooha, 'Existing and alternative policy towards Arabs in Israel', *Ethnic and Racial Studies* 5, no. 1 (January 1982), p. 74.
16. Sabri Jiryis, *The Arabs in Israel* (New York: Monthly Review Press, 1976), p. 4.
17. Segev, *1949*, p. 46.
18. Ibid.
19. Quoted in ibid., pp. 46–47.
20. Quoted in ibid., p. 47.
21. Ibid.
22. Ibid., p. 47. See Also Tzvi Shiloah, *Ashmat Yerushalayim* [The Guilt of Jerusalem] (Tel Aviv: Karni Press, 1989), p. 252.
23. Cited in Tawfiq Zayyad, 'The Fate of the Arabs In Israel', *Journal of Palestine Studies* 6, no. 1 (Autumn 1976), p. 97.

Chapter 1
Evolving Israeli Policies, 1948–67

In the post-1948 period, most important Israeli leaders thought that a *total* transfer of the Arab minority was no longer necessary because transfer had been largely achieved by 1948. However, it is necessary to explain why mass expulsions of peaceful, unarmed rural and urban Arab communities continued, despite the possession of Israeli residency papers, throughout the 1950s. Moreover, why did David Ben-Gurion, Moshe Sharett, and other leaders back, in principle, Operation Yohanan? The answers to these questions lie, in part, in the widespread sentiment (described below) among Israeli leaders and army commanders that 'too many Arabs' remained in Israel in the post-1948 period, a sentiment derived from Zionist premises and fundamentals, particularly the principle of a demographically homogenous Jewish state with 'more land (under Jewish control) and less Arabs'.

Reflecting the general attitude toward the Arab minority in the post-1948 period, Interior Minister Moshe Shapira referred to the Arab citizens as 'foreigners' in a Knesset debate on the citizenship law of 1950.[1] Other leading figures considered the Arab minority as a fifth column. 'The Arab minority is a danger to the state, in time of peace just as much as in time of war,' Yigael Yadin, the army Chief of Staff (1949–1952), told Prime Minister Ben-Gurion in August 1950.[2] The notion that Israel's Arab minority was a fifth column was also expressed by Ya'acov Meridor, a Knesset member from the Herut Party who had been a prominent Etzel-Irgun commander in the 1940s. Meridor pronounced that Stalin's action during World War II provided a justification for Israel to expel the Arab minority:

Soviet Russia knew how to solve the problem of the Volga Germans during the war. There were 800,000 Germans in that region. They

1

transferred them to the east, beyond the Urals. If there should be a second round of fighting, where shall we transfer this fifth column? With the coastal region being only 10 miles wide, how shall we do it?[3]

The same notion of a fifth column was held strongly by the leadership of the governing Labour party. Shmuel Dayan, a veteran Labour leader and Knesset member (and the father of Moshe Dayan), told a caucus of his party in 1951 that Israel could not allow the Arab fifth column in the state to become powerful. Golda Meir (then Minister of Labour in the Ben-Gurion Cabinet) remarked at the same Labour meeting that she felt 'sick' whenever she heard an Arab swear allegiance to the state of Israel three times a day.[4] These statements demonstrate that the Israeli elite barely reconciled itself to the existence of an Arab minority in the Jewish state in the post-1948 period. In fact, the possibility of finding a way to rid Israel of its Arab minority occupied a long discussion by the Labour Knesset faction and party secretariat on 9 July 1950. At this meeting some participants were very much in favour of the idea. However, there was a minority that opposed transfer on moral and practical grounds. Yitzhak Ben-Tzvi, although in favour of expelling 'disloyal' Arab citizens, thought that a total mass expulsion in time of peace was unrealistic for domestic and international reasons, and therefore the Israeli government should aim at obtaining Arab 'loyalty' to the state.

> Do we want [the Arabs] to remain in the state, to be absorbed in the state, or to get out of the state. But even if some of them would get out, it is necessary to formulate this thing from a socio-political point of view or in principle. A distinction should be made between a lover and an enemy. To encourage the former [to remain] and drive out the latter. Here, for example, is the question of liquidation. In my view, total liquidation [i.e., removal of the Arab minority] would not cross one's mind.[5]

David Hacohen, a Histadrut leader and Labour Knesset member, denounced incidents of brutality against Israeli Arabs and reassured his colleagues that Israel's Arabs would leave the state in any case, without enacting discriminatory laws against them because they would not be able to adjust to the new state of Israel, with its high levels of education, taxation, and living standards.[6] Another Labour leader, Nahum Verlinsky (who was also a member of the Histadrut's Council and the head of Tnuva Marketing Company), said at the same meeting that it would not be possible to uproot 180,000 Arabs in time of peace and that Israel cannot form its policies toward the Arab minority on the basis of the assumption that war would break out – implying that it would be possible to carry out expulsion during war time.[7] In summing up the discussion, Foreign Minister Sharett said that it would be better not to have Arabs in the state, implying that those who were willing to emigrate should be encouraged to do so. However, Sharett suggested that a policy decision ought to be taken on whether it was preferable to carry out systematic harassment designed to encourage Arabs to emigrate. Sharett thought that a policy based on minimal fairness should be adopted toward Arabs who were not inclined to leave.[8]

Several months later, the idea that Israel should exploit a propitious moment – such as a future war situation – to expel its Arab minority was at the centre of a discussion of the Labour Knesset faction. With his characteristically hard-line thinking, Ben-Gurion said:

> These [Israeli] Arabs should not reside here in the same way that the American Jews should not reside in America . . . I think that we must do everything so that an [Israeli] Arab would reside in an Arab state because the [Israeli] Arabs have countries . . . If war breaks out all [Israeli] Arabs would flee, either out of fear that we would slaughter them, or because they would think that they would help their Arab states to slaughter us.[9]

Yosef Nahmani, a senior executive of the Jewish National Fund (JNF) and a close friend of Ben-Tzvi, sent a memorandum to Ben-Gurion (a copy was also sent to Ben-Tzvi) on 11 January 1953, expressing anxiety that the Arabs had remained in significant numbers in the Galilee after the establishment of Israel:

> Western Galilee has been occupied, but it has not been freed of its Arab population, as happened in other parts of the country. Fifty-one

3

unabandoned villages and the town of Nazareth remain in it. In all, its Arab inhabitants are 84,002 (not counting Acre), controlling 929,549 dunums of land . . . Its Arab population, mostly agricultural, makes up approximately 45 per cent of the Arab minority in our state, and is concentrated in a homogenous continuous area, bordering Arab Lebanon. This concentrated Arab minority presents a continual threat to the security and integrity of the state. 1) [This minority] is likely to add to the burdens of the government and to create problems when the boundaries of our state are finally defined. The very existence of a homogenous group in this part of the country is a factor strengthening the claim of Arab states to the area . . . in accordance with the UN [partition] resolution of November 1947; 2) At a suitable opportunity [this Arab minority is likely] to play a role similar to the one played by the Sudeten Germans in Czechoslovakia at the outbreak of World War II; 3) [It is likely] to be a motivating factor for the crystallization of an Arab nationalist movement, influenced by the nationalist movements in the neighbouring countries, and guided and used by them to undermine the stability of the state.[10]

The so-called German 'example' in Czechoslovakia had been repeatedly cited in the Jewish Agency Executive's discussions of 7 and 12 July 1938, which were largely devoted to the transfer solution. During these discussions as well as in the discussions of the Jewish Agency's Transfer Committees between 1937 and 1944, in which Nahmani took part, many leading Zionists used the so-called German 'precedent' to justify their advocacy of Palestinian removal. In January 1953, Nahmani (and his JNF colleague Yosef Weitz) still viewed Arab citizens of Israel from the same perspective as that from which he had viewed the Palestinians in the 1930s and 1940s before the creation of Israel:

> [It is] essential to break up this concentration [of Arabs in the Galilee] through [Jewish] settlement . . . There is no doubt that after peace is achieved with neighbouring countries, those Arab residents who have not reconciled themselves to the existence of the state of Israel will leave the country, and for that a policy of encouraging [departure] should be pursued.[11]

Similar proposals were repeated in Nahmani's letters to President Ben-Tzvi, dated 27 July 1953 and 21 December 1955.[12]

The situation of the Palestinian minority in Israel was anomalous: a Palestinian minority inside a state that was founded for the Jews at the expense of the Palestinian people and following the partial destruction of the Palestinian society by the Zionist military in 1948. In such an anomalous situation the Palestinian minority was bound to be regarded with suspicion by the government of Israel as well as the Jewish majority. The Israeli Palestinian leader 'Abdul-'Aziz al-Zu'bi wrote in 1957:

> The natural attachment of Israel Arabs to the rest of the Palestine Arab nation and to the Arab peoples in general . . . became the basis of an organized regime of suspicion and distrust which regarded the Arab minority as an 'internal danger' if not as 'the enemy within'.[13]

Two years later, in 1959, influential Labour leader Yigal Allon (later deputy prime minister) wrote in his book *A Curtain of Sand*:

> To this day, there has not been a clear, explicit policy regarding the Arab population in the country. On the one hand there has not been a policy to bring the majority of the Arab citizens to decide in favour of emigration to some other country, and there has not been a policy aimed at . . . encouraging them to integrate 'socially' in the state of Israel, on the other.[14]

Allon put delicately that the Jewish National Fund should play 'a big role' in assisting the voluntary departure of those Arab citizens who were not prepared 'to link their fate with the fate of the state of Israel'.[15]

While Israel faced real security problems which were largely a consequence of Zionist premises and fundamentals, history has shown that the Palestinian minority in Israel never has been a fifth column. Yet, even though Israeli Jews have become more realistic in their attitudes toward the Arab minority, many of them still consider it disloyal. This perception of the Jewish majority combined with the Zionist character of the state as well as the above-described anomalous situation have had a disorientating effect on the younger generation of Palestinians growing up in Israel because they feel like foreigners in their own land. Reflecting on this anomalous situation, the Israeli-Palestinian novelist Anton Shammas said: 'I sometimes think that we are neither real Arabs nor real Israelis, because in the Arab countries they call us traitors, and in Israel, spies.'[16]

Clearly, in dealing with a small Palestinian minority in the post-1948 period, most Israeli leaders were no longer obsessed with transfer (in the same way that the Yishuv's leadership had been in the 1930s and 1940s), since this had largely been achieved in the 1948 war. Furthermore, the total transfer of a peaceful, unarmed, and subdued minority was not an option in the 1950s because the establishment of the state of Israel had introduced domestic and international constraints with regard to total transfer. Moreover, even in the pre-1948 period, the Zionist leadership had not ruled out the existence of an Arab minority in the projected Jewish state, as long as this minority remained small and did not challenge the domination of the would-be Jewish majority and the Zionist mission of the state. In the post-1948 period, Zionist-dominated party politics was far from being monolithic, and some political groups, such as the small Mapam party, were committed, at least rhetorically, to the integration of the Arab minority into Israel.

However, due to a phenomenally high birth rate, this Arab minority grew rapidly in the post-1948 period even as the Zionist striving for land and demography ('more land and less Arabs') continued. While the establishment of the state added domestic constraints with regard to the transfer issue, it nevertheless opened the way for a massive seizure of Arab lands for Jewish benefit in a perfectly 'legal' manner and with the authority of legislation enacted by the Israeli Knesset. This chapter will show how the Zionist striving for land and demography continued in the post-1948 period. It will demonstrate that the main focus of Israel's policies toward the remaining Palestinian minority in the post-1948 period was land seizure, economic dependence, political control/domination, and demographic containment.

'Less Arabs': Expulsions in the 1950s

After 1948, Israeli use of force continued in an attempt to induce some of the remaining Arabs to leave the country. Wholesale expulsions of Arabs, many with Israeli citizenship, across the border continued well into the late 1950s. In fact, as late as 1959 – eleven years after the establishment of the state – Bedouin tribes were expelled from the Negev to the Sinai Peninsula in Egypt and to Jordan; only after United Nations intervention was this 1959 action reversed.[17] Over ten thousand Israeli Arabs were expelled by the Israeli army across the border in the early years of the state (together with many thousands of other Palestinian refugees who had managed to 'infiltrate' back to their villages and towns). The continuation of expulsions was underpinned by traditional Zionist premises: the drive to 'redeem' Arab-owned land and the dream of setting up a homogenous and exclusive Jewish state.

The several instances of collective expulsion of Israeli Arab residents in the post-1948 period need to be reviewed. For instance, on 31 May 1950 the Israeli army transported about 120 Palestinians in two crowded trucks to a point near the edge of Wadi Araba, a hot desert wasteland astride the Israeli-Jordanian frontier between the Dead Sea and the Gulf of 'Aqaba. The Palestinians were ordered to cross to Jordan, with the soldiers 'firing bursts over their heads to urge them forward'. While most of the expellees made it, as many as thirty-six 'may be assumed . . . [to have] perished from thirst and starvation', the British Minister to Amman, Kirkbride, wrote.[18] The survivors, who were questioned in Jordan, were found to be:

> Members of divided families who infiltrate[d] across the line to find their relatives, or who fled from what is now Israel territory when the Jews arrived there, abandoning money and valuables in their homes; . . . Refugees caught *en route* from Gaza to Jordan; . . . [and] Arabs living in their homes in Israel, with whom the Jews have become displeased for some reason or other.[19]

This incident shows that in the process of expelling Palestinian refugees who had managed to 'infiltrate' back into their villages and towns, some Israeli Arabs were also driven out. In the wake of this incident, which triggered an internal debate within the ruling Mapai party about the policy of expelling 'infiltrators' (returning refugees), Foreign Minister Sharett, while supporting the general policy of expelling 'infiltrators', also expressed his attitude toward Israel's Arab minority at a meeting of the Mapai Knesset faction and party secretariat on 18 June 1950:

> If there is a possibility of reducing the Arab minority, if there is a poss-
> ibility of prompting some [Arab] village or community, a certain num-
> ber of Arabs, to leave the country, to send them on their way by peaceful
> means – this must be done . . . If there is a possibility today of reducing
> the Arab minority, which numbers some 170,000, by one thousand – it
> should be done, but it depends on how one does it . . . One must not
> strive to do this by a wholesale policy of repression and discrimination.
> First of all, by such [means] the objective will be missed . . . I say that we
> must adopt a dual policy, we must stand firm as a wall against infiltration
> and not be deterred from using harsh measures, but at the same time we
> must understand that the Arabs who remain in Israel . . . must be assured
> a minimum.[20]

At the same meeting, Moshe Dayan, the Commanding Officer of the Southern Command, expressed his extremist views on Israel's Arabs, whom he regarded as a fifth column:

> I hope that there will perhaps be another opportunity in the future to
> transfer these Arabs from the Land of Israel, and as long as such a
> possibility exists, we must do nothing to foreclose the option . . . It is
> possible that the moment a way of resettling the 700,000 [Palestinian]
> refugees is found, the same method will also prove good for the
> resettlement [outside Israel] of these Arabs [i.e., the Israeli Arab minor-
> ity]. It is possible that when there is an Arab state . . . which, with world
> agreement, is ready to resettle Arabs in other places, then that same
> agreement will be [extended] to the transfer of this [i.e., Israeli Arab]
> population as well.[21]

In another Mapai internal debate a few weeks later on 9 July 1950, the moderate Mapai MK and novelist Yizhar Smilansky criticized the assumptions underlying Sharett's and Dayan's thinking: 'It is bad that Arabs remained [in Israel] . . . It were better that Arabs had not stayed.'[22]

Dayan was not alone in supporting the expulsion of Israel's Arab minority. According to Benny Morris, 'During the immediate post-1948 period, talk of "transferring" Israel's Arab minority was relatively common in Israel.'[23] Army Chief of Staff, Yigael Yadin, supported implicitly the 'transfer' of Israel's Arabs. In consultation with Ben-Gurion on 8 February 1950, he described the Israeli Arabs as 'a danger in time of war, as in time of peace'.[24] The head of the military government, Lieutenant Colonel 'Emmanuel Mor (Markovsky), stated in 1950 ('with probably only marginal exaggeration', according to Benny Morris), that 'the entire nation [i.e., Jews] in Zion [i.e., Israel], without exception, does not want Arab neighbours'.[25] About the same time, in the summer of 1950, almost two years after the 1948 war, the remaining 2,700 inhabitants of the southern Arab town of al-Majdal (now called Ashkelon) received expulsion orders and were transported to the border of the Gaza Strip over a period of a few weeks. The town, which on the eve of the war had 10,000 inhabitants, had been conquered by the Israeli army on 4 November 1948. From that time and throughout 1949, the Commanding Officer of the Southern Command, General Yigal Allon, had 'demanded . . . that the town be emptied of its Arabs'.[26] A government 'Committee for Transferring Arabs' had decided in February 1949 in principle to remove the remaining 2,700 inhabitants of al-Majdal. A year later, in the spring of 1950, General Moshe Dayan, Allon's successor in the Southern Command, had decided to direct the clearing of al-Majdal's residents to Gaza. Authorization for this action was given by Ben-Gurion on 19 June 1950.[27] A day earlier, on 18 June, Dayan had appeared before the Mapai Secretariat and stated that he supported the *total* transfer of all the Israeli Arabs out of the country.[28]

Some 700,000 Jews arrived in Israel between its proclamation as an independent state in May 1948 and the end of 1951. The state's leaders believed that al-Majdal and its lands were needed for rehousing and settling these new immigrants. Na'im Gila'adi, a newly arrived Iraqi Jew, was put together with other Iraqi immigrants in a *ma'abarah*, a transit camp, near al-Majdal. According to Gila'adi, several important figures in the Jewish Agency came to reassure them: 'Be patient: soon we shall drive the Arabs out of Majdal and you will be able to have their houses.' Gila'adi recalled many years later:

> For us this was a shock. Majdal was a nearby little town, and we knew nothing of its inhabitants. One night, five or six of us crossed the barbed wire that surrounded Majdal to go and speak to the inhabitants, to see who they were, and why they wanted to drive them out. Talking to them, we discovered that they were very peaceful people, very hospitably disposed towards us, and ready to behave as loyal citizens of the state that had just been founded. And it was those people they wanted to drive out to settle us in their houses![29]

The Israeli authorities had in fact considered the option of relocating al-Majdal's residents to other Arab localities inside Israel, but they opted for 'less Arabs', transporting the Majdalites to the Gaza border, which then was controlled by Egypt. Israeli historian Benny Morris explained:

> the absence of public or even internal party political debate and backbiting during and in the wake of the Majdal transfer seems to indicate that the operation in effect enjoyed a broad political consensus. Moving the Majdal Arabs to Gaza was in all likelihood perceived by most if not all the ministers as a clear, important Israeli interest, in terms of demography (less Arabs), day-to-day security (less infiltration and smuggling back and forth), strategy (no Arab concentration to serve as a way station between Gaza and Tel Aviv for potential invaders from the south), and immigration absorption and town planning (more space for Jewish immigrant settlers . . .).[30]

The Negev was an early focus of expulsion activities. According to the 1947 UN Partition Plan, the Negev had been included in the areas allotted to the Jewish state. But during negotiations in the UN General Assembly part of the Negev was transferred to the areas allotted to the Palestinian Arab state. After its occupation, Prime Minister Ben-Gurion in particular had been anxious to populate the Negev with Jews.

In November 1949, some 500 Arab Bedouin families (2,000 people) from the Beersheba area were forced across the border into the West Bank. Jordan complained about this expulsion.[31] A further expulsion of 700–1,000 persons of the 'Azazmeh or Jahalin tribes to Jordan took place in May 1950.[32] On 2 September 1950 the Israeli Army rounded up hundreds of 'Azazmeh tribesmen (a United Nations Truce Supervision Organization – UNTSO – complaint spoke of 4,000) from the Negev 'and drove them . . . into Egyptian territory'.[33] A week later further expulsion of the 'Azazmeh tribesmen was carried out. UNTSO chief of staff Major-General William Riley put the total number of Bedouin at Qusaima in Sinai in mid-September 1950 at 6,200, the majority having been recently expelled by the Israeli army from the Negev. Riley also wrote that the Israeli army killed 13 Bedouin during these expulsion operations.[34] (The Israelis claimed that the 'Azazmeh tribesmen were crossing back and forth continually between the Negev and Sinai.) In September 1952 the Israeli army expelled some 850 members of the Al-Sani' tribe from the northern Negev to the West Bank. 'Subsequently,' Morris writes, 'several thousand more 'Azazme [sic] and other Bedouin tribesmen were expelled to Sinai.'[35]

Morris quotes an Israel Foreign Ministry report as stating during 1949–53 'Israel expelled all told "close" to 17,000 Negev Bedouin, not all of them alleged infiltrators.'[36] The Arabs of the Negev had been reduced through expulsion and flight from 65,000–95,000, at the end of the British Mandate, to 13,000 by 1951.[37] In fact, the remaining Arabs of the Negev were not granted Israeli identity cards until 1952, a situation which made it easier for the Israeli army to push them out. A year later, in 1953, it was reported in the United Nations that 7,000 Arab Bedouin, approximately half of them from the 'Azazmeh tribe, had been forcibly expelled from the Negev.[38]

Two years later, in March 1955, members of the 'Azazmeh tribe, including women and children, suffered a massacre at the hands of the notorious 'Unit 101' of the Israeli army, which had been created by Chief of Staff Moshe Dayan in 1953.[39] Commanded by Ariel Sharon and patronized in particular by Ben-Gurion, Unit 101 was considered the 'bayonet' of the army and carried out numerous raids against Arab targets across the border. The tactics used by the unit were debated widely in Israel. Its expulsive action against Bedouin tribes of the Negev in the mid-1950s was described in the daily *Haaretz* in November 1959:

> The army's desert patrols would turn up in the midst of a Bedouin encampment day after day dispersing it with a sudden burst of machine-gun fire until the sons of the desert were broken and, gathering what little was left of their belongings, led their camels in long silent strings into the heart of the Sinai desert.[40]

A shaykh of a Negev tribe, Tarabin al-Sani', recalled in a conversation with a journalist in 1985:

> Those were the days of military government and do you know what that means? It meant that they could kill people as if they were stray dogs out there in the desert with no witness to record their atrocities.[41]

Expulsion activities were also carried out in the Little Triangle after its annexation to Israel in May 1949, following the Rhodes agreement signed with Jordan on 3 April 1949. For instance, in late May or early June 1949, 4,000 'internal refugees' were expelled by the military government from the Little Triangle across the border into the West Bank. The military governor of the central area, Lieutenant Colonel 'Emmanuel Markovsky, reported to the head of the military government, General Elimelech Avner, on 30 June 1949:

> Upon our entry into the area [the Little Triangle] and the proclamation of [Israel's] rule in it, we announced that we will not recognize the [internal] refugees as being entitled to reside in the area or any aid and benefit. We prohibited their employment in any work . . . we banned organizing permanent aid for them. When we received authorization to transfer them across the border, the action was implemented in full within a week.

Markovsky also added that after the military government put pressure on 'representatives' of the Little Triangle's villages (possibly certain *mukhtars*), the latter had agreed to assist in the process. In conclusion, Markovsky wrote: 'In retrospect, this action proved that a fair and forceful rule in the [Israeli Arab] villages gives the possibility of implementing tasks in full, and fortifies Israel's rule.'[42]

In the same year (1949), some 1,000 people from the village of Baqa al-Gharbiyyah in the Little Triangle were expelled by Israel across the border into the West Bank.[43] In early February 1951, the residents of thirteen small Arab villages in Wadi 'Ara were expelled over the border. Later, on 17 November of the same year the inhabitants of the village of Khirbat al-Buwayshat in the Little Triangle also were expelled and their houses were dynamited by the army.[44] Zalman Lifschitz, adviser on land affairs in the Prime Minister's Office – who also had been a member of the 1948 (Israeli government) 'Transfer Committee' – reported to the Prime Minister, the Foreign Minister, and the Finance Minister on 3 July 1950 that it would be possible to persuade the 1,760 residents of the village of Kafr Qare'a near Wadi 'Ara to cross to the West Bank on condition that they would be compensated for their property left behind. Lifschitz strongly recommended that the government should bear the financial cost of these transfer activities and pay the would-be evacuees 10 Israeli lira for each dunum left behind:

> Such activities were carried out in the past and being undertaken and carried out in the [Little] Triangle also now . . . It seems to me that we have a great interest in encouraging the process of departure [of Israeli Arabs] and in reducing the Muslim Arab minority, on the one hand, and in solving the problem of land itself, on the other.[45]

Earlier in 1949 some 700 people from Kafr Yassif village in the Galilee were trucked to the Jordanian border and ordered to cross it. These villagers had not left the Galilee during the war, but simply fled their homes in adjoining villages and moved to Kafr Yassif.[46] In a Knesset debate on 8 March 1949, Communist Knesset Member Tawfiq Tubi strongly protested against this large single expulsion. He stated:

> The forced evacuation of Arab villages has also been carried out by the

Israeli authorities. Only a few weeks ago 700 people who had taken refuge in the village of [Kafr] Yasif [sic] during the [1948] war were taken to the Iraqi front [on the northern West Bank border with Israel] in trucks and forced to cross the lines to Abdullah . . .[47]

In mid-April 1949, the U.S. consul in Jerusalem reported that 'several hundred' Galilee Arabs – 'all Israeli citizens' – had been expelled by the Israeli army across the border, together with some Palestinian refugees who had 'infiltrated' back to their villages.[48] Such expulsions were often carried out with brutality, as one Kibbutz woman wrote anonymously to the newspaper 'Al-Hamishmar of witnessing such 'infiltrators', men, women and children blindfolded, being trucked out:

Those of us standing nearby had witnessed no bad behaviour on the part of the Arabs, who sat frightened, almost one on top of the other. But the soldiers were quick to teach us what they meant by 'order'. 'The expert' jumped up and began to . . . hit [the Arabs] across their blindfolded eyes and when he had finished, he stamped on all of them and then, in the end, laughed uproariously and with satisfaction at his heroism. We were shocked by this despicable act. I ask, does this not remind us exactly of the Nazi acts towards the Jews?[49]

Resettlement Schemes

To some extent the actual transfer activities described above were an extension of Israel's expulsion policy of 1948[50] into the mid-1950s. Only this time the victims were Israeli Arabs, many with Israeli residency papers. However, the main focus of Israel's policies toward the remaining Palestinian minority gradually shifted from mass expulsion to demographic containment, political control, exclusionary domination, and a whole constellation of government policies – military rule, blatant discrimination, land confiscation. The last wholesale expulsion of Israeli Arabs was in 1959, eleven years after the establishment of the state.

As far as most important Israeli leaders were concerned, expulsion was no longer a serious option by the mid-1950s. Thus, most of the remaining Arabs were granted Israeli citizenship. Approximately 30,000 internal refugees (also referred to as the 'present absentees'), who were not allowed to return to their homes and property, most of which had been confiscated by the state, also received Israeli citizenship. The policies of the Labour governments focused in the initial stage on obliterating the Arab minority's Palestinian identity by fragmenting it and attempting to create loyal 'non-Jewish minorities' (Druze, Bedouin, Christians, Muslims, etc.), who, if they did not identify with the state and its Zionist mission, at least would be loyal subjects.

Not all Israelis accepted the permanency of the Arab minority during the 1950s. Leaders such as Yosef Weitz, director of the Jewish National Fund's Land Settlement Department, remained obsessed with voluntary transfer, principally because of its perceived connection with the land issue and the need to take over more land from the Arab minority for prospective Jewish immigrants (again 'more land and less Arabs'). Operation Yohanan, which was backed by the prime minister and most important ministers, vividly demonstrates Weitz's obsession in connection with the remaining small Arab minority. Operation Yohanan originated in 1950 as a plan to transfer over 20 Christian Arab families from a village in the Galilee to Argentina. As he wrote in a June 1951 letter to Ya'acov Tzur, Israel's ambassador to Argentina:

The chief purpose of this matter [Operation Yohanan] is the transfer of the Arab population from Israel. I have always, and already before the establishment of the state, feared the Arab minority in our midst [i.e., Israel], and these fears still exist, not in theory but in practice. In addition to this, we lack land, and if not now, we will feel its shortage after a short time, when the objective of 'curtailing the exiles' [reducing Jewish diaspora through immigration to Israel] is realized. By the transfer of the Arab minority from Israel through mutual agreement, we will achieve a solution for the two [above-stated] problems, and the more we make progress in this [objective], the better it will be for the state. From this viewpoint I see the wish of one group from the village of Gush Halav [Jish] as the beginning of the way to realize the idea.

This extraordinary letter implied the *total* transfer, 'through mutual agreement', of the peaceful, small Arab minority and reflected Weitz's continuing obsession with transfer. Weitz's attitude toward the Israeli Arab citizens, who had been allowed to vote and be elected to the Knesset, is revealed in his diary. When three Arabs (out of a total of 120 members) were elected to the First Knesset in 1949, one of the Arab MKs appeared in the parliament wearing a tarboosh and another a traditional *kafiyyah*. Weitz, who was among the guests attending the first session, recorded his feelings: '[I felt] cold in [my] heart and angry in [my] soul . . . I do not want [the Arabs] to be many' [in the Knesset]. On the same page, Weitz recorded that he told General Yosef Avidar 'about the letter I had sent to Moshe Dayan in connection with the granting of citizenship to [the 30,000] Arabs who live here [in the Little Triangle], a matter which has prevented us from settling this Triangle [with Jews]. The Chief of Staff [Dayan] replied to me that he, like me, also regrets this measure which was taken contrary to his opinion.'[51] In the end, Operation Yohanan 'melted away like morning clouds in spring time' because the Palestinians who initially had expressed interest in the transfer had lost interest by early 1953.[52]

The 'Libyan Operation', 1953–58

After the failure of Operation Yohanan, Weitz became involved in a plan to resettle Palestinians in Libya. This 'Libyan Operation' was conceived as a combined operation that would include the inducement of emigration of Israeli Arabs to Libya while exchanging their properties in Israel with those of North African Jews who would be encouraged to immigrate to Israel. In the context of the Israeli scheme for resettling Palestinians in Libya two points are relevant. First, there was a tendency among Israeli ministers and officials to link the fate of the Palestinian transferees/refugees to that of the Jewish communities in Arab countries. This tendency had been revealed in the Zionist institutions' 'transfer' debates as early as the mid-1930s. Second, the Israelis wanted to exploit the fact that the Sanusi monarchy, set up in Libya in 1951, was heavily dependent on and under the indirect control of Britain and the United States.

Libya was granted formal independence by the United Nations on 24 December 1951, following eight years of temporary British and French administration, imposed on the country after the removal of Italian colonial rule in 1943. At the head of the new monarchy was King Idris, who was patronized and guided by the British and the Americans. The Zionists believed that this indirect Western influence could be brought to bear on what they termed the 'Libyan Operation', a plan concerned with the resettlement of Palestinian refugees in Libya and the encouragement of emigration among Israeli Arabs to Libya.

On 13 March 1952, Eliahu Sasson's son, Moshe Sasson, a senior diplomat and Arabist of the Foreign Ministry Middle East Department (later to become a prime ministerial adviser on the Palestinians of the West Bank and Gaza, 1967–69; Ambassador to Italy, 1973–77; and Ambassador to Egypt, 1981–88), who was then serving as vice-consul at the Israeli embassy in Athens, wrote a secret letter to Foreign Minister Sharett outlining 'A Combined Proposal for the Settlement of Arab Refugees in Libya, the Rescue of Jewish Property [in Libya] and the Emigration of Arabs from Israel to Libya'.[53] Moshe Sasson explained that there were still 3,500 Jews 'lingering' in Libya who did not feel in a hurry to emigrate to Israel.[54] Most of these Jews owned property. Sasson stated that a modest estimate of their real estate property only was six million pounds sterling, while a generous estimate was 40 million pounds sterling. According to Sasson, there were Arabs in Israel, who owned property, who would be interested in emigrating from Israel on condition that they would be allowed to take their capital with them, and among those Arabs there were some who would be prepared to exchange their property with those of Jews in Arab countries. Sasson explained that 'the emigration of these [Arabs] from Israel falls into line with the immigration of Libyan Jews to Israel in the course of a mutual exchange of properties'.

Sasson cited the name of Muhammad Nimr al-Hawwari as an Israeli Arab who had expressed a wish to emigrate to Libya. Al-Hawwari had been the commander of the Palestine Arab Youth Organization until 1948. In 1952 he published in Nazareth a book entitled *The Secret Behind the Catastrophe* (Sir al-Nakbah), in which he

17

claimed that the Arab leadership was largely responsible for the 1948 Palestinian catastrophe. According to Sasson, al-Hawwari claimed that he would be able to persuade certain circles of Palestinian refugees in Arab countries to emigrate to and settle permanently in Libya. (It is hard to establish the truth about this claim of willingness on the part of al-Hawwari to collaborate in such a scheme. In 1953 al-Hawwari sent a memorandum to the President of the State of Israel – which was also published in *Al-Rabitah*, the organ of the Arab Greek-Catholic community in Israel – in which he condemned the transfer proposal as violating basic international principles.)[55] Sasson also claimed that a Palestinian refugee named Daud al-Dajjani, who was in Lebanon, would collaborate in carrying out this scheme.

Sasson asserted that 'poor Libya would willingly receive intellectual and technical Arab [human] resources, which were of a much higher standard than those existing in Libya';

> the success of this small scale settlement in Libya depends on the agreement, in principle, of Britain and the local Libyan authorities and the ensuring of means for its financing, on the one hand, and the advance planning and organization, on the other. Diplomatic activity at high level in London . . . and negotiation with UN institutions on the permanent settlement of the refugees (in order to finance the settlement of those who would emigrate from Arab countries [to Libya] – would ensure one side of the coin, and the JNF (which agrees to be in charge of the exchange of properties between Israeli Arabs and Libyan Jews) would ensure the other side of the coin. The JNF is prepared to [carry out] this task only after the Foreign Ministry [grants it the sole right] to talk to those concerned in Israel [as a first step in] implementation.[56]

Sasson believed that 'the political and propagandistic reward that would stem from the emigration of Arabs from Israel, after they had been living there, and the lesson for the refugees, who are still demanding to return, is great'. Sasson suggested that if

> the proposal as a whole, or in part, were to be approved, we [the Foreign Ministry Middle East Department] would be able to work out a detailed

plan which would be implemented in stages. It is worth emphasising here that the first stage would be directed towards the emigration of three to four Arabs from Israel and a similar number of refugees from Arab countries [to Libya].

Sasson concluded his letter to Foreign Minister Sharett by pointing out that Yehoshu'a Palmon, Prime Minister Ben-Gurion's Adviser for Arab Affairs, 'approves of the plan and would be prepared to assist in its implementation'.

Although Sharett's response to this specific proposal coming from one of his senior officials in the Foreign Ministry is not known, it is most likely that he approved of it. First, he had been fully behind 'Operation Yohanan'. Second, he provided strong encouragement for his senior officials to pursue the Libyan Operation, both during his premiership (1954–November 1955), as well as during his last six months in office as Foreign Minister until his resignation in June 1956. Sharett advocated an active approach aimed at 'dissolving' the refugee problem and removing it from the heart of the Arab–Israeli conflict. The Libyan Operation apparently appealed to Sharett as a plan that promised to resolve the problem of both Palestinian refugees and the Arab minority in Israel. Thus, the plan was approved at a meeting held on 13 May 1954 with the participation of Finance Minister Levi Eshkol; Peretz Naftali, the Agriculture Minister; Pinhas Sapir, Director General of the Ministry of Finance; Mordechai Shattner; Shmuel Divon, adviser on Arab affairs; and Yosef Weitz. As to 'the question of exchanging properties of the Arabs here [that is, Israeli Arabs] with the properties of Jews in other countries, to which the farmers [Israeli Arabs] would emigrate – a positive answer was given', by the participants, who concluded that 'this way is desirable'.[57] According to Weitz, Sharett, who did not ask many questions, said that 'the matter is respectable and serious and must be carried out'. The participants also approved Weitz's proposal that Yoav Tzuckerman and Weitz should travel to 'North Africa to investigate the possibility of the exchange of properties of Jews in [countries such as] Tunisia [and] Algeria',[58] presumably with those of Palestinian refugees and Israeli Arab citizens who would be offered financial incentives for departing to North Africa. A second meeting for detailed discussions on these proposals, with the participation of 'Ezra Danin, was set for the Monday of the following week. Either at this second meeting of mid-May or shortly after, Sharett entrusted Danin with the task of dealing with the Libyan scheme.[59]

Weitz and Danin worked together for nearly four years to bring the Libyan plan to fruition. Their efforts included numerous hours of secret meetings to raise money for the purchase of Libyan agricultural land from Italian colonialists who had returned to Italy. This land was to be provided to Palestinians who agreed to farm it with the help of hired Libyan workers. The prospects for the Libyan Operation succeeding were dimmed by political developments in the Middle East between 1954–58. However, what really aborted the plan was sudden and unexpected publicity. The revelations about the plan and its source of financing occurred in 1958 while Danin was in Italy seeking to register the transfer of the first 100,000 dunums from the control of former Italian settlers in the Tripoli region to Zionist control.[60] At that time, the operation, which until then had been kept strictly confidential, was leaked to an Israeli news reporter, who treated it as a journalistic scoop and passed it on to *The Sunday Times* in London and to *Ma'ariv* and *Lamerhav* in Israel. The whole operation collapsed as a result of this leak. Danin wrote: 'our men in Libya were immediately persecuted by the men of the Mufti [Haj Amin al-Husayni], and some of them were detained and tortured'. In summing up his efforts Danin wrote that, although the actual implementation of the project had not been tested, there was no certainty that it would have succeeded even had the whole operation remained confidential and the leakage to the press had not occurred.[61]

The collapse of the Libyan operation did not bring an end to the efforts by Israeli Foreign Ministry officials to try to 'dissolve' the refugee problem and disperse the Palestinians through economic means and employment projects. Moreover, the Libyan scheme would resurface ten years later, after the Israeli occupation of the West Bank and Gaza, in conversations and correspondence between Danin, then retired from the Foreign Ministry, and Yitzhak Rabin, then Israel's ambassador to Washington. In 1968 Rabin and Danin appear to have discussed the idea of 'infiltrating' skilled Palestinians – not necessarily refugees – from the newly occupied territories to Libya. These would then attract Palestinian immigration to that country, which would result in thinning out the Arab population in the West Bank and Gaza.[62]

In summary it is clear that these official, though secret, Israeli schemes such as Operation Yohanan and the Libyan Operation ended in failure. However, they are significant in the sense of showing how the Israelis wanted to remove the refugee problem from the centre of the Arab–Israeli conflict and remove any possibility of Palestinian return in the future. These schemes also constituted a background against which other Israeli schemes were attempted by the governments of Eshkol and Golda Meir in the aftermath of the conquest of the West Bank and Gaza Strip in June 1967. Faced with what they termed a 'demographic problem' and the existence of hundreds of thousands of refugees in the newly acquired territories, Eshkol and Meir – both had been involved in the schemes of the 1950s – carried a plan (known as the Moshe Dayan plan) between the summer of 1967 and 1970 that aimed at thinning out the population of the refugee camps, particularly in Gaza. This secret scheme and other Israeli transfer plans and proposals from June 1967 onward will be discussed in subsequent chapters.

Operation Hafarferet

The most dramatic expulsion plan was the secret Operation Hafarferet in 1956. The plan was aborted after Israeli soldiers massacred 49 Palestinian civilians in the village of Kafr Qassim. On 25 October 1991, 35 years after this infamous massacre, the Hebrew newspaper *Hadashot* revealed for the first time an expulsion plan that stood behind the massacre. The essence of this secret plan was to expel the Arab inhabitants of the 'Little Triangle' (over 40,000 Israeli Arab citizens), apparently to Jordan. The investigator, Rubik Rosenthal, interviewed several officers connected with the episode and used material from the IDF's archives as well as the trials of army commanders and soldiers involved in the massacre. *Hadashot* established that the slaughter was carried out against the background of a plan devised by the Israeli army on the eve of the 1956 war.[63]

On 29 October, the day the Israeli army launched its attack on Egypt in the south, the Israeli Border Guard carried out a large massacre in the Israeli Arab village of Kafr Qassim, in the Little Triangle bordering the West Bank (a long way from the fighting in the south). This episode underlined the fact that the disproportionate use of force formed an important element in Israel's policy towards the Arab citizens throughout the period of the Military Government, which lasted until 1966. Ostensibly, the cause of this well documented massacre was the breaking of a curfew by the victims, who were not aware that a curfew had been imposed on their village and neighbouring Arab communities. In his book *The Arabs in Israel*, Sabri Jiryis, a former Israeli Palestinian lawyer, hints at a possible role played by the army Chief of Staff, Moshe Dayan, and the Commanding Officer of the Central Command, General Tzvi Tzur, in the orders given to the army and the Border Guard.[64]

A description of the events at Kafr Qassim was recorded by the Israeli military court:

> On the eve of the Sinai War . . . a battalion [brigade] attached to the Central Area Command was ordered to prepare itself to defend a section of the Israeli-Jordanian frontier . . . a unit [battalion] of the Frontier [Border] Guard was attached to the said battalion [brigade] and the commander of this Frontier Guard unit, Major Shmuel Melinki [Malinki], was placed under the orders of the battalion [brigade] commander, Brigadier [Colonel] Yshishkhar [Issachar] Shadmi. In the morning of 29 October 1956, the Commander of the Central Area, Major General Zvi Tsur [*sic*] informed Brigadier Shadmi and the other battalion commanders of the policy it had been decided to adopt toward the Arab population.
>
> The area commander went on to emphasize to the battalion commanders that the safeguarding of the operation in the south [the Suez campaign] required that the area coterminous with Jordan be kept absolutely quiet.
>
> . . . Brigadier Shadmi requested that he be empowered to impose a night curfew in the villages of the minorities in the area under his

command in order to: a) facilitate the movements of his forces, and b) prevent the population being exposed to injury by the reserve troops. These arguments convinced the area commander, who empowered Brigadier Shadmi to impose a curfew . . .

On the same day Brigadier Shadmi summoned Major Melinki [*sic*] to his headquarters, informed him of the duties of the unit under his command, and gave him instructions about the execution of these duties. One of the duties of this Frontier Guard unit was to impose the curfew . . . The two commanders agreed that the curfew should be enforced between 5 P.M. and 6 A.M.

The battalion [brigade] commander [Shadmi] also told the unit commander [Malinki] that the curfew must be extremely strict and that strong measures must be taken to enforce it. It would not be enough to arrest those who broke it – they must be shot. In explanation he said, 'A dead man [or according to other evidence "a few dead men"] is better than the complications of detention.'

When Melinki [*sic*] asked what was to happen to a man returning from his work outside the village, without knowing about the curfew, who might well meet the Frontier Guard units at the entrance to the village, Shadmi replied: 'I don't want any sentimentality' and 'That's just too bad for him.'[65]

A similar order was issued by Major Malinki to the reserve forces attached to his battalion, shortly before the curfew was enforced: 'No inhabitant shall be allowed to leave his home during the curfew. Anyone leaving his home shall be shot; there shall be no arrests.'[66] Explicit instructions were given by Malinki to his officers and policemen-soldiers to 'shoot to kill all who broke the curfew', including women and children.[67]

The evidence produced by *Hadashot* shows that it would be impossible to comprehend fully the extent of the massacre without knowing about the expulsion plan within which the slaughter was carried out. 'Operation Hafarferet' was a contingency plan formulated under the direction of Dayan, who six years earlier had stated before the Secretariat of Mapai that he supported the transfer of all Israeli Arabs out of the country.[68] This military plan was designed on the eve of the 1956 Sinai War to evacuate the Arab population of the Little Triangle by force, within the framework of a possible war with Jordan. Zionist mainstream thinking had always considered a Jewish state from the Mediterranean to the Jordan River as its ultimate aim. Throughout the early 1950s, leading establishment figures such as Dayan continued to speak of an opportunity that might enable Israel to conquer the West Bank.[69]

The destination of the would-be Arab evacuees cannot be ascertained absolutely; however, it is most likely that they were earmarked for removal to Jordan. Dan Horowitz (whose influential father, David Horowitz, was the Governor of the Bank of Israel), who, as a young journalist, had covered the trial of the officers involved in the Kafr Qassim massacre for the daily *Davar*, said that during the trial the main topic of conversation in the Jerusalem court's corridors had been 'Operation Hafarferet'. In his opinion, formed on the basis of the conversations and rumours then circulating in the court's corridors,

> Operation Hafarferet was designed to create a provocation among the Arab population, to force it to carry out illegal acts, and then to expel it. To frighten them and then to evacuate them. And it seems there were yearnings for this way of expelling Arabs.[70]

The Arab areas were under the Military Government, which usually imposed a nightly curfew from 8 P.M. until the next morning. Yet everything seemed to have been done by the army and the Military Government to make sure that the local villagers would not know about the altered time of the curfew, which had been brought forward, until a very short time before its coming into effect. The *mukhtar* of Kafr Qassim was informed of the new time of the curfew at 4.30 P.M., on the very day it was applied. When it came into effect half an hour later, the authorities must have known that dozens of villagers were still in different places of work outside the village, unaware of the fact that it had been imposed. Moreover, the very extreme instructions given by top commanders for enforcing the curfew and the brutal way in which these instructions were carried out give rise to the impression that the army had been preparing for something out of the ordinary toward the Arab residents of the

Little Triangle. The head of the Military Government's department on the army's General Staff, Mishael Shaham, testified at the trial of one of the commanders involved in the massacre:

> It was discussed on the morning [of 29 October] that if the curfew were to be brought forward, people would not know about that, since if the curfew were to be announced at a time sufficiently before its coming into effect, it would lose its impact.[71]

Only 30 minutes separated the announcement of the curfew from its harsh enforcement, and the villagers had been deliberately given no cause for the treatment they received. Within an hour of the curfew, between 5 and 6 P.M., forty-seven villagers returning from work were killed. The forty-three killed at the western entrance of Kafr Qassim included seven boys and girls and nine women between the ages of 18 and 61. The victims, returning from work mostly on bicycles, mule carts, or trucks (and a few on foot), through the main road, were stopped by Border Guard soldiers, who ordered them to get out of their transport and then shot them at a close range with automatic weapons and rifles. Several other villagers were wounded.[72]

Major Shmuel Malinki, the commander of the Border Guard battalion, which was attached to the army brigade of Colonel Issachar Shadmi and sent to the area to enforce the curfew, was given this contingency plan which had been worked out in anticipation of the outbreak of the 1956 war. This plan, named in the army's official records as plan 'S-59', was referred to by all army commanders involved as 'Operation Hafarferet'. The plan included the imposition of a general curfew on the Arab villages of the Little Triangle in the first stage, to be followed by the total evacuation of the inhabitants of these villages in the case of war with Jordan. In the course of the preparation for the 1956 war, 'Operation Hafarferet' was taken off the shelf, and army officers down to the level of company commanders were drilled in connection with its implementation. At the same time ordinary Border Guard policemen-soldiers learned about its existence through whispering and private conversations. Also significantly, the curfew which was ordered by the Commanding Officer of the Central Command, General Tzvi Tzur, was part of this contingency plan. During the trial of Shadmi, which opened on 2 November 1958, Colonel Haim Hertzog (later President of Israel), who in 1956 had been Commanding Officer of the Jerusalem District, testified that 'the order of [General] Tzur for the curfew was correct in the light of S-57, S-58, and S-59. The order for Shadmi's sector was logical. Although S-59 was cancelled, the background remained.'[73] Also, Dayan testified at the same trial of Shadmi that he 'knows about the above-mentioned documents [including S-59], and therefore he sees the order [for the curfew?] as certainly reasonable'.[74]

The implementation of Operation Hafarferet was apparently cancelled at the highest level in conjunction with the cancellation of the war plans against Jordan and 'Hafarferet' was put back on the shelf. It is not clear, however, when Operation Hafarferet was returned to the shelf and when Major Malinki, whose battalion was given the task of enforcing the curfew and was subsequently involved in the atrocities, received the cancellation notice. In any event, no alternative plan was made available to local commanders to replace Operation Hafarferet. Consequently, these commanders went along with the order imposing the strict, early curfew, which was an integral part of Operation Hafarferet. At his trial, Shadmi testified:

I had not requested that the curfew be brought forward. I had requested a curfew which had already been planned, and had been presented to me as a given fact according to a certain planning. I mean 'Hafarferet', which had been presented to me as a solution, and at a certain moment they told me that this would not be fulfilled.[75]

Without having an alternative plan, both Colonel Shadmi and Major Malinki still saw Operation Hafarferet as the right framework within which to impose the 5 P.M. curfew on the Little Triangle's villages on 29 October 1956. On the initiative of Malinki, in particular, Operation Hafarferet in fact had become the only framework for the curfew. In his instructions to his officers and policemen–soldiers, Malinki pointed out that the curfew was to be imposed according to Operation Hafarferet, although its accompanying stages, including 'arrests, confiscations and transfer of villages', would not be implemented.[76] Explicit orders were given by Malinki: to 'shoot to kill all who broke the curfew', including women and children; 'No inhabitant shall be allowed to leave his home during the curfew. Anyone leaving his home shall be shot; there shall be no arrests.'[77] In the circumstances, Malinki later testified in Shadmi's trial, Operation Hafarferet was most suitable, because the cancellation of the war situation in the Jordanian sector was not absolute:

> Shadmi said that our role is defensive, but there is room for change . . . If Shadmi was saying that the policy of [people] in high level was not to harm the Arab minority, and that the Arabs should be treated as citizens of the state, I would have cancelled my orders immediately. But there was no trace of these words [in Shadmi's orders].[78]

In the trial of Malinki, his defence counsel claimed that, in the atmosphere created by Operation Hafarferet, it was possible to interpret the extreme orders issued by Colonel Shadmi to Malinki as a preparation for expulsion, and this found its expression in the preparation of the military forces assembled at Kafr Qassim.[79]

It is most likely that the destination of the would-be Arab expellees was Jordan. According to David Rotlevi, the lawyer for Shalom 'Offer, a section commander who had been found directly responsible for murdering 41 Arab citizens at Kafr Qassim and sentenced on 16 May 1958 to fifteen years,

> 'Hafarferet' was a shelf plan that was taken off the shelf and put back on it. We referred to the operation as part of our defence line [in the trial], to show that it is possible to perceive the order [to shoot to kill all who broke the curfew?] as something that came from higher up within the tendency to expel Arabs . . . ['Hafarferet' was aimed at] setting up detention camps for the Arabs, so as not to cause chaos in a time of war and to enable them to flee eastward.

According to Rotlevi's version, there was an additional objective for the operation:

> 'Hafarferet' was designed to disrupt the transport system of the Jordanians across the border [on the West Bank] . . . by a movement of Israeli Arabs in these lines. In the material reaching my hands, components of Operation Hafarferet are mentioned explicitly: transfer of residents, confiscations, transfer of villages, concepts which are incompatible with temporary evacuation for security needs.[80]

Shalom 'Offer himself read a written statement in court in 1958: 'I understood that the order [to shoot to kill all who broke the curfew?] was right and it ought to be carried out, because the state wants to frighten the Arabs and perhaps to remove them.'

In an interview in 1991, 'Offer had this to add:

> In conversations we had in the [army] company [in 1956] in connection with the problems of the Arabs, operations which had been carried out against the Arab population in 1948 were very often mentioned, and it was explained that it was the policy of the government to remove the Arabs from their villages, in order that the state would not suffer from an internal enemy. Therefore actions were carried out in which forces entered Arab villages, and they were firing salvos at them, killing people and causing others to flee.[81]

The testimonies of both defendants and witnesses, in the trials which followed the Kafr Qassim massacre, quoted from the open sections of the military court protocols, make it clear that the curfew imposed on 29 October 1956 was understood in Malinki's Border Guard battalion as a preparation for the expulsion of the Arab inhabitants of the Little Triangle to Jordan. David Goldfield, a soldier in the platoon of Lieutenant Gabriel Dahan (who also was found guilty of murdering many villagers from Kafr Qassim and was sentenced to 15 years), testified in court: 'There were whisperings that they think to conquer the [Big] Triangle [the northern part of the West Bank, including the towns of Tulkarm, Qalqilyah, Jenin, and Nablus], and that the movement [of the Arabs] would be towards Transjordan. It was clear that the curfew was for military purposes.'[82] Benyamin Kol, a platoon commander in the battalion of Malinki, also testified in court:

> My feeling was that, in the light of the things said in the [army] leaflet, we were going here to [attack] Jordan, and that we here must give a 'flick', a blow to somebody, so that they would flee across the border, [there] they can do what they like.

Gabriel Dahan, the commander of the platoon that carried out the Kafr Qassim massacre, testified in court: 'The battalion commander said the next morning [after the massacre] at 6 A.M. we are leaving the place and letting the residents do as they wish. I understood that the intention was that they would flee to Jordan.'[83]

All the evidence produced in *Hadashot* points to the conclusion that Operation Hafarferet was designed to drive the Arab inhabitants of the Little Triangle out of the country. There is only one claim at variance with all the evidence presented to the Jerusalem court in 1958. Reserve General Avraham Tamir, who in 1956 was a Lieutenant Colonel in the army and OC (Officer Commanding) Operations of the Central Command and had taken part in working out the details of Operation Hafarferet, claimed in a 1991 interview that:

> Operation Hafarferet was prepared, under the direction of the Chief of Staff, in case a war broke out. The intention was to remove the villagers of the Little Triangle away from the border line, to take them behind and put them in detention camps, closed places. This is a normal action, which was used in the past also by the Americans and the Japanese. 'Hafarferet' was a plan which related to the question what do we do until the war begins . . . The people of Kafr Qassim should have been evacuated 10 kilometres behind . . .[84]

However, there is no evidence to substantiate Tamir's version. On the contrary, advocate Yosef 'Azran, who together with advocate Asher Levitzki acted as defence counsel for Major Malinki in 1958, said in a 1991 interview: '"Hafarferet" included the setting up of detention camps in which the residents would be concentrated, and then it would be possible to cause their expulsion eastward.' 'Azran said that he did not hear during the 1958 trials about the possibility of evacuating the Arabs to other locations inside Israel.[85]

Ben-Gurion, who was also the mentor of Dayan, must have been aware of Operation Hafarferet. It is not known, however, whether this secret military plan was discussed at cabinet level prior to the massacre of Kafr Qassim. It also would be difficult to gauge the extent of domestic and public opposition to this plan had the operation been implemented in full. What is known, however, is that when the Israeli army did succeed in exploiting the 1956 war to carry out a mass expulsion of Israeli Arabs from the Galilee to Syria at the same time no domestic opposition was recorded (see discussion below).

It seems that Ben-Gurion was already aware of the Kafr Qassim massacre and its gruesome details on the night of 29–30 October. His adviser, Shmuel Divon, met with the Commanding Officer of the Central Command, General Tzvi Tzur, a few hours after the massacre, at 2 A.M. on 30 October. Initially, efforts were made to hush up the matter and questions asked by Communist Knesset Member Tawfiq Tubi were expunged from the records. The massacre was kept secret for two weeks, but soon the news of the atrocities leaked out. Even as the Ben-Gurion government tried to cover up the extent of the massacre from the Jewish population, certain circles in Israel were spreading the news of the atrocities among the Arab citizens with the aim of 'encouraging' them to leave the country.[86] Ben-Gurion was against bringing the commanders responsible for the massacre to trial; only after realizing the extent of the publicity the news of the atrocities was attracting, did he acquiesce in the holding of the trials. For many years afterward he remained unhappy with these trials and their outcome.[87]

Eleven officers and soldiers of the Border Guard were court-martialled by the army. The trial was conducted in camera. However, according to the Hebrew newspaper *Haaretz* of 11 April 1957,

the eleven officers and soldiers who are on trial for the massacre of Kafr Qasem [*sic*] have all received a 50% increase in their salaries. A special messenger was sent to Jerusalem to bring the checks to the accused in time for Passover. A number of the accused had been given a vacation for the holiday.

In court, *Haaretz* went on:

> the accused mingle freely with the spectators; the officers smile at them and pat them on the back; some of them shake hands with them. It is obvious that these people, whether they will be found innocent or guilty, are not treated as criminals, but as heroes.[88]

Major Shmuel Malinki and Lieutenant Gabriel Dahan were found guilty of the killings and sentenced to 17 and 15 years respectively, a relatively light punishment for the major crime committed. Other officers and soldiers involved in the massacre also were given light sentences of various prison terms. The court placed the blame on one army unit alone, failing to trace up the chain of command those who had issued the orders and devised Operation Hafarferet. The official Israeli attitude to these convictions was even more telling. Various authorities made great efforts to lighten and reduce the sentences. The convicted men were soon pardoned, apparently with Ben-Gurion's blessing, and the last person had been released from prison by the end of 1959, about three years after the massacre. Equally remarkable, in September 1960 the municipality of Ramle was about to appoint Gabriel Dahan as an officer for Arab affairs; only after pressure from some local councillors was his appointment cancelled. However, the Jewish Agency later gave Dahan a job as manager of the sale of Israel's government bonds in a European capital.[89] Interviews thirty years later with the perpetrators of the massacre showed that some of them still felt little remorse.[90]

Perhaps the most revealing of all was the sentence given to the army commander, Colonel Shadmi. He earlier had been described by the first military court, which tried other commanders, as responsible for the killing to a greater extent than any of the other persons involved. However, the second court which tried Shadmi found him guilty (on 26 February 1959) of a mere 'technical error' and sentenced him to a reprimand and a fine of one piastre, perhaps as a symbol of exoneration for any person higher up. Shadmi was also a member of the Ahdut Ha'avodah party, a partner in the Mapai coalition, and apparently with influential supporters in the cabinet. Since 1959, 'Shadmi's piastre' has become proverbial among the Arab citizens of Israel.[91]

A mystery surrounded the attitude of Ben-Gurion and the special treatment he accorded Major Malinki. Although the court found Malinki guilty of murdering 43 Arab citizens, and sentenced him to 17 years in prison, he served only three years. He was pardoned and left prison in November 1959. Malinki, who was stripped of his rank by the court, was reinstated due to Ben-Gurion's personal insistence. Malinki's widow, Nehama, revealed many years later that while the trial was in progress her husband was released from prison to meet Ben-Gurion who told him that he was a 'living victim of the state', and pleaded with him not to reveal orders he was given by his superiors lest this implicate the cabinet and the general staff, and that he was promised an early release and reinstatement. As a result, Mrs Malinki said her husband agreed to take responsibility on himself.[92] Ben-Gurion not only treated Malinki respectfully and warmly and reinstated him; soon after his release, Malinki was invited to meet the prime minister who offered him a very important post: security officer of the new, top secret nuclear plant at Dimona, in the Negev. Malinki held this post for several years. Malinki also returned to serve in the army from which he retired in 1964 with the rank of colonel. After his release from prison, Malinki talked about a message he had received from Ben-Gurion, in which he had been requested to maintain silence in return for being granted a pardon.[93] However, in spite of the special treatment he had received, Malinki remained until his death in 1978 very bitter at the fact of having been brought to trial in the first place and having been made a scapegoat for the state's plans toward the Israeli Arabs.

Operation Hafarferet, although resulting in the infamous massacre of Kafr Qassim, was never implemented fully. Jordan gave Israel no pretext for action and the expulsions did not occur. It must be seen, however, as part of a general tendency among the politico-military establishment in Israel to exploit the 1956 war to carry out large-scale expulsions of Israeli Arab communities, particularly those situated along the borders, in the name of security. Although this operation was put back on the shelf and the Kafr Qassim massacre failed to drive the inhabitants of the Little Triangle to flight, the Israeli army did succeed in carrying out a mass expulsion at the same time in another part of the country. On 30 October 1956, only one day after the Kafr Qassim massacre, General Yitzhak Rabin, then Commanding Officer of the Northern Command, exploited the attack against Egypt in the south to carry out a mass expulsion of Israeli Arabs across the northern border into Syria. This little-known episode, which was revealed by Rabin himself in his 'Service Notebook', involved the expulsion to Syria of 2,000–5,000 inhabitants of the two villages Krad al-Ghannamah and Krad al-Baqqarah, to the south of Lake Hulah. These people had already been evicted from their native villages by the Israeli army in 1951 in the course of water diversion projects. Then (in 1951) the UN Security Council had passed a resolution calling on Israel to halt work on the water diversion projects and to enable the villagers to return to their homes. In the meantime, however, the Israeli army had blown up all the houses in the two villages in order to block their return. In his memoirs, Rabin wrote:

> I solved one problem in the north by exploiting the fighting against the Egyptians [in the south] and, in co-ordination with the United Nations, we [the army] transferred about 2,000 Arabs, who had been a burdensome security problem [across the Jordan River into Syria].[94]

It is not clear what Rabin meant by the phrase 'in co-ordination with the United Nations'. The UN Security Council earlier in 1951 had called on Israel to allow the return of these villagers to their homes. It seemed obvious, however, that he wished to justify publicly his role in this mass expulsion of Israeli Arabs by implying that it was not a unilateral action on the part of the Israeli army.

Referring to the same episode in an interview in early November 1982, on the 26th anniversary of the Sinai war, Rabin (then a member of the Knesset) said that 'during Operation Kadesh [the code name of the Sinai operation] in 1956, the IDF expelled between 3,000 and 5,000 Arab villagers, residents of the Galilee, to

Syria'. Rabin also claimed that Syria agreed to receive them. When Rabin was asked by the interviewer what was the reaction of the villagers to their expulsion, he replied: 'I did not take in this matter a democratic decision.'[95]

There were no international repercussions to this 1956 episode in the Galilee. International attention was focused on the fighting in the south and the Suez Canal crisis. It is likely that a single plan underlay this mass expulsion from Galilee and Operation Hafarferet: to exploit the war situation in the south and the invasion of Sinai for carrying out mass expulsions of Israeli Arabs in the name of security. Of course, the expulsion of over 40,000 residents from the Little Triangle would have been far more difficult than was the case of the few thousand people in the north, who were confined to an isolated area along the Syrian border and cut off from the outside world since their eviction from their villages by the Israeli army in 1951.

In 1964, eight years after the events of October 1956, the expulsion issue apparently resurfaced in a minor way, when Colonel Ariel Sharon (who earlier in the mid-1950s had been a protégé of Chief of Staff Dayan and Prime Minister Ben-Gurion), then Head of Staff of Northern Command, reportedly asked his staff to research the number of buses and trucks that would be required in case of war to 'transport' some 300,000 Israeli Arab citizens out of the country. According to Sharon's biographer, 'Uzi Benziman, the political editor of the Hebrew daily *Haaretz,* who exposed Sharon's secret plan, most of Sharon's subordinates refused to co-operate with him unless he showed them written orders from the army General Staff in Tel Aviv. They feared that if Sharon's plan ever were to be exposed it would greatly embarrass Israel.[96]

Very little is known about Sharon's plan. However, it seemed to have a number of things in common with Operation Hafarferet: it perceived the Israeli Arabs as a potential fifth column and 'superfluous people'. (In his book *Memalei Hapekudot* [The Executors] [1990], the Israeli historian Yigal 'Elam summed up the Kafr Qassim episode: 'In the Israeli consciousness [the Israeli Arabs] were seen as superfluous people.')[97] The plan originated with a very influential commander in the military establishment, a commander who had been closely associated with Ben-Gurion and Dayan throughout the 1950s. Sharon meant it to be a contingency plan that would be prepared and kept ready on the shelf to implement in case of war. In other words, Sharon intended to exploit a situation of war with an Arab country in order to drive Israeli Arab citizens out of the country in the name of security.

The 1956–57 Occupation of the Gaza Strip

The Gaza district is the southernmost section of the coastal plain of Palestine. Under the 1947 partition plan, this district was to form a part of the Palestine Arab state, but during the 1948 war much of the district was seized by, and annexed to, Israel. The Egyptians held Gaza City together with two other towns and several villages forming what came to be known as the Gaza Strip. The Strip is about 25 miles long and varies in width from four miles in the north to eight miles in the south. Its population trebled from eighty thousand in 1947 to nearly two hundred and forty thousand at the end of the 1948 war, creating a massive humanitarian problem of tens of thousands of refugees crammed into a tiny area. To provide for the needs of Palestinian refugees, the United Nations General Assembly in December 1949 established the United Nations Relief and Works Agency for Palestine Refugees (UNRWA).

The Palestinian refugees clung stubbornly to the right of return that was embodied in UN Resolution 194 (III) of 11 December 1948 and reaffirmed almost yearly by the General Assembly, the essence of which called for repatriation of, or compensation to, the refugees. However unfeasible repatriation may have seemed to outsiders, the refugees themselves believed they eventually would return to their homes and villages in what became Israel. Throughout the early 1950s, refugees continued to cross the armistice lines, 'infiltrating' back to their villages either to collect possessions and pick up unharvested crops or, in some cases, to raid Israeli settlements adjacent to the Strip.[98] In an effort to combat this persistent Arab 'infiltration', the Israelis carried out 'retaliatory' attacks against 'infiltrators' in general and civilian targets in the Gaza Strip in particular. These attacks resulted in many civilian deaths. According to the Israeli historian Benny Morris:

Israel's defensive anti-infiltration measures resulted in the death of several thousand mostly unarmed Arabs during 1949–56, the vast majority between 1949 and 1952 . . . Thus, upward of 2,700 Arab infiltrators, and perhaps as many as 5,000, were killed by the IDF, police, and civilians along Israel's borders between 1949 and 1956. To judge from the available documentation, the vast majority of those killed were unarmed 'economic' and social infiltrators.[99]

One major reason for the insistence with which Israel prosecuted its 'retaliatory' policy during these days, according to Livia Rokach,

was the desire of the Zionist ruling establishment to exercise permanent pressure on the Arab states to remove the Palestinian refugees of the 1948 war from the proximity of the armistice lines and to disperse them throughout the interior of the Arab world. This was not due, in the early fifties, to military considerations.[100]

The Egyptians, in fact, undertook strong repressive measures to suppress 'infiltration'.[101] Moreover, in 1954, against the background of escalating Israeli attacks for these 'infiltrations', the Egyptian President, Gamal 'Abdul Nasser (who had little wish to hang on to Gaza and its refugee population), fearing a potentially explosive situation in the Gaza Strip and the consequences of provoking the Israelis into a war for which he still was unprepared, considered a United States-UNRWA plan to settle the refugees in Sinai. However, following strong protests against this leaked scheme from the refugees, which culminated in two days of demonstrations and rioting in Gaza and the besieging of Egyptian government buildings and the burning of Egyptian vehicles, Nasser was forced to discard this Sinai scheme.[102]

Two years later, on 29 October 1956, the Israelis invaded the Gaza Strip and Sinai, holding both areas for four months before strong international, and especially American, pressure eventually forced them to evacuate both areas. Originally, the Israelis had every intention of staying in what their government considered to be an integral part of the Land of Israel. Foreign Minister Golda Meir told a

Mapai Party rally on 10 November 1956 that 'the Gaza Strip was an integral part of Israel'.[103]

Israel went to war in 1956 against Nasser's Egypt for several reasons which are beyond the scope of this discussion. For instance, in September 1955, after Egypt signed an arms deal with Czechoslovakia intended to secure its self-defence, the director of the Mossad, Isser Harel, proposed, according to Moshe Sharett's personal diary [entry for 3 October 1955],

> seriously and decisively . . . that [we] now carry out [our] plan for the occupation of the [Gaza] Strip . . . Today the situation has changed and new factors have emerged in favour of 'time for action'. First of all, there is the [recent] discovery of oil near the Strip . . . Its defence requires the occupation of the Strip . . . this consideration alone is sufficient for deciding [in favour of occupying the Strip] against the [consideration of potential] turbulence among the refugees.[104]

However, the strategic thinking of Israeli 'hawks' – those who agreed with Ben-Gurion's policy toward the Arabs – was an integral part of the decision to invade the Gaza Strip and Sinai in October. Already on the eve of the tripartite attack on Egypt, Ben-Gurion presented to the French Prime Minister Guy Mollet a far-reaching secret plan for creating a 'new order' in the Middle East.[105] The plan included, apart from the occupation and annexation of Sinai and the Gaza Strip, the overthrow of the Egyptian President, Nasser, the dismantling of Lebanon and the annexation of southern Lebanon to Israel and the creation of a Christian state in other parts of the country, and the partitioning of Jordan between Israel and Iraq: Israel would annex the West Bank and Iraq the East Bank, on condition that Iraq signed a peace accord with Israel and absorbed the Palestinian refugees in the camps on both banks of the Jordan River. According to Ben-Gurion's secret plan, the Suez Canal would be internationalized and Israel should control the access to the Gulf of Aqaba. He also believed that such a solution suited the interests of the British and the French and would consolidate their colonial positions in the Middle East and North Africa. However, after Israel captured the Gaza Strip and Sinai in early November

1956, Ben-Gurion was clearly disappointed with the demographic outcome of the war. Of the then 300,000 inhabitants of the Gaza Strip, 215,000 were listed as refugees, living in eight large camps. Gaza had nearly one-fourth of the total of about 900,000 Arab refugees from historic Palestine. According to Ben-Gurion's biographer Michael Bar-Zohar:

> Ben-Gurion was thrilled by this spectacular victory of the IDF. But when he visited the towns and refugee camps in Gaza and northern Sinai, a new reality was revealed before his eyes, which shocked him deeply: the Palestinians did not flee from the IDF as they had in 1948.[106]

According to *The New York Times* of 2 November 1956, some 1,000 Palestinians were thought to have fled from the Gaza Strip to Jordan and Syria. The true figure of the 1956 evacuees, however, may have been much higher, although clearly far smaller in comparison to the 1948 exodus, or even the subsequent 1967 one. *The Times* (London) correspondent had reported from Gaza on the evening of 1 November about Israeli bombing aircraft:

> darkly flashing Spitfires and Mustangs dived over Gaza and violet dust rose where shells and bombs had just burst . . . the Israelis were . . . putting the defences of Gaza out of action; . . . Earlier this afternoon that narrow gateway [the old road between Gaza and El Arish] was choked with fleeing Arab refugees, barefooted or riding distracted donkeys. Many of the refugees had taken to the sea in frail little boats. From this correspondent's point of vantage Gaza itself, seen through failing light and a screen of smoke, looked as if it had been emptied of the refugee multitude that was lodged inside it or in camps along the dunes after the Israel-Arab war of 1948.[107]

The vast majority of the refugees and other residents in the Strip, however, stayed put.

The Israeli military victory was swift and complete. The Israeli forces entered the Gaza Strip on 1 November, and Gaza City fell after a three-hour fight on the morning of 2 November. At 10 A.M. that morning Gaza was surrendered by the general commanding the 8th Division of the Egyptian army. By 3 November Israel's lightning conquest of Egypt's Sinai Peninsula and the Gaza Strip was almost complete. Arab resistance was neither strong nor organized. However, there is ample evidence to suggest that the Israeli occupation of 1956–57 was characterized by widespread brutality, especially in its early days, perhaps in order to terrorize the Palestinians into fleeing from the teeming refugee camps. In fact, the goal of dispersing the residents of the refugee camps was much in evidence throughout the 1956–57 occupation. Several hundred civilians were massacred by the Israeli army, the worst incidents of which were at Khan Yunis and Rafah on 3 November and 12 November 1956 respectively. Local residents believed that the motive behind these atrocities was the same one as at Dayr Yassin in 1948 – to intimidate the population of the Gaza Strip into fleeing.[108] One of the worst incidents took place at Khan Yunis on 3 November (four days after the Kafr Qassim massacre), when the Israeli army occupied the town and its neighbouring refugee camp. On the same day a twenty-four hour curfew was declared by the army, officially to check looting or disorder. A Khan Yunis resident, Abu Talal, recalled:

At dawn, just before 5 A.M., we heard voices in the street and the next thing I knew, someone was kicking our door down. All my family was gathered in the back room; my mother, my wife who was seven months pregnant, three brothers, two sisters and my two daughters, aged six and four . . . When the soldiers came in, we did not even know which country they were from. We had heard talk about British and French troops. One of the soldiers shouted in Arabic 'Stand still!' Then he opened fire on me with his rifle, hitting me in the elbow. I ran back into the room and my family held the door open for me. The soldiers fired again and my younger brother was killed instantly. My third brother was shot in the legs as he tried to climb out of the window. A second soldier then came into the room, took one look around and then emptied his rifle at random round the room. I was hit again in my leg and chest. Then they took all the women outside leaving the injured, myself and my brother, inside. My mother started to curse the soldiers and I remember one of them beating her with his rifle butt shouting 'Don't curse the Israelis, you should be cursing Abdel Nasser.'

39

I don't know why they chose my house. I wasn't anyone special. I heard later that the same thing had happened in many houses in our quarter alone. People were just chosen at random – ordinary people who had no connection with politics or the fedayeen. Outside I could hear a lot of shouting and shooting coming from the Khan in the town centre. Later, I heard that dozens of people had been lined up against the wall and shot in cold blood. Some say thousands were killed, but I think that 600 is probably nearer the truth. There were corpses everywhere, and because of the curfew, no-one could go out to bury them for about four days. This all took place that first morning. So much killing in such a short space of time. I heard that it was stopped by a senior officer.

I lay on my back on the floor of the bedroom in my house for 30 hours with blood everywhere . . . We couldn't get out to the clinic because of the curfew . . . When the curfew was finally lifted, I was able to get to the clinic on a stretcher. That's when I saw all the bodies in the streets.[109]

More accurate figures were produced by a subsequent investigation made by UNRWA officials who found that 275 Arab civilians were killed by the Israeli army at Khan Yunis and the adjacent refugee camp on 3 November and 111 other civilians were killed at the Rafah refugee camp, mostly on 12 November. UNRWA officials lodged a strong protest over these civilian deaths, in particular the murder of eight of their local employees.[110]

A correspondent for *The New York Times* reported from Gaza City on 26 November, a few weeks after the atrocities described above had taken place:

The Arab population of Gaza, still aching from the shock and wounds of war, appeared indifferent today to the effort of Israeli authorities to restore normal life to the Gaza Strip and integrate its economy with Israel. Arab shopkeepers, schoolteachers, students and idlers questioned during a tour of the town said they hoped the United Nations Emergency Force would soon replace Israeli occupation authorities and restore the Gaza Strip to Egypt. Many asked why International Red Cross personnel had not yet come to Gaza. The main reason the Gaza population is embittered against Israel is the loss of life and property that occurred in the three days following occupation of the region.[111]

The initial estimate of civilian casualties made by United Nations truce personnel seemed inaccurate. According to the same account in *The New York Times* of 2 December, 'United Nations truce personnel said their information indicated that 400 to 500 persons were killed at Khan Yunis during the first days of the occupation, 700 at Rafah and thirty to fifty in the town of Gaza.' UN truce officers explained that their information was gathered indirectly because the Israeli army restrictions prevented them from carrying out on-the-spot investigations. These officers also added that 'physicians of the United Nations Relief and Works Agency had compiled a list of eighty-four civilians known to have been killed in Rafah'. Moreover, Dr James Young, Director of the American Baptist Hospital in Gaza, said that his 'institution had treated 165 civilians wounded by Israeli troops, including 118 men, thirty-six women and eleven children. Eight have died of wounds, including two children.'[112]

The Israeli authorities claimed that many of the Arab deaths in the Gaza Strip resulted from the army's response to Palestinian resistance in the Gaza Strip in general and to disturbances at the Rafah refugee camp on 12 November in particular, and that the initial estimate of civilian casualties given by UN truce personnel was too high.[113] The refugees, on the other hand, asserted that local resistance had ceased when the Israelis arrived and that the victims were largely unarmed civilians.[114] On 28 November 1956, an Arab member of the Knesset (MK) asked for a debate on the Rafah incident. This motion was defeated by 62 votes to three. Although the ruling Mapai party blocked any debate on the Rafah killings, Prime Minister Ben-Gurion, speaking in the Knesset on the same day, said that the incident was the result of 'disturbances in which Israeli soldiers, after firing into the air, had been compelled to fire into the rioting mob. Forty-eight refugees had been killed and a number wounded.' Ben-Gurion accused the Communist Party MKs of being 'traitors'.[115] In March 1957, after the Israelis withdrew from the Strip, a mass grave was unearthed at Khan Yunis containing the bodies of forty Arabs who had been shot in the back of the head after their hands had been tied.[116]

There were other atrocities committed by the Israeli army during the 1956 war or shortly after. On 4 August 1995, the Hebrew daily

Ma'ariv revealed some details of large-scale atrocities for the first time. An extensive investigative report by Israeli journalist Ronal Fisher, based on Israeli academic research, exposed atrocities that had been committed by the elite paratroop battalion 890 commanded by Raphael Eitan. (Eitan was to become army Chief of Staff from 1978 to 1983, and was criticized by the Israeli Kahan Commission of Inquiry for his failure to try to prevent the September 1982 massacres at Sabra and Shatilla in Beirut. He is currently the leader of the right-wing Tzomet Party and Minister of Agriculture and Environment in the Likud cabinet of Binyamin Netanyahu.) Apparently in late October and early November 1956 Eitan gave the order that resulted in his troops murdering some 273 unarmed Egyptian prisoners during the Sinai War. This figure included 49 Egyptian civilian road workers, who happened to be in the wrong place at the wrong time. They all were executed by a platoon headed by Captain Arie Biro, who subsequently became a brigadier general in the Israeli army.[117] In an interview published in *Ma'ariv* on 4 August 1995, Biro provided further details about these atrocities, talking openly and even unrepentantly about his personal involvement in them.[118] The 49 Egyptian road workers, all dressed in white *galabias* (the loose, shirt-like garment that is typical dress for the male population of Egypt), were picked up by Battalion 890 on the eastern side of the Mitla Pass on 29 October and were taken prisoner. On 30 October their hands were tied and they were all executed by a platoon headed by Captain Biro.[119] At Ras Sudar, another 56 Egyptians were shot dead, including 20 unarmed prisoners murdered with their hands tied behind their backs. Army Chief of Staff Moshe Dayan apparently knew about the Ras Sudar incident but did nothing to punish the perpetrators.[120] During the last stages of the war, on the road from Ras Sudar to Sharm El-Shaykh another 168 unarmed Egyptian and Sudanese soldiers were shot dead, many of them in the back.[121]

During the five-month occupation, the Israelis had every intention of staying in the Gaza Strip. Within four days of taking over the area, *The New York Times* reported, 'Israel has started integrating the conquered territory into the nation'; workmen were busy laying new railroad tracks between Israeli territory and Gaza. At the same time plans were being formulated by the occupation authorities in Gaza to make the switch over from Egyptian currency to Israeli money.[122] Even shortly before their evacuation, they managed to form a new Municipal Council composed of notables who were amenable to their policies.[123] Also during the brief occupation of 1956–57, a secret committee was set up by Prime Minister Ben-Gurion to consider proposals for resettling elsewhere hundreds of thousands of refugees from the Gaza Strip. Little is known about the ideas put forward by this committee, which was headed by 'Ezra Danin, who, at the same time, was deeply involved in the Libyan resettlement scheme. In a letter to Eliahu Sasson, Israel's ambassador to Italy (who was at the time involved in the scheme of purchasing the lands of former Italian settlers in Libya for resettlement of Palestinian refugees in that country), dated 10 December 1956, Danin explained that Prime Minister Ben-Gurion approved the appointment of the committee and that Finance Minister Levi Eshkol approved the allocation of financial resources for the work to be carried out by the committee, the members of which would be Haim Gvati (Director General of the Ministry of Agriculture and later to be Minister of Agriculture), Yitzhak Levi (Secretary General of the Prime Minister's Office), Shmuel Divon (Prime Minister Ben-Gurion's adviser on Arab affairs), Yitzhak 'Elam (Director General of the Ministry of Labour, 1951–1958), and Ra'anan Weitz (Yosef Weitz's son), director-general of the Jewish Agency's Land Settlement Department.[124] It is not clear whether there was any direct link between this committee and Danin's Libyan operation. Only patchy information is available on the Israeli intention to remove Palestinian refugees from the Gaza Strip during this short period. Yosef Nahmani, the top Jewish National Fund executive in Galilee, who had been involved in the 'Operation Yohanan' transfer scheme, wrote to his senior colleague Yosef Weitz on 22 December 1956:

> You certainly know that a committee headed by 'Ezra Danin is considering proposals to resettle the refugees of Gaza. If Gaza remains in Israeli hands together with its refugees this would put a great burden on

the economy, development and security of Israel ... Your absence denies the JNF representation on the committee.[125]

The official Israeli position had always been that there could be no returning of the Palestinian refugees to Israeli territory, and that the only solution to the problem was their resettlement in the Arab states or elsewhere. If Israel intended to annex the Gaza Strip in late 1956, the official Israeli reasoning was that a solution must be found to the critical refugee problem. Indeed, the idea of relocating the refugees residing in Gaza to the Sinai Peninsula was raised in internal debates. For instance, on 23 December 1956 Premier Ben-Gurion cut short a cabinet session in Jerusalem to have a lunch meeting with President Yitzhak Ben-Tzvi and his wife Rahel Yanait. The latter was a prominent Mapai leader, who would subsequently join the Whole Land of Israel movement advocating the annexation of the West Bank and the Gaza Strip to Israel. The 23 December conversation at the presidential residence, which focused on the future of the Gaza Strip and the Sinai Peninsula, contained the following exchange between the Prime Minister and Rahel Yanait:

> **Ben-Gurion:** 'We will hold on to Gaza. However we have no need of the 300 thousand refugees, it would be better that UNRWA deals with them.'
>
> **Rahel Yanait:** 'You should propose a constructive settlement.'
>
> **Ben-Gurion:** 'These things are abstracts. Would you suggest the resettlement of the refugees of Gaza in Israel?'
>
> **Rahel Yanait:** 'We would settle them in El Arish [in Sinai].'
>
> **Ben-Gurion:** 'Do you know that in 1920 an expedition went to investigate whether or not El Arish was suitable for [Jewish] settlement and the conclusion was negative. How would we settle them in El Arish if the land is not suitable?'
>
> **Rahel Yanait:** 'But things have changed since. Today there are new and modern methods for discovering water and improving the soil.'

Rahel Yanait and the president also tried to persuade Ben-Gurion not to yield to Eisenhower's pressure and evacuate the Sinai Peninsula. An implied threat by the United States of economic sanctions against Israel had already forced Premier Ben-Gurion to agree to withdraw from Sinai when a United Nations force moved into the Suez Canal zone. In his speech to the nation, broadcast on 9 November 1956, Ben-Gurion even conceded that one of the main objectives of the offensive against Egypt – the 'liberation of homeland' territory – had not been achieved.[126] Ben-Gurion replied to Ben-Tzvi and Rahel Yanait that Israel could not fight two superpowers – the United States and the Soviet Union – and therefore would be forced to evacuate Sinai. However, he still regarded Gaza as part of the 'homeland' and wanted, he said, to hold on to the Gaza Strip.[127] Judging by his past record before and during 1948 and his previous vigorous advocacy of Palestinian transfer, it seems that Ben-Gurion's scepticism towards Yanait's argument in favour of relocating the refugees from the Gaza Strip to Sinai had more to do with political realism and the need to evacuate Sinai, in the face of the strong American-Soviet pressure, than with any fundamental rejection of the idea of removing the refugees from the Gaza Strip, away from Israel and the 1949 cease-fire lines.

The same idea of dispersing the refugees residing in the Strip was frequently raised by top officials of the Foreign Ministry, which at the time was headed by Golda Meir.

In his personal diary entry for 20 November 1956, former Foreign Minister Moshe Sharett cited a cable sent to him in India by Walter Eytan, Director General of the Foreign Ministry. Eytan explained in his cable that 'the problem of the refugees [in Gaza] is very pressing . . . there is a need now for more far-reaching actions with the aim of ensuring the future'. In response Sharett – who was then bitter about having been manoeuvred out of office by Ben-Gurion and had opposed the occupation of Gaza largely because of the hundreds of thousands of refugees in it – recorded in the same entry of his diary his amazement at the content of Eytan's cable: 'What is a far-reaching action – the transfer of the refugees to Iraq or their resettlement in Israel? The two solutions are impractical'; neither Iraq nor Israel was prepared to accept them.[128] Eytan did not explain what he meant by 'far-reaching actions'; it seems that in Jerusalem Ben-Gurion and Golda Meir were determined to keep Sharett in the dark, mainly because of his known opposition to the

1956 war. Sharett, on the other hand, felt deceived and humiliated for not being informed about the impending attack on Egypt, and this might also explain his amazement at the suggestion of 'far-reaching actions' in connection with the refugees in the Gaza Strip.

About the same time, another senior official of the Foreign Ministry and Minister plenipotentiary to the Scandinavian countries, Haim Yahil, wrote a secret letter from Stockholm to Walter Eytan in Jerusalem. He strongly advocated the annexation of the Gaza Strip to Israel. Yahil, at the same time, totally rejected a proposal that Eli'ezer Livneh, a Mapai colleague and member of the First and Second Knessets of 1949-55, put forward in *Haaretz* on 22 November, calling for the annexation of the Gaza Strip to Israel together with all of its Palestinian residents, including the refugees. Describing Livneh's proposal as totally impractical, Yahil instead suggested that the refugees in the Gaza Strip be divided into three groups: the first group should be relocated to and settled in Sinai; the second group would be settled in Israel, outside the Gaza Strip; and the third group should be settled in Gaza itself. No specific figures were mentioned in Yahil's proposal as to how many refugees should be included in each category.[129] A month later, Yahil returned to the proposal in another secret letter to Eytan, dated 26 December. After the annexation of the Gaza Strip to Israel, Yahil explained, Israel then would absorb some of the refugees residing in the Strip 'and the rest of them would be settled in Sinai or some other Arab country through the payment of compensation on our part'. No less important, for Yahil,

a solution to the refugee problem is necessary not only for political and humanitarian reasons – as our contribution to a settlement – but also for [Jewish] settlement reasons. Here the incorporation of Gaza to Israel would be secure and durable only if certain Jewish settlements would also be in this area, and how could we carry out settlement in the area if it was full of refugee camps.[130]

In private and internal discussions, senior officials of the Foreign Ministry and the Prime Minister's Office, including members of the committee set up to deal with the Palestinian refugees in the occupied Gaza Strip, emerged as the strongest advocates of en- couraging the refugees to emigrate from Gaza to countries overseas. The same officials also realized that neither Egypt nor Syria had any intention of opening their borders for the masses of refugees in Gaza. There were three men at the centre of these discussions: 'Ezra Danin, a senior adviser on Arab affairs at the Foreign Ministry and head of the Gaza Strip's refugee committee; Shmuel Divon, a member of the same refugee committee and Ben-Gurion's adviser on Arab affairs; and Ya'acov Hertzog, the son of the Chief Rabbi of Israel and a brother of Haim Hertzog, who later served as president of Israel, 1983–1993.

During the 1956–57 occupation of Gaza, Ya'acov Hertzog, in his official capacity as Israel's minister plenipotentiary in Washington, as well as other officials of the Foreign Ministry in Jerusalem and the Israeli embassy in Washington, were involved in the efforts to encourage the emigration of refugees from Gaza to countries over- seas, including the United States and Latin American countries. It is inconceivable that Ya'acov Hertzog's boss in the Washington embassy, Abba Eban, Israel's ambassador to Washington (later to be foreign minister), was not privy to these official efforts that were presided over by Walter Eytan and his boss Foreign Minister Golda Meir. Gershon Avner, director of the Foreign Ministry's U.S. Division, wrote a secret letter to Hertzog, dated 24 January 1957, telling him about 'a new attempt in dealing with the problem of refugees': the 'rehabilitation' of Gaza's refugees through 'the Inter- governmental Committee for European Migration (ICEM)'.[131] Avner had been the director of the Foreign Ministry's West Europe Division between 1948 and 1952. (He subsequently became ambassador to Norway, 1962–63; ambassador to Canada, 1963–67; Secretary to the Israeli Cabinet, 1974–77; and President of Haifa University, 1977–81.) In December 1951 the ICEM had been set up, on the initiative of the United States, at a meeting in Brussels in which sixteen nations took part, to be 'responsible for the move- ment of migrants, including refugees, for whom arrangements could be made with the governments of the countries concerned'. In his letter to Hertzog, Avner explained that ' 'Ezra Danin was en- thusiastic about this plan which fits in with Israel's effort to move a

number of refugees to resettle permanently, in the hope that this example would encourage others [refugees to emigrate].' Avner added:

> As is known, we are prepared to pay compensation to refugees who [take
> advantage of] this possibility. Assuming that it [were] possible to reach an
> agreement with the ICEM, there would be a need for a gentle whisper-
> ing activity in order to move initially a number of families to take this
> road, but it is still early [to know whether this would work].

The key to success, according to Avner, was to secure the support of
the U.S. representative on the ICEM and his government's influence on this organization. Avner also suggested that the Israeli
embassy in Washington should discuss exploiting these ideas to the
full.[132] At this stage the Israeli government was still insisting that
under no circumstances could it agree to the return to Egypt of the
Gaza Strip.

A few weeks later Moshe Bartur, Director of the Economic
Department of the Foreign Ministry (later to be Deputy Director
General of the Foreign Ministry, 1958–61; Ambassador to the
UNO European Bureau, 1961–65; and Ambassador to Japan,
1966–72), wrote a strictly secret memorandum, dated 10 February
1957, suggesting the following:

> Since we are determined to stay in the Strip in one way or another, we
> have in fact taken responsibility for the 200,000 refugees. It cannot be
> assumed that we would be able to cause their departure except through
> an orderly process of resettlement in and outside Israel. For the sake of
> that we need the assistance of the UN and USA.

To achieve this aim, Bartur went on, the Israeli administration in the
Strip should assume a joint responsibility with UNRWA for the
refugees in Gaza (an Israeli-UN 'condominium', in his words) and
set up an international committee, the composition of which would
remain private, for working out a final solution to the problem
through resettlement. Bartur did not specify how many refugees
would be resettled in the Gaza Strip after its annexation by Israel or
how many of them would be resettled overseas.[133]

By March 1957, Israel, under intense international pressure, was preparing to withdraw from Gaza. Reporting to the Knesset on 7 March, Prime Minister Ben-Gurion stressed that under any administration 'the Gaza Strip would be a source of trouble as long as the refugees had not been resettled elsewhere'.[134] By this stage, the United Nations had agreed to station an emergency force (UNEF) between Israel and Egypt in the Gaza Strip.

On 12 March 1957, shortly before Israel was forced to evacuate the Strip, the U.S. Division of the Foreign Ministry received an undated memorandum from Yehuda Harry Levine, a counsellor at the Israeli embassy in Washington who was also in charge of information, suggesting that Israel should undertake a unilateral, practical, and dramatic measure which would demonstrate that the Arab leaders were deliberately preventing a solution to the Palestinian refugee problem. The Oxford University-educated Levine (who had been Palestine [and later Middle East] correspondent for the *Daily Herald* [London], 1929–47; and Director of the English Propaganda Department of the Jewish National Fund, and subsequently became Director of the Information Department of the Foreign Ministry and ambassador to Denmark) explained that he had just met the editor of *Harper's* magazine, John Fisher, who had expressed an opinion in favour of a similar proposal. According to Levine, Fisher assumed that for the first time since 1948 the refugees in Gaza were now free of pressures from Arab leaders, and consequently as a first step and gesture of goodwill, Israel should offer compensation to a number of refugees in Gaza – he mentioned 5,000 people – that would enable their relocation to and resettlement in other countries, with the UN's assistance.[135] In May 1949, during the last stage of the Palestinian refugee exodus, *Harper's* published an article by Eliahu Ben-Horin, a Zionist Revisionist publicist and advocate of Arab transfer since the early 1940s, entitled 'From Palestine to Israel'. The then editor of *Harper's* noted that in an earlier article of the magazine's December 1944 issue, Ben-Horin had advocated a plan that at the time 'looked far-fetched . . . that the Arabs of Palestine be transferred to Iraq and resettled there. Now, with thousands of Arab refugees from Palestine facing a dismal future, the transfer idea appeared to be a likely bet . . . in view of the sound

49

character of Mr Ben-Horin's earlier judgements and prophecies, we feel we can bank on his word about present-day Israel: 'It works.' '[136]

Two days later, on 14 March 1957, another senior foreign ministry official, Hanan Bar-On (later to be Consul General in Ethiopia), wrote a secret letter to Hertzog and Divon:

> Following-through our conversation, the outlines of the plan for encouraging the emigration of refugees from the [Gaza] Strip are as follows:
>
> 1) the setting up of an organization in the United States or Latin America, whose aim is to encourage the emigration of refugees to countries of the world, including countries of the American continent, without becoming involved in the political problems of the Middle East;
>
> 2) the organization must be based first of all on the leaders of Arab migrants in Latin America and the United States; however this could also include in it other elements, such as Christian clergy and perhaps even Jewish factors who are not publicly known as distinguished sympathizers of Israel (Lessing Rosenwald?);[137]
>
> 3) the organization should operate on a scale similar to that of HIAS [the Hebrew Immigrant Aid Society] and the JOINT [American Jewish Joint Distribution Committee] in the years before the Second World War, that is to say, it should not only try to concern itself with the matter of financing the emigration as such, but first of all to conduct negotiation with governments and various bodies in the world for finding absorption places in various countries. The proposed body should operate as a political body based on humanitarian principles, without pretending to represent the refugees or any other Middle Eastern community. In addition to this the body should work in order to bring about the emigration of refugees without religious distinction, in spite of the fact that most of the activists of the organization would, undoubtedly, naturally be Christians;
>
> 4) Notwithstanding that the financing of the first steps of such an organization would, undoubtedly, have to come from our own sources, it is possible to assume that with the help of various fund-raising appeals it would be possible, in time, for these to finance the lion's share of the organization's expenditure. Clearly this could not include the cost of rehabilitating the refugees in their new countries of residence, but

perhaps it would be possible to find solutions for this in the framework of UNRWA;

5) Despite the fact that the proposed organization should be based first of all on Arab elements, the action of organization and guidance must, undoubtedly, be made by Israeli and Jewish bodies and personalities jointly, of course with adequate camouflage and concealment.

In summing up the outlines of his proposed plan, Bar-On wrote:

The above are only few initial thoughts, and it is possible, no doubt, to find impractical flaws in them, but it seems to me that the central idea, that is to say, the setting up of an organization which would attempt by various means to persuade governments to open their borders for emigration, even if limited, is likely to give us not insignificant advantages in the sphere of our dealing with the refugee problem in general and the Arab refugees in particular.[138]

In the same month in which Israel was forced to evacuate the Gaza Strip, Danin, the head of the official committee set up to consider relocation and resettlement of the Gaza refugees, complained in a letter to David Shaltiel, Israel's ambassador to Brazil, that 'it was possible to operate a great deal in Gaza, but we did not receive permission and money for it'.[139] Perhaps, because the 1956–57 occupation was short-lived and uncertain, the Israeli goal of dispersing the refugees under their control through transfer and resettlement schemes was not prosecuted vigorously. Still, after the withdrawal from Sinai and the Gaza Strip, Danin and other Foreign Ministry officials were back dealing with the Libyan scheme, which envisaged the transfer of Israeli-Palestinians and Palestinian refugees to Libya. The Israeli goal of dispersing the hundreds of thousands of refugees residing in the Gaza Strip – constituting over three quarters of the Strip's population – would indeed remain constant for many years.

Notes to Chapter 1

1. Quoted in David Gilmour, *Dispossessed: The Ordeal of the Palestinians* (London: Sphere Books Limited, 1982), p. 92.
2. Segev, *1949*, p. 44. Yadin served as chief of operations during the 1948 war. In 1977 he entered politics, founding the 'Democratic Movement for Change' which obtained seats in the Knesset, thus enabling Yadin to become deputy premier in Menahem Begin's government.
3. Quoted in ibid., p. 89. Knesset debate, 8 January 1949.
4. Cited in Benziman and Mansour, *Dayarei Mishne*, pp. 19, 51–57; Amos Elon, 'The Jews' Jews', *The New York Review of Books*, 10 June 1993, p. 16.
5. Quoted in 'Uzi Benziman and 'Atallah Mansour, *Dayarei Mishne* [Subtenants] (Jerusalem: Keter Publishing House, 1992), pp. 19, 51–7. See also Reinhard Wiemer, 'Zionism and the Arabs after the Establishment of the State of Israel', in A. Schölch (ed.), *Palestinians Over the Green Line* (London: Ithaca Press, 1983), p. 36.
6. Benziman and Mansour, *Dayarei Mishne*, pp. 56–57.
7. Ibid., p. 57.
8. Ibid.
9. Quoted in ibid., p. 57.
10. Quoted in Yosef Weitz, *Yosef Nahmani: Ish Hagalil* [Yosef Nahmani: Man of the Galilee] (Ramat Gan: Massada, 1969), pp. 118–19, 134.
11. Ibid. See also pp. 15–16 on Yosef Weitz and 'Operation Yohanan'.
12. Ibid., pp. 121 and 134.
13. See *New Outlook* 1, no. 1 (July 1957), p. 15.
14. Yigal Allon, *Masakh Shel Hol* [A Curtain of Sand] (Tel Aviv: Hakibbutz Hameuhad Press, third edition, 1968), p. 324.
15. Ibid., p. 334.
16. Quoted in Baruch Kimmerling and Joel S. Migdal, *Palestinians: The Making of a People* (New York: The Free Press, 1993), p. 183.
17. Sabri Jiryis, *The Arabs in Israel* (New York: Monthly Review Press, 1976), p. 82.
18. Quoted in Morris, *Israel's Border Wars*, pp. 157–58.
19. Quoted in ibid., p. 158.
20. Quoted in ibid., pp. 162–63.
21. Quoted in ibid., pp. 163–64.
22. Quoted in ibid., p. 164.
23. Ibid., note 160, p. 164.
24. Cited in ibid., p. 164.

25. Ibid.
26. Cited in Benny Morris, *1948 and After* (Oxford: Clarendon Press, 1990), p. 257.
27. Morris, *1948 and After*, pp. 258–59.
28. Cited by Yehuda Litani in *Hadashot*, 7 December 1990.
29. Quoted in Ilan Halevi, *A History of the Jews* (London: Zed Books, 1987), pp. 203–204.
30. Morris, *1948 and After*, p. 269.
31. Morris, *Israel's Border Wars*, p. 154.
32. Ibid.
33. Ibid., p. 155.
34. Ibid., pp. 155–56.
35. Ibid., p. 157.
36. Ibid.
37. Cited in Maddrell, *The Beduin of the Negev*, p. 6.
38. Cited in Christina Jones, *The Untempered Wind: Forty Years in Palestine* (London: Longman, 1975), p. 218.
39. On this little known massacre, see also Adnan Amad (ed.), *Israeli League for Human and Civil Rights – The Shahak Papers* (Beirut: Near East Ecumenical Bureau for Information and Interpretation, n.d.), p. 99, cited by Kurt Goering, 'Israel and the Bedouin of the Negev', *Journal of Palestine Studies* 9, no. 1 (Autumn 1979), p. 5.
40. Quoted in Jiryis, *The Arabs in Israel*, p. 258, n. 32.
41. Quoted in Maddrell, *The Beduin of the Negev*, p. 7.
42. For Markovsky's very secret report, dated 30 June 1949, see ISA, Foreign Ministry, 2401/19a.
43. See Segev, *1949*, p. 33.
44. Jiryis, *The Arabs in Israel*, p. 82.
45. Much of Lifschitz's report dealt with the question of land ownership in Kafr Qare'a. According to his report, 80 per cent of the 12,000 dunums of land previously belonging to the village now were considered legally as 'absentees' property', despite the fact that the village inhabitants had never left their homes. For Lifschitz's report, see ISA, Foreign Ministry, 2402/5. In the event, however, Kafr Qare'a was not evacuated, although some of its residents may have left for Jordan.
46. Segev, *1949*, p. 61.
47. For Tubi's statement, see Natanel Lorch (ed.), *Major Knesset Debates, 1948–1981*, vol. 2 (London: University Press of America, 1993), p. 415.

48. Segev, *1949*, p. 61.
49. MM to *'Al-Hamishmar*, and *'Al-Hamishmar* to Mapam Knesset faction, 20 June 1950, cited in Morris, *Israel's Border Wars*, p. 148.
50. Masalha, *Expulsion of the Palestinians*, chapter 5.
51. Weitz's Diary, 12 November 1954, p. 271.
52. Weitz, *Yomani*, vol. 4, appendix no. 5, p. 365. Although the 22 families from Jish in the Galilee had lost interest in the emigration scheme to Argentina in early 1953, Weitz himself was still attempting in 1954 to promote the scheme in internal discussions with senior officials. For instance, Weitz met Prime Minister Moshe Sharett on 4 May 1954 and reported to him on his efforts to encourage the emigration of Palestinians from Israel, and more specifically the inhabitants of Jish in the Galilee, the residents of al–Tira and Qalansawa, two villages in the Little Triangle, and various categories of townspeople. During this meeting Weitz suggested that the sum of 400,000 dinars be paid in compensation for the land and property of those (mainly townspeople) willing to emigrate from Israel. See Moshe Sharett, *Yoman Ishi* [Personal Diary], vol. 2 (Tel Aviv: Sifriyat Ma'ariv, 1978), p. 481.
53. See from M. Sasson, Foreign Ministry Middle East Department, to Foreign Minister, Most Secret letter, dated 13 March 1952, in ISA Foreign Ministry, 2402/5. Copies of the letter were also sent to Foreign Ministry Director General (Walter Eytan); Prime Minister's Adviser for Arab Affairs (Yehoshu'a Palmon) and Israel's ambassador to Turkey (Eliahu Sasson).
54. Ibid. In 1950 the number of Jews in Libya was estimated at 8,000. See Shukri Ghanem, 'The Libyan Economy Before Independence', in G. Joffe and K. S. McLachlan (eds.), *Social and Economic Development of Libya* (London: Menas Press, 1982), p. 148.
55. *Al-Rabitah*, nos. 9–10.
56. Sasson's letter to Foreign Minister Sharett, dated 13 March 1952.
57. Weitz, *Yomani*, vol. 4, entry for 13 May 1954, p. 285.
58. Ibid.
59. 'Ezra Danin, *Tzioni Bekhol Tnai* [Zionist in All Conditions], vol. 1 (Jerusalem: Kiddum, 1987), p. 323.
60. Ibid., p. 324.
61. Ibid., p. 325.
62. Ibid., pp. 346–47, citing his letter to Rabin, Israeli ambassador to Washington, dated 20 July 1969.
63. See Rubik Rosenthal, 'Operation Hafarferet: Or How the Massacre

of Kafr Qassim was Really Born', *Hadashot*, Supplement, 25 October 1991.

64. Jiryis, *The Arabs in Israel*, p. 151.

65. Quoted in Jiryis, *The Arabs in Israel*, pp. 140–41. Some of the inaccuracies found in this book concerning army ranks and units may have been the result of the fact that this book originally was translated from Hebrew into Arabic and then from Arabic into English.

66. Quoted in ibid., p. 141.

67. Ibid., p. 142.

68. See Yehuda Litani in *Hadashot*, 7 December 1990, p. 4.

69. Morris, *Israel's Border Wars*, pp. 11–12. There was another indication that an attack on Jordan, in conjunction with the attack on Egypt, may have been considered by influential circles within the Israeli establishment. On 9 July 1956 the Israeli newspaper *Lamerhav*, the official organ of the Ahdut Ha'avodah party (which was represented in the Knesset by 10–12 members and participated in the coalition government of Ben-Gurion and later in 1965 formed with the Mapai party the Labour Party), published an editorial describing the Hashemite kingdom of Jordan as an artificial entity, which had been carved out of the 'Land of Israel' by British imperialism, and incapable of surviving. More importantly and ominously, *Lamerhav* denounced, as a major 'crime' committed against the Jewish people, 'the annexation of large and vital lands from the western Land of Israel (i.e., the West Bank) to the Jordanian kingdom'. The editorial went on:

> All the indications point to the nearing of the decisive hour for the fate of this [Jordanian] state, and it should be known that Israel cannot stand with arms crossed, and it ought not do that, in the face of possible developments and the possibility of bringing about great changes to the border, on its eastern frontiers, through the escalation of conflict among the powers in the region.

70. Quoted in Rosenthal, 'Operation Hafarferet'.

71. Quoted in ibid.

72. Jiryis, *The Arabs in Israel*, pp. 143–47.

73. Quoted in Rosenthal, 'Operation Hafarferet'.

74. Ibid.

75. Ibid.
76. Ibid.
77. Quoted in Jiryis, *The Arabs in Israel,* pp. 141–42.
78. Quoted in Rosenthal, 'Operation Hafarferet'.
79. Ibid.
80. Ibid.
81. Quoted in Rosenthal, 'Operation Hafarferet'.
82. Quoted in ibid.
83. Ibid.
84. Quoted in ibid.
85. Ibid.
86. Jiryis, *The Arabs in Israel,* pp. 147–48.
87. Rosenthal, 'Operation Hafarferet'.
88. Quoted in Sami Hadawi, *Bitter Harvest* (New York: Olive Branch Press, 1991, fourth edition), p. 156.
89. See Daliah Karpel in *Ha'ir,* 10 October 1986; Rosenthal, 'Operation Hafarferet'; Jiryis, *The Arabs in Israel,* pp. 149–50.
90. Karpel in *Ha'ir,* 10 October 1986.
91. Jiryis, *The Arabs in Israel,* pp. 152–53. *The New York Herald Tribune* of 27 February 1959 reported that Shadmi was sentenced to 'a token fine of two cents for exceeding his authority by imposing an absolute curfew on an Arab village in Israel in 1956'.
92. *Ha'ir,* 10 October 1986.
93. Rosenthal, 'Operation Hafarferet'.
94. Yitzhak Rabin, *Pinkas Sherut* [Service Notebook; memoirs, written in collaboration with Dov Goldstein] (Tel Aviv: Sifriyat Ma'ariv, 1979), vol. 1, p. 97.
95. See Eli Tabor in *Yedi'ot Aharonot,* 2 November 1982, p. 7.
96. See Yossi Melman and Dan Raviv, 'Expelling Palestinians', *The Washington Post,* 7 February 1988; Yossi Melman and Dan Raviv in *Davar,* 19 February 1988. Sharon himself denied the Benziman account in a letter published in *Davar.* However, as we shall see, this episode appears to be consistent with Sharon's record in the eviction of Arab communities from the Rafah area in 1969–1972 and his general advocacy of Arab transfer from the Palestinian territories occupied in 1967.
97. Quoted in Morris, *Israel's Border Wars,* p. 417, note 3.
98. On Arab refugee 'infiltration', see Morris, *Israel's Border Wars,* pp. 28–68.
99. Morris, *Israel's Border Wars,* pp. 135 and 137.

100. Livia Rokach, 'Israeli State Terrorism: An Analysis of the Sharett Diaries', *Journal of Palestine Studies* 9, no. 3 (Spring 1980), p. 21.

101. Rokach, ibid., citing Ehud Ya'ari's *Mitzrayim Vehafedayeen*.

102. Michael Palumbo, *Imperial Israel* (London: Bloomsbury, updated edition, 1992), p. 28; Paul Cossali and Clive Robson, *Stateless in Gaza* (London: Zed Books, 1986), pp. 13–15.

103. Cited in *The New York Times,* 11 November 1956. Menahem Begin, the leader of the Herut Party, which was the second largest in Israel, said in an interview on 27 November that 'he could not countenance withdrawal from the Gaza Strip under any terms because the area belonged to Israel by right'. Cited in *The New York Times,* 28 November 1956.

104. Moshe Sharett, *Yoman Ishi* [Personal Diary], vol. 4 (Tel Aviv: Sifriyat Ma'ariv, 1978), pp. 1186–87, entry for 3 October 1955.

105. See Michael Bar-Zohar, *Mool Hamarah Haakhzarit: Yisrael Berega'a Haemet* [Facing a Cruel Mirror: Israel's Moment of Truth] (Tel Aviv: Yedi'ot Aharonot Books, 1990), p. 27; Mordechai Bar-On, *Itgar Vetigrah: Haderekh Lemivtza'a Kadesh* [Challenge and Quarrel: The Road to Sinai 1956] (Beersheba: The University of Ben-Gurion, 1991), pp. 252–53; *Yedi'ot Aharonot,* 3 April 1986.

106. Bar-Zohar, *Mool Hamarah Haakhzarit*, p. 27.

107. *The Times* (London), 2 November 1956.

108. Cossali and Robson, *Stateless in Gaza*, p. 17.

109. Quoted in ibid., pp. 17–18.

110. Palumbo, *Imperial Israel*, p. 31.

111. See *The New York Times,* 2 December 1956.

112. Ibid.

113. Ibid.

114. Palumbo, *Imperial Israel*, p. 30.

115. Cited in *The Times* (London), 29 November 1956.

116. Palumbo, *Imperial Israel*, p. 32.

117. See Ronal Fisher in *Ma'ariv*, 4 August 1995; and *Ma'ariv*, 18 August 1995.

118. *Ma'ariv*, 4 August 1995; and Haim Baram in *Middle East International*, 25 August 1995, p. 9.

119. *Ma'ariv*, 4 August 1995.

120. Ibid.

121. Ibid.

122. *The New York Times,* 6 November 1956.

123. Cossali and Robson, *Stateless in Gaza*, p. 16.

124. Danin, *Tzioni Bekhol Tnai*, vol. 1, pp. 328–29.

125. Weitz, *Yosef Nahmani*, p. 139.

126. See *The New York Times*, 10 November 1956.

127. Quoted in Yosef Carmel, *Yitzhak Ben-Tzvi: Metokh Yoman Bevet Hanasi* [Diary of President Yitzhak Ben-Tzvi's bodyguard] (Ramat Gan: Massada, 1967), p. 92.

128. Moshe Sharett, *Yoman Ishi* [Personal Diary], vol. 7, entry for 20 November 1956 (Tel Aviv: Sifriyat Ma'ariv, 1978), p. 1866.

129. ISA, Foreign Ministry, 3085/16, from Israel's Minister to Stockholm, Haim Yahil, to Foreign Ministry's Director General, Walter Eytan, secret and personal letter no. ST/101, dated 28 November 1956.

130. ISA, Foreign Ministry, 3085/16, from Dr Haim Yahil, Stockholm, to Walter Eytan, Foreign Ministry's Director General, secret letter, dated 26 December 1956.

131. ISA, Foreign Ministry, 3085/16, G. Avner, to Y. Hertzog, Israel's minister to Washington, secret letter dated 24 January 1957. Abba Eban is also brother-in-law of Haim Hertzog.

132. Avner to Hertzog, letter dated 24 January 1957, ibid.

133. ISA, Foreign Ministry, 2448/8.

134. David Ben-Gurion, *Israel: A Personal History* (New York and Tel Aviv: Funk & Wagnalls and Sabra Books, 1971), p. 534.

135. ISA, Foreign Ministry, 3085/16, from Y.H. Levine, to Y. Hertzog, memo no. YHL/114.

136. CZA, A 300/54, Ben-Horin's file.

137. Lessing Rosenwald was an American non-Zionist Jewish merchant and philanthropist. In 1943 he led the foundation of the American Council for Judaism and was its first president. Before 1948 the Council was against the establishment of a Jewish state in Palestine. It is not clear whether Rosenwald would have been interested in cooperating with an Israeli plan for transferring Palestinian refugees from the Gaza Strip to the United States or Latin America. His younger brother William, a financier, served as chairman of the National United Jewish Appeal campaign, and vice-chairman of the Joint Distribution Committee, American Jewish Committee, and United HIAS Service. Although generally non-Zionists, the Rosenwalds contributed modestly to Jewish educational and agricultural institutions in Palestine.

138. ISA, Foreign Ministry, 3085/16, Hanan Bar-On, to Ya'acov Hertzog and Shmuel Divon, personal and secret letter, dated 14 March 1957. The American Joint Distribution Committee (AJDC), an American

Jewish relief organization, had its beginning in 1914. In August 1954 the Hebrew Sheltering and Immigrant Aid Society (HSIAS) merged with United Service for New Americans and the migration service of the AJDC to establish the Hebrew Immigrant Aid Society (HIAS). HIAS is the international migration agency of the organized American Jewish community. It assists Jewish migrants and works with various agencies to increase Jewish immigration opportunities.

139. Danin, *Tzioni Bekhol Tnai*, vol. 1, p. 251, citing a letter to Shaltiel dated 21 March 1957.

Chapter 2
The Revival of the Transfer Concept after June 1967

The June War of 1967 marks a decisive turn in the history of Zionism, the Israeli State and the Palestinians, particularly those living in the occupied West Bank and Gaza Strip. Zionism had at last reached its aim of controlling the whole of Palestine. Moreover, the overwhelming Israeli victory in the war, the seizure of the remainder of Palestine with its sizeable Arab population, the resultant outburst, and later upsurge, of Messianic Zionism and the growing Israeli confidence all contributed to the prompt and inevitable revival of the 'transfer' concept. In the wake of the 1967 conquests, the perception of Eretz Yisrael (the Land of Israel) as a whole was found not only in the maximalist Revisionist camp of Herut (later Likud), but increasingly gained ground in all mainstream Zionist parties, particularly the traditionally pragmatic ruling Labour Party. Given the fact that ideological/historical and security claims to the occupied areas were to be put forward, action had to be taken to 'redeem the land' – through Jewish settlement without which the 'redemption' process was impossible. At the same time, official and public concern at being faced with what is called 'the demographic problem', that is, the problem of absorbing too many non-Jews within the Jewish state, became manifestly stronger. Although nearly 300,000 Palestinians fled or were expelled in the course of hostilities or shortly after, the Palestinian inhabitants of the territories – contrary to the 1948 exodus – remained in situ. The number of Palestinians living within the new cease-fire lines – including those citizens of Israel – was over 1.3 million in 1967,[1] and given the high Arab birthrate, the prospect of the Palestinians becoming at least 50 per cent of the population – a Zionist/Israeli nightmare – was perceived as a feasible reality. The 'conquest of the land' (Kibbush Haadamah) always had been Zionism's central task. The

Zionists needed, as in 1948, to hold the land they had conquered, to people it and 'develop' it, and to 'transfer', or otherwise to keep down, the natives who might oppose them. Indeed, for the Israeli leaders one of the key questions from June 1967 onwards was not whether Israel should maintain a presence in the newly acquired territories, but how it could be maintained without adding over one million Palestinians to the Arab minority of Israel. The old Zionist dilemma of non-Jews in a Jewish state had to be resolved. Against this background of Zionist expansionism, transfer ideas were revived in public debates, in popular songs, in articles in the Hebrew press and, most importantly, in cabinet discussions and government schemes.

'A Land without a People': 'Jerusalem of Gold'

For the settler who is coming 'to redeem the land', the native inhabitants earmarked for dispossession are usually invisible. The natives, marked for uprooting and dislocation, are simultaneously divested of their human and national reality and classed as a marginal nonentity. Indeed, Zionist historiography provides ample evidence suggesting that from the very beginning of the Zionist Yishuv (settlement) in Palestine the attitude of the majority of the Zionist groups toward the native Arab population ranged from a mixture of indifference and patronizing superiority, to outright denial of their national rights, accompanied by uprooting and transferring them to neighbouring countries. Leading figures such as Israel Zangwill, a prominent Anglo-Jewish writer, a close lieutenant of Theodor Herzl (the founder of political Zionism) and propagator of the transfer solution, worked relentlessly to propagandize the slogan that Palestine was 'a land without a people for a people without a land'. A reference to the same notion of an 'empty country' was made in 1914 by Chaim Weizmann, later president of the World Zionist Congress and the first president of the State of Israel: 'In its initial stage, Zionism was conceived by its pioneers as a movement wholly depending on mechanical factors: there is a country which happens to be called Palestine, a country without a people, and, on the other hand, there exists the Jewish people, and it has no country.

What else is necessary, then, than to fit the gem into the ring, to unite this people with this country?'[2]

More revealing, however, is the anecdote Weizmann once told to Arthur Ruppin, the head of the colonization department of the Jewish Agency, about how he (Weizmann) obtained the Balfour Declaration in 1917. When Ruppin asked what he thought about the indigenous Palestinians, Weizmann said: 'The British told us that there are some hundred thousand Negroes ['kushim'] and for those there is no value.'[3] A few years after the Zionist movement obtained the Balfour Declaration, Zangwill wrote: 'If Lord Shaftesbury was literally inexact in describing Palestine as a country without a people, he was essentially correct, for there is no Arab people living in intimate fusion with the country, utilising its resources and stamping it with a characteristic impress; there is at best an Arab encampment.'[4] This and other pronouncements by Weizmann and other leading Zionists embodying European supremacy planted in the Zionist mind the racist notion of an empty territory – empty not necessarily in the actual absence of its inhabitants, but rather a kind of civilizational barrenness – justifying Zionist colonization, and obliviousness to the fate of the native population and their eventual removal.

The same axiom of 'empty territory' ('a land without a people for a people without a land') runs through Zionist state education in Israel and finds strong expression in children's literature. One such work for children contains the following excerpt:

> Joseph and some of his men thus crossed the land [Palestine] on foot, until they reached Galilee. They climbed mountains, beautiful but empty mountains, where nobody lived . . . Joseph said, 'We want to establish this kibbutz and conquer this emptiness. We shall call this place Tel Hai [Living Hill] . . . The land is empty; its children have deserted it [reference is, of course, to Jews]. They are dispersed and no longer tend it. No one protects or tends the land now.'[5]

In a similar vein, Israel's leading satirist, Dan Ben-Amotz, observed in 1982 that 'the Arabs do not exist in our textbooks [for children]. This is apparently in accordance with the Jewish-Zionist-socialist principles we have received. "A-people-without-a-land-returns-to-a-land-without-people." [6]

These images and formulae of empty and untended land gave those who propounded them a simple and self-explanatory Zionism. These contentions not only justified Zionist settlement but also helped to suppress conscience-pricking among Israeli Jews for the dispossession of the Palestinians before, during, and after 1948: if the land had been empty, then no Zionist wrongdoing had taken place. [7]

A few weeks after the June 1967 War Israel's leading novelist, 'Amos 'Oz, wrote an article in the Hebrew daily *Davar* in which he drew attention to the revival of transfer thoughts in Israel: 'One often hears talk about pushing the Palestinian masses back to rich Kuwait or fertile Iraq.' [8] 'Oz tried to explain this 'talk' about transfer against the background of the deep-seated inclination among Israeli Jews to see Palestine as a country without its indigenous inhabitants:

> When I was a child, some of my teachers taught me that after our Temple was destroyed and we were banished from our country, strangers came into what was our heritage and defiled it. The desert-born Arabs laid the land waste and let the terraces on the hillsides go to ruin. Their flocks destroyed the beautiful forests. When our first pioneers came to the land to rebuild it and to redeem it from desolation, they found an abandoned wasteland. True, a few backward, uncouth nomads wandered in it.
>
> Some of our first arrivals thought that, by right, the Arabs should return to the desert and give the land back to its owners, and, if not, that they (the Zionists) should 'arise and inherit', like those who conquered Canaan in storm: 'A melody of blood and fire . . . Climb the mountain, crush the plain. All you see – inherit . . . and conquer the land by the strength of your arm . . .' (Tchernichovsky, 'I Have a Tune'). [9]

'Oz also drew attention to Na'omi Shemer's song 'Jerusalem of Gold', which encapsulated this deep-seated inclination among Israeli Jews to see Palestine as a country without its Arab inhabitants. The song 'Jerusalem of Gold', which came to be defined as a kind of 'national anthem of the Six-Day War', [10] was commissioned by the municipality of Jewish Jerusalem, was written for a music festival held on the eve of the war,[11] and became a national hit after the Israeli seizure of Arab East Jerusalem, the West Bank, and Gaza Strip. It is the most popular song ever produced in Israel and in 1967 it swept the country like lightning, genuinely expressing Israeli national aspirations following the new conquests. Na'omi Shemer herself received the Israel Prize for her unique contribution to the Israeli song. The song contains the following passages:

> Jerusalem of Gold . . .
> How did the water cisterns dry out, the market-place is empty,
> And no one visits the Holy Mount [Al-Haram al-Sharif] in the Old City.
> And through the cave within the rock winds are whining,
> And no one descends down to the Dead Sea en route for Jericho . . .
> Jerusalem of Gold . . .
> We have returned to the water cisterns, to the market-place and the square.
> A shofar[12] sounds on the Holy Mount in the Old City.
> And in the caves within the rock a thousand suns do glow,
> We shall again descend to the Dead Sea en route for Jericho.[13]

In his *Davar* article, 'Oz offers a liberal Zionist explanation of the connection between the 'land without a people' formula, the popularity of Shemer's song 'Jerusalem of Gold', and the emergence of the transfer 'talk' after the war:

> It seems that the enchantment of 'renewing the days of old' is what gave Zionism its deep-seated inclination to see a country without inhabitants before it . . . How fitting would it have been for the Return to Zion to have taken the land from the Roman legions or the nations of Canaan and Philistia. And to come to a completely empty country would have been even better. From there, it is only a short step to the kind of self-induced blindness that consists in disregarding the existence of the country's Arab population, or in discounting it and its importance on the dubious grounds that it 'has created no valuable cultural assets here', as if that would permit us to take no notice of its very existence. (In time, Na'omi Shemer would express this state of mind in her song 'Jerusalem of Gold': '. . . the marketplace is empty/And no one goes down to the Dead Sea/By way of Jericho.' Meaning, of course, that the marketplace

is empty of Jews and that no Jew goes down to the Dead Sea by way of Jericho. A remarkable revelation of a remarkably characteristic way of thinking.)[14]

This 'characteristic way of thinking' echoes strongly the deep-seated formula of 'land without a people' and naturally leads to the revival of the transfer concept, a fact illustrated by the attitude of Na'omi Shemer, the poet laureate of Greater Israel's supporters, toward the indigenous inhabitants of Palestine. In January 1979 one of the famous heroes of the Israeli army, Meir Har-Tzion,[15] who owns a large cattle ranch situated on the lands of the destroyed Arab village of Kawkab al-Hawa in the Beisan Valley (the inhabitants of which were driven out in 1948), stated: 'I do not say that we should put them [the Arabs] on trucks and kill them . . . We must create a situation in which for them it would not be worth living here, but [to leave] to Jordan or Saudi Arabia or any other Arab state.'[16] Har-Tzion was promptly applauded by Shemer in an article in the Histadrut (Labour controlled) daily *Davar*: 'Arab emigration from Israel, if it is done with mutual respect and positive will . . . is likely to be the right solution . . . it is possible that it will be recognized as a most humane possibility after much suffering and only after hard and bitter civil war – but talking about it is permitted and must be now'; 'why is the exodus of one million French from Algeria a progressive and humane solution and the exodus of one million Arabs from Israel' is not?[17] Shemer and Har-Tzion are not marginal figures in Israel. Shemer is Israel's most famous and popular song-writer and Har-Tzion, who fought in the Ariel Sharon-commanded 'Unit 101', set up by the army in the 1950s to carry out 'retaliatory' attacks against Arab targets, was described by the late Moshe Dayan as 'the brightest soldier in Jewish history since Bar-Kohkva'.[18]

The argument that support for the 'transfer' concept does not come only from a fringe group is also illustrated by the fact that other veterans of 'Unit 101' and the paratroop corps, the elite force of the Israeli army which carried out most of the 'retaliatory' oper-ations against Arab targets in the 1950s and the 1960s, have emerged in the 1970s and the 1980s among the most persistent public

exponents of Arab 'transfer'. The most important veteran commanders of the paratroopers were Ariel Sharon – Defence Minister
1981–82; Raphael Eitan – Chief of Staff 1978–83; and Colonel
Aharon Davidi – a former head of the Paratroop Corps, who
became a senior lecturer in Geography at Tel Aviv University.
Davidi replied in an interview in the mass-circulation daily *Ma'ariv*
how he would solve the Palestinian problem: 'In the simplest and
most humane manner: the transfer of all the Palestinians from their
present locations to the Arab countries.' When interviewer Dov
Goldstein remarked that the Arabs would not accept such a solution, Davidi responded: 'They will. The transfer is very important
for both the Jews and the Arabs. They will accept it, if they have no
choice. The Arab states are spread out over a territory of more than
ten million square kilometres. The density of the Arabs is the lowest
in the world. Would it be a problem to absorb one million there, and
to arrange housing and employment for them, with the help of their
great wealth?'[19]

Davidi's assertions echoed classical mainstream Zionist arguments in justification of Arab removal. The argument that support
for the 'transfer' concept does not come only from a fringe group is
also illustrated by the fact that some of the nation's leading authors,
novelists, and poets, such as Natan Alterman, Haim Hazaz, Yigal
Mossenson, and Moshe Shamir (all of whom supported Israel's
retention of all the territories seized in 1967), publicly supported
the idea of transfer in the post-1967 era. These leading literary
figures were also closely associated with mainstream Labour or left-
wing Zionism in the pre-1948 period and the first two decades of
the State of Israel.

Natan Alterman (1910–1970), whose poetry had a powerful
impact on Jewish society during the Yishuv period and the first
three decades of the State of Israel, wrote in an article in the mass-
circulation daily *Ma'ariv* shortly after the 1967 War, that the transfer
'solution is only possible in an ideal peace situation between us and
Arab states, which will agree to co-operate with us in a great project
of population transfer'. Alterman had served on the editorial board
of the liberal daily *Haaretz* from 1934 to 1943, when he joined the
Histadrut daily *Davar*, virtually the mouthpiece of the ruling Mapai

Party, and he had been closely associated with the two most important leaders of Mapai, David Ben-Gurion and Berl Katznelson, the
founder of *Davar* and the hero of Labour Zionism in the mandatory
period.

In justification of his views on the morality of Arab removal in
the post-1967 period, Alterman cited statements made by Berl
Katznelson in 1943 (the year Alterman joined *Davar*):

> Our contemporary history has known a number of transfers . . . [for
> instance] the U.S.S.R. arranged the transfer of one million Germans
> living in the Volga region and transferred them to very distant places . . .
> one could assume that this transfer was done against the will of the
> transferees . . . there could be possible situations that would make [Arab]
> population transfer desirable for both sides . . . who is the socialist who is
> interested in rejecting the very idea beforehand and stigmatizing it as
> something unfair? Has Merhavyah not been built on transfer? Were it
> not for many of these transfers Hashomer Hatza'ir [which later in 1948
> founded the Mapam Party] would not be residing today in Merhavyah,
> or Mishmar Ha'emek or other places . . . and if what has been done for a
> settlement of Hashomer Hatza'ir is a fair deed, why would it not be fair
> when it would be done on a much larger and greater scale, not just of
> Hashomer Hatza'ir but for the whole of Israel?[20]

Haim Hazaz (1898–1973) was another example of a leading author
who supported the 'transfer' concept in the post-1967 era. As a
prolific Hebrew novelist, his works have won him numerous awards,
including the Bialik Prize and the Israel Prize, the top prize awarded
by the State of Israel. Hazaz, in an article published in *Davar* on
10 November 1967, echoed the Labour Zionist apologia of the
pre-1948 period:

> There is the question of Judea and Ephraim [the West Bank], with a
> large Arab population which must be evacuated to neighbouring Arab
> states. This is not an exile like the exile of the Jews among the Gentiles
> . . . They will be coming to their brothers, to large and wide and little
> populated countries. One culture, one language and religion. This is
> 'transfer' such as that which took place between Turkey and Greece,

between India and Pakistan . . . putting the world aright in one place through exchanging [the Arab population] to its designated place. We will assume responsibility for this task and assist in planning, organizing and financing.[21]

Hazaz repeated his transfer proposal in a simplistic way in an interview in 1968: 'the [1967] war cost us 3 billion [Israeli] pounds – let's take three billion more pounds and give them to the Arabs and tell them to get out'.[22] Hazaz was willing to allow a small Arab minority to remain in Israel provided it 'would not disrupt or change the Jewish character of the Land of Israel'.[23]

Also among the well-known and influential authors who expressed support for the transfer solution in the post-1967 era was Yigal Mossenson, who was an officer in the Palmah (the elite strike force of the Haganah from 1941 to 1948) during the 1948 war. He was also a military judge and has written 25 children's books, 20 plays for screen and theatre and has received top Israeli prizes, including the Ussishkin Prize, the Kinor David Prize, and the Prime Minister's Creative Prize. Mossenson published an article in the mass-circulation daily *Ma'ariv* in 1985 in which he expressed support for the non-compulsory transfer of Arabs from Israel.[24]

Another prolific and prominent Hebrew novelist who served in the Palmah was Moshe Shamir. A former member of Hashomer Hatza'ir, he joined Kibbutz Mishmar Ha'emek (1941–47), and between 1944 and 1948 he served in the Palmah and edited several of its literary publications. In 1948 he was awarded the Ussishkin Prize for literature. He also was a member of Mapam (Israel's Zionist socialist party, later part of the ruling Labour Alignment) for nearly two decades after the establishment of Israel. Following the 1967 conquests, he quit the Zionist left and joined the nationalist right, and in 1973 he became a leader of the La'Am wing of the Likud party bloc, serving in the ninth Knesset as a Likud member. In 1979 he resigned from the Likud and was a founding member of the Tehiya Party, supporting Israel's retention of all the territories occupied in 1967. Moshe Shamir, like the above-mentioned leading authors, supported the concept of transfer in the post-1967 era. In a recent book published by Tzvi Shiloah (another La'Am-Likud member of the ninth Knesset, 1973–77), entitled *The Guilt of Jerusalem*, which dwells on the justification of Arab transfer, Shiloah explains that the novelist Moshe Shamir has read the manuscript of the book and has made a significant contribution to it.[25] In his recent book *The Green Place* (1991), Moshe Shamir comes out openly in favour of Arab population transfer, which he describes as an 'actual' solution.[26]

The argument that support for the 'transfer' idea does not come only from a fringe is further illustrated by the fact that some of the ideologists, public figures, and old-timers of the ruling Mapai party, men such as Eli'ezer Livneh, Dr Haim Yahil, Tzvi Shiloah, and Dr Dov Yosefi, publicly supported the transfer concept in the post-1967 period.

Eli'ezer Livneh (1902–1975), who headed the Political and Educational Department of the Haganah in the mandatory period and was a Mapai Knesset member of the first and second Knessets (1949–1955), and who served on the influential foreign affairs and defence committee between 1951 and 1955 (during which period he was closely associated with Ben-Gurion), put forward in the summer of 1967 a plan for the transfer of 600,000 Palestinian refugees from the West Bank and Gaza Strip. In an article in the mass-circulation daily *Ma'ariv* of 22 June 1967 (less than two weeks after the June war conquests), Livneh wrote: 'They [the refugees] will choose, willingly, resettlement in whatever Arab country, or emigration to countries overseas. The Prime Minister of Australia has already suggested co-operation.' A few weeks later Livneh reiterated the proposal:

> The refugees are now within our boundaries. We could rehabilitate some of them in our country [in Sinai], and transfer others for productive life overseas or resettle them in neighbouring countries with which we will come to an arrangement . . . Jordan . . . is likely to be the chief beneficiary [to be able] to populate its wide territories.[27]

Livneh developed his proposal further into a fully-fledged plan in an article in the liberal daily *Haaretz* on 28 August 1967 (p. 2). Livneh wrote that in the last 19 years tens of thousands of refugees have crossed . . . to Saudi Arabia, Kuwait, Bahrain, Qatar, Abu Dhabi, Dubai and the [other] oil principalities. Tens of thousands of their families, who have remained in the camps [in the West Bank and Gaza] have lived off money remitted by their distant relatives . . . Just as half a million Jews immigrated to the Land of Israel from Arab countries . . . hundreds of thousands of 'Palestinian' Arabs were crossing to Arab countries. The parallel is amazing . . . What is happening in the refugee camps in a sporadic and limited way without the support of a governmental body [in Arab states] should be widened and developed by us from the side of dimensions and means. This means: a) constructive emigration should be directed to all the countries in need of a work-force including the United States, Canada, Australia and Latin America; b) the emigrants should be entitled to financial support from Israel . . . ; c) the implementation must be planned for a prolonged time, let us say 18 years; d) the number of countries designated for migration and resettlement should be as large as possible.

'If these Arabs [would-be transferees] would want to maintain their Arabness in the United States, Canada, Brazil and Australia', it is up to them, Livneh wrote. Livneh made another little 'concession':

To the extent that there might be a number of refugees who want, in spite of everything, to experience striking agricultural roots in a landscape close to their spirit and tradition, it is worth offering them settlement in north Sinai . . . in the opinion of cautious experts there are there water, land and other conditions for the settlement of tens of thousands (approximately 60,000 persons).

Livneh argued that the 'carrying out of the [transfer] task' depended mainly on Israel and on the conditions it could create:

a) the allocation of large sums; b) patience. If we spend 5,000 dollars on the emigration of a family of 6–7 persons on average (1500 dollars on the journey, and the rest [under] the exclusive control of the emigrating family) we would be able to finance every year the emigration of tens of thousands of families, or 60–70,000 persons by 50 million dollars (or 150 million Israeli Lira, 3% of our state budget). There would be no lack of candidates and they would increase when encouraging information from abroad on the settlement of the first ones arrived . . . if we placed such encouraging sums . . . within 8–9 years about 600,000 persons would be likely to emigrate at this pace, meaning all the refugees from the [Gaza] Strip, the Hebron mountain, the mountains of Ephraim [in the West Bank] and the Jordan valley.

Although in his earlier proposal Livneh had suggested that the world powers should finance the transfer and resettlement, in the August 1967 plan he proposed that Israel and world Jewry should shoulder 'financing the project':

There is no need to explain its importance from the national, security and propaganda point of view. It should be placed at the top of our national priorities. Insofar as we need for it [financial] means greater than the estimate given here, we are entitled to appeal to the world Jewry. This is more justified and blessed than the use of fund-raising to raise the standard of living [of Israelis] . . . The Jews of the Diaspora will respond to this in understanding, and even in enthusiasm.

For Livneh, the success of the 'project' would depend on its

planning in a long breath. In the beginning there will certainly be various difficulties of running it . . . Our reckoning should not be for one month or one season. We will develop the project on our responsibility, without making it conditional upon the participation of other elements. To the extent that we carry it out we will gain the co-operation of others. The United Nations action in the refugee camps (UNRWA) would then assume constructive and purposeful meaning . . . the training in the schools of UNRWA would be adjusted to the needs of emigration and resettlement.

From other references, it is obvious that Livneh was not content with the removal of 600,000 Palestinian refugees from the West Bank and Gaza, as he put forward his euphemistically termed 'emigration project', but he sought to transform the demographic and political reality of the occupied territories by clearing out other residents as well.[28] What is also noticeable is the absence of any discussion in his plan of the resistance the Palestinians would be likely to put up to foil such a mass removal. Such a deliberate attempt to ignore Palestinian resistance to transfer is – as will be seen again – common to other transfer proposals put forward publicly in the euphoric period following the spectacular conquests of the 1967 war.

Another example of a prominent Mapai public figure who supported the concept of transfer in the post-1967 era was Dr Haim Yahil (1905–1974), a former senior government official who served as director of the Histadrut's Education Department in Haifa (1939–42) and then as a member of the Histadrut's Executive Committee (1942–45); between 1949 and 1951, he was director of the Jewish Agency's Department of Immigrant Absorption; from 1951 to 1952, he served as head of the Foreign Ministry's Information Department; from 1956 to 1959 he served as Minister to the Scandinavian countries; from 1960 to 1964 he served as Director General of the Foreign Ministry; and in 1965 he became Chairman of the state-controlled Israel Broadcasting Authority; for several years he also served as head of the Centre for the Diaspora of the Jewish Agency in Jerusalem.

In the post-1967 period, Dr Yahil, a Labour Party man, supported the annexation of the West Bank and Gaza to Israel, and saw in 1972 'in principle . . . in population exchange or in the transfer of minorities an efficient, just and in the final consideration, the most humane solution to conflicts between nations'. He realized, however, that a large-scale outright removal of the Palestinians, which 'few [Israelis] are talking about but not a few are contemplating', could only be carried out under circumstances of war, and therefore 'officially' should not be adopted as part of a political programme 'not because of moral reasons but for political considerations . . . such a plan would be received by [Arab, Western?] public opinion as a conspiracy for expulsion and would increase the enmity' towards Israel. According to Yahil, mass transfer 'would only be possible as an agreed solution in the framework of a peace agreement . . . or in the opposite case, that is a solution implemented in the midst of war'.[29]

Tzvi Shiloah, a senior veteran of the Mapai Party and a former deputy mayor of the town of Hertzliyah, was another open advocate of the transfer solution in the post-1967 period. He was appointed by Prime Minister Ben-Gurion as Acting Editor of the Mapai daily *Hador*, serving from 1949 to 1954; he was a member of the Central Committee of the ruling Mapai Party between 1949 and 1965. Between 1965 and 1968 he joined the Rafi List which was headed by Ben-Gurion and Defence Minister Moshe Dayan, and together with Haim Hertzog (later to become President of Israel), was a member of its country-wide Secretariat; in 1968 he rejoined the ruling Labour Party. On 3 July 1967 (less than four weeks after the June war), Shiloah (while he was *still* a member of the Secretariat of the labour Rafi faction, an important partner in the Labour coalition cabinet) published an article in the Histadrut daily *Davar* (an official organ of the Labour Party) arguing for the annexation of the West Bank and Gaza Strip to Israel and for mass Arab transfer:

> [H]undreds of thousands of Arabs are residing in the liberated territory ... the inclusion of this hostile population within the boundaries of the State of Israel is considered as a time-bomb in the heart of the state ... Leaving them in these territories endangers the state and its national Jewish character ... the only solution is to organize their emigration to, and settlement in, Arab countries abundant in land and water such as Syria and Iraq.

Shiloah also reminded the readers that the transfer of Palestinian Arabs as a Zionist solution had already been advocated by Zionist leaders in the pre-1948 period, citing the transfer proposal to Iraq and the al-Jazirah province in Syria put forward by 'Akiva Ettinger, who headed the Land Settlement Department of the Zionist Executive (1918–25) and the Land Acquisition Department of the Jewish National Fund (1926–36). Moreover, shortly after the June 1967 war, in private conversations with his Labour colleagues, which included former mayor of the town of Kfar Saba and member of Knesset Mordechai Sorkis, Shiloah expressed the view that Israel had lost the June war because we didn't follow the Rambam advice regarding an enemy city under siege, and we didn't leave one exit open for population exodus from the besieged city, and first of all from the capital Jerusalem . . . it was clear to me . . . that we were receiving a hostile Arab population that we wouldn't be able to digest in our state, and especially in our capital.[30]

In his book *A Great Land for a Great People*, published in 1970, two years after rejoining the ruling Labour Party, Shiloah discusses the application of the transfer solution to the Arab–Israeli conflict, while reviewing, and drawing inspiration and legitimacy from, those earlier proposals put forward by mainstream and 'socialist' Zionist leaders such as Dr Max Nordau, Dr Arthur Ruppin, Berl Katznelson, David Ben-Gurion, and 'Akiva Ettinger. He also castigates the dovish Mapam faction (a partner in the Labour coalition), for making 'demography' an argument for returning the occupied territories ('liberated', in Shiloah's words, to Arab sovereignty). According to Shiloah, 'the entire history of Zionism is a continuous struggle to change the face of demography in this country. To this all trends in Zionism agreed, including Brit Shalom.'[31] Shiloah also cited Berl Katznelson's polemics against the Hashomer Hatza'ir movement – which later founded the Mapam Party – in the pre-1948 period as the standard Labour Zionism apologia in justification of transfer.[32]

In spite of the Arab states' opposition to transfer, Shiloah writes, 'in the end the transfer idea will materialize, either within a peace settlement or as a result of war'.[33] He interpreted the announcement of the late Prime Minister Levi Eshkol immediately after the June 1967 War that the problem of the refugees residing in the West Bank and Gaza could only be solved through regional co-operation as leading naturally to transfer. Shiloah wrote in 1970:

the only meaning of these things is that when peace comes [with the Arab states] . . . the refugees of the Land of Israel will be settled, for the benefit of all sides, in a sparsely populated Arab state abundant in land, water and oil, such as Iraq. And what is good for the refugees, is desirable – under conditions of peace! – also for most of the Arab population of the Land of Israel.[34]

Shiloah's self-confessed advocacy of compulsory transfer was reiterated two decades later: 'some claim that I have spoken for voluntary transfer: Who wants to leave his home voluntarily?' In justification of outright expulsion, he wrote: 'in 1948, we deliberately, and not just in the heat of the war, expelled Arabs. Also in [19]67 after the Six-Day War, we expelled many Arabs.'[35]

Another long-time Labour Zionist and an advocate of the transfer concept in the post-1967 period was Dr Dov Yosefi, a publicist and journalist and a former senior Israeli diplomat. Born in Chile, Yosefi first joined the Hashomer Hatza'ir Zionist 'socialist' movement. He immigrated to Israel shortly after its establishment at the age of 43 and was among the founders of the Mapam-affiliated Kibbutz Ga'ash. He also held central positions in the Mapam Party, including being Secretary of the Mapam international movement and the editor of its Yiddish-language organ *Yisrael Stimme*. After leaving Mapam in the early 1960s, Yosefi joined the ruling Mapai Party and later the Israeli diplomatic service in Latin America where he stayed until 1970. In the late 1960s, while he was still a serving diplomat, Yosefi expressed support for the annexation of the West Bank and Gaza Strip to Israel. Yosefi's advocacy of Arab transfer was articulated later in a 1977 article entitled 'A Humane Solution to the Demographic Problem', in which he came up with the following conclusions. First,

> If we want to prevent mutual and continuous bloodshed, there is only one solution – the transfer of the Arab population of the Land of Israel to Arab States . . . True, this is a little painful (who knows this like us the Jews), but it is inevitable and preferable to cumulative poisoning which undermines the whole body. There is no doubt that this solution will come sooner or later. The question is only whether it will be by peaceful ways through regional planning and international assistance, or, God forbid, as a result of bloody events.

Second,

> The State of Israel has to show political courage at an opportune

moment . . . and to announce that according to experiences in other places and similar situations there is no other solution but population transfer . . . The problem of the Arab minority in the Land of Israel remains without a solution because this [minority] has not been transferred to Arab states.

Third,

We should also not be deterred from repeating time and again in the ears of the world nations that Jordan (or the combination of Jordan and Syria) actually constitutes a Palestinian homeland and only in it will the Arabs of the Land of Israel have self-determination . . . This should be the central Israeli demand in any negotiation with Arab countries. The author does not overlook the fact that this solution is not easy to implement in no-war situations. Because most cases of population transfer in the world were in time of battle or shortly after. In any case, this is a humane solution . . .[36]

Dr Yosefi's position appears to have hardened further since the mid-1970s, as demonstrated in the more extremist version of his article 'A Humane Solution to the Demographic Problem' in the autumn 1987 issue of the periodical *Haumah* (*The Nation*). Published by Misdar Jabotinsky, *Haumah* is the most important ideological organ of the Likud Party.[37] In this version Yosefi asserts that the 'Arab minority [including the Arab citizens of Israel] is already endangering, and will endanger with greater vigour in the future, the sovereignty and even the existence of the State of Israel'.[38] He elaborates: 'the main objective, so long as Judea and Samaria are in our hands, there exists the hope that in a political or military-political-regional, or international constellation the ideal solution of population transfer will be made possible. And in the region in which we are living such a constellation is a permanent possibility.' Although Yosefi explicitly raises the 'military' solution for Arab removal, he proposes, in the interest of the two parties,

not to wait for painful and even tragic opportunities . . . but to plan in good time the transfer of the Arab population from the West Bank to

Arab countries – with the understanding and assistance of the world nations, if possible. Yet for that purpose the government of Israel must set up, as early as possible, a special information department, which would conduct a worthy information/propaganda [campaign] – with the assistance of experts on the mentality of the Arab leaders and the interests of Arab states, on the one hand, and the political, strategic and economic interests of European states, and especially of the two superpowers, on the other. In question is an adequate information campaign which clearly proves that the solution proposed here is the only humane solution for the two parties.[39]

Mainstream Zionism rejected the views of a liberal minority – to which 'Amos 'Oz belongs – which argued that Palestine is also the homeland of the Palestinian people. Therefore one needs to go beyond 'Oz's explanation to understand the background against which 'transfer' thoughts and debates promptly resurfaced after 1967. This background consists of the standard mainstream Zionist 'solution for the Palestinian problem', which was predicated on the claim for monopolized Zionist/Jewish ownership and Israeli/Jewish domination of Eretz Yisrael/Palestine. This being the case, Zionism was bound to base its conception of Jerusalem upon a non-existent entity, Jerusalem of Gold, and to involve abstract historical and ideological rights in the newly acquired territories, as well as resting its claim on territorial expansion and domination and the actual 'redemption of land' through settlement. One implication of the claim for monopolized ownership of a country shared by another people is the 'transfer' solution. Against this background transfer proposals and plans were inevitably put forward by mainstream labour leaders – including ministers – immediately after the 1967 victory.

Yosef Weitz's Transfer Proposal, September 1967

Yosef Weitz, the then retired leading Zionist proponent and practitioner of transfer with experience in dealing with the 'Arab problem' spanning four decades, realized immediately after the war that the 'Arab problem' had acquired a new quality. On 29 September

1967 he published an article in *Davar* in which he quoted his 1940 proposal to transfer all the Palestinians, and urged the public to consider the notion in the wake of the new conquests. The article was based on a six-page memorandum written by Weitz 12 days earlier,[40] and possibly submitted to the Israeli government for consideration.

> Amongst ourselves it must be clear that there is no room for both peoples in this country. . . . With Arab transfer the country will be wide-open for us. And with the Arabs staying the country will be narrow and restricted . . . the only solution is the Land of Israel, or at least the Western Land of Israel [i.e., the whole of Palestine], without Arabs. The Zionist work . . . must come all simultaneously in the manner of redemption (here is the meaning of the Messianic idea); the only way is to transfer the Arabs from here to neighbouring countries, all of them, except perhaps Bethlehem, Nazareth, and old Jerusalem. Not a single village or a single tribe must be left. And the transfer must be done through their absorption in Iraq and Syria and even in Transjordan. For that goal money will be found and even a lot of money. And only then will the country be able to absorb millions of Jews . . . There is no other solution.[41]

From this perspective, Weitz explained in his *Davar* article, a solution of 'transfer' was advocated in the early 1940s and was supported by Berl Katznelson,[42] Yitzhak Volcani[43] and Menahem Ussishkin,[44] and 'investigations were undertaken to put this concept into effect'.[45] Weitz argued that 'any suggestion for the settlement of the liberated territories (the West Bank and Gaza Strip) must be subjected necessarily to a definite policy which addresses and solves three fundamental problems rendered more acute' by the June war: regional security, the demographic problem and the 'resettlement of the refugees'.

> [As to] the demographic problem, there are some who assume that non-Jewish population, even in high percentage, can be more effectively under our surveillance if it is within our boundaries, and there are some who assume the contrary . . . The author of this article tends to support

the second assumption and has an additional argument to support his position: the need to sustain the character of the state, which will henceforth and obviously in the near future be Jewish, by the majority of its inhabitants, with a non-Jewish minority limited to 15%.[46]

Early on, Israeli leaders realized that the refugee communities in the West Bank and Gaza[47] presented in more than one way the most serious problem for Israel. The refugee camps were – and still are – the most overcrowded parts of the territories, and are therefore the most difficult parts to control. In addition, because the refugees did not accept their sojourn in the territories as an indefinite one, Israeli leaders saw a greater long-term challenge from them than from the indigenous population. In his *Davar* article, Weitz referred to a memorandum drawn up by 'Ezra Danin, Zalman Lifschitz and himself – all members of the Israeli government Transfer Committee of 1948 –called 'Memorandum On Settlement of the Arab Refugees', dated October 1948, 'the composition of which was preceded by investigations, surveys and research based on data considered reliable at the time'.[48] In 1967 Weitz believed that 'the logical and possible way of rehabilitating the refugees in the Arab countries is blocked by their rulers, and will be blocked for a long time to come; with no alternative the way leads, at least initially', to the West Bank side of the Jordan Valley. In this region the arable lands could be increased by means of desalination and some of the refugees could be settled there. However, for Weitz, the solution for too many residents in the territories' refugee camps remained transfer. Although willing to cede some of the heavily populated regions of the territories to Jordan, Weitz argued that forestalling the Arab 'demographic problem . . . should [be] consider[ed] as an essential action towards the solution of the refugee problem making financial assistance available to families who are prepared to emigrate to countries outside the Arab world. Every financial investment in these [transfer] activities will be of great blessing to our state today and in the future.'[49]

It should be pointed out that not everyone in Israel was satisfied with mere financial incentives and encouragement of the kind proposed by Weitz. An opinion poll carried out three weeks after the 1967 victory showed 28 per cent of the Israeli Jewish electorate in favour of expelling the Palestinian citizens of Israel, and 22 per cent favouring expulsion of Palestinians from the occupied territories.[50]

In a way Weitz's practical and usually discreet approach to Arab transfer activities characterized the pragmatism of Labour Zionism and its handling of this very prickly and explosive issue. Although in 1940 he had advocated 'total' Arab removal from the whole of Palestine, in 1967 he opted for 'partial' transfer. It is likely that four decades of immersion in the attempts to implement secret plans for Arab transfer taught Weitz to take pragmatic constraints into consideration, including opposition among the Palestinians themselves, rejection from Arab states as well as the sensitivity of Western public opinion. All these factors rendered the transfer task exceedingly difficult. Weitz's experience and 'expertise' in this regard may have been taken into account by the Labour government while working for the promotion of a secret transfer plan – known as the Moshe Dayan Plan – between 1967 and 1970.

The Israeli Government's Transfer Schemes and Operations, June 1967–1972

In the course of hostilities and in the immediate aftermath of the June 1967 War, with its rapidly changing circumstances, and particularly given the fact that most Western governments applauded the overwhelming Israeli victory, Defence Minister Dayan and other army generals (including 'Uzi Narkiss, Haim Hertzog, and Shlomo Lahat) found an ideal opportunity to drive out tens of thousands of Arabs from their villages, towns and refugee camps in the West Bank and Gaza Strip. In their article in *Davar* of 19 February 1988 entitled 'This is the History of Transfer', the Israeli journalists Yossi Melman and Dan Raviv pointed out that the Israeli conception of 'exploiting opportunities to transfer Arab population, which was first employed in 1948, resurfaced shortly after the 1967 War: Commanders in various ranks of the army believed that the wind blowing from the political echelon was calling for exploiting the opportunity to thin out the Palestinian population'.

Among the first evictees were the residents of the ancient al-Magharbeh quarter in East Jerusalem. They were turned out of their homes on 11 June, two days after the capture of Arab East Jerusalem, on a few minutes' notice.[51] The order to evict the quarter and destroy its houses was given by Shlomo Lahat, then the Commander of Jerusalem, with the express approval of 'Uzi Narkiss, Commanding General of the Central Command, whose approval was given at a meeting with Lahat on 9 June.[52] Apparently, the quarter was demolished because it was located immediately adjacent to the southern part of the Western Wall of al-Haram al-Sharif. Its inhabitants, about 135 families (or some 1,000 persons), were the beneficiaries of an ancient Islamic Waqf foundation originally established in 1193 by al-Malik al-Afdal, the son of Salah al-Din. Its obliteration in June 1967 resulted also in the destruction of several historic religious sites the quarter contained.[53]

The evictees of the al-Magharbeh quarter were dispersed in West Bank villages close to Jerusalem (such as Shu'fat, Bayt Hanina, and Silwan) as well as in the Muslim quarter of the Old City of Jerusalem. Like the eviction of the three villages in the Latrun salient, this removal should be treated as an internal expulsion rather than transfer out of the occupied territories. However, it is extremely important to remember that these cases of internal expulsion had a psychological effect on the 1967 exodus from the West Bank to Jordan, helping (almost certainly) to precipitate and encourage further exodus out of the country, especially in the first few weeks following the war.

The evictions and levelling of the al-Magharbeh quarter were only the beginning of the sweeping changes carried out by the Israeli authorities. In Jerusalem's Jewish Quarter and its surrounding districts, some 4,000 Palestinians were evicted to make possible the reconstruction of a vastly enlarged and completely 'Jewish' quarter, excluding its former Arab residents.[54]

Also among the first to go were the 10,000 inhabitants of the villages of Bayt Nuba, 'Imwas, and Yalu, situated near the Green Line in the strategic Latrun salient north-west of Jerusalem. On orders from Commanding General of the Central Command 'Uzi Narkiss, the army bulldozers moved in and wiped out the three villages.[55] Narkiss (who later became Director General of the Jewish Agency's (JA) Department of Immigration and Absorption and is in 1995 chairman of the JA's Department of Information) also commanded the troops who captured Jerusalem and clearly approved of the order to evict the al-Magharbeh quarter.[56]

'Amos Kenan, a well-known Israeli journalist, who took part in the war, revealed, in graphic detail, the story of Bayt Nuba:

> We were ordered to block the entrances of the villages and prevent inhabitants returning to the village from their hideouts after they had heard Israeli broadcasts urging them to go back to their homes. The order was to shoot over their heads and tell them not to enter the village. Beit Nuba is built of fine quarry stones; some of the houses are magnificent. Every house is surrounded by an orchard, olive trees, apricots, vines and presses. They are well kept. Among the trees there are carefully tended vegetable beds . . . At noon the first bulldozer arrived and pulled down the first house at the edge of the village. Within ten minutes the house was turned into rubble, including its entire contents; the olive trees, cypresses were all uprooted . . . After the destruction of three houses the first column arrived from the direction of Ramallah . . . some Arabic-speaking soldiers went over to notify them of the warning. There were old people who could hardly walk, murmuring old women, mothers carrying babies, small children. The children wept and asked for water. They all carried white flags.
>
> We told them to go to Beit Sura. They told us that they were driven out everywhere, forbidden to enter any village, that they were wandering like this for four days, without food, without water, some dying on the road. They asked to return to the village, and said we had better kill them . . . We did not allow them to enter the village, and take anything . . . More and more columns of refugees arrived, until there were hundreds of them . . . The platoon commander decided to go to headquarters and find out if there were any orders about what to do with them, where to send them, and whether it was possible to arrange transport for the women and food for the children. He returned saying that there were no orders in writing, simply that they were to be driven out.
>
> We drove them out. They go on wandering in the south like lost cattle. The weak die. In the evening we found that they had not been

taken in, for in Beit Sura too bulldozers had begun to destroy the place and they were not allowed to enter. We found out that not only in our sector was the border [the Green Line] straightened out for security reasons but in all other sectors too.[57]

According to General Narkiss, the evictees of the 'four [sic] villages of the Latrun area' were evacuated to Ramallah and some of them crossed the river to Jordan.[58] In his book *The Liberation of Jerusalem*, Narkiss wrote: 'I was determined that the Latrun enclave, that years-old thorn in our flesh, would never be returned [to Arab sovereignty].'[59]

Canada Park was created with the help of the Canadian Jewish National Fund on the site of the three bulldozed villages and their 20,000 dunums of agricultural lands.[60] More recently plans were announced to plant another section of the same site with trees and name it 'Scharansky Hope Forest' after Nathan Scharansky, the well-known Zionist activist and former Soviet prisoner,[61] who is Minister of Trade and Industry in the Likud cabinet of Binyamin Netanyahu.

In the same year four other Arab villages, Bayt Marsam, Bayt 'Awa, Habla, and Jifliq, were cleared and razed to the ground,[62] and only the intervention of a group of liberal Israeli intellectuals and academics saved the West Bank town of Qalqilyah from a similar fate when an order by Defence Minister Dayan for the expulsion of the inhabitants and the destruction of the town was cancelled.[63] Attempts to 'thin out' the teeming population of Gaza were also made in the summer of 1967, as a resident of the Strip, Abu Hassan, recalled:

A few weeks after the Strip had been occupied, the Israelis embarked on a programme of forced deportation. On one occasion, the Israeli army rounded up all the men from my quarter and herded us into Jaffa school. The Israelis had two local mukhtars with them who told the officer in charge each man's profession – 'he's a labourer, that one's a teacher' and so on. The Israelis picked out the ones they wanted, put them on trucks and sent them to Jordan. I remember another time the army arrived in trucks early in the morning and grabbed all the young men they could find. Those of us who were around began protesting, but the Israelis told us not to worry because they were only taking the youths for a few hours to help in the disposal of those killed in the Sinai during the war. We never saw those young men again. As soon as the work had been done, their identity papers were confiscated and they were forced to cross the canal into Egypt.[64]

The 'Transfer' Operation of Haim Hertzog, Shlomo Lahat, and 'Uzi Narkiss, June 1967

Haim Hertzog was the army's first Military Governor of the West Bank after the June 1967 War. Hertzog had been a political and military broadcaster during the war and published *Israel's Finest Hour* (1967). He was also a regular radio and television commentator in Israel and abroad and managed to amass honorary doctorates from several universities in Israel and other countries.[65] At a public debate on the Palestinian issue held in Jerusalem on 3 April 1970, this first Military Governor of the West Bank and an influential figure of the Labour establishment did not refrain from revealing openly his heart's wishes: 'if we had the possibility of taking one million Arabs [from the territories] and clearing them out, this would be the best'.[66] However, it was only 21 years later in early November 1991, a few days after the Madrid Peace Conference, that President Hertzog revealed publicly and proudly one of Israel's little known secrets: that he, as the first Military Governor of the West Bank, efficiently organized and carried out, in cooperation with Shlomo Lahat, the commander of Jerusalem, the operation of transferring 200,000 Palestinians from the West Bank in the immediate aftermath of the war. According to a statement confirming that this operation was indeed carried out, the President's office said: 'his [Hertzog's] considerations were that in the departing wave many of the PLO men would leave, and this would make it easier for the military administration. For days and weeks lines of buses ran from the Damascus Gate [in East Jerusalem] to the Allenby Bridge [on the River Jordan]. Altogether during this period 200,000 Palestinians left Judea and Samaria voluntarily, including 100,000 refugees whose camps were in the Jericho valley.'[67]

Hertzog claims that he had been prompted to organize this operation during a meeting with Anwar al-Khatib, the former Arab
governor of the Jerusalem district, at the Ambassador Hotel in Jerusalem on Friday 9 June 1967. According to Hertzog, al-Khatib
raised at this meeting, *inter alia*, the problem of the families of Arab
consuls stranded in Jerusalem and the problem of the families of the
Jordanian officers, who fled and left their dependants behind, and
asked the Israeli Military Governor to allow these families to leave
Jerusalem for Jordan via the Allenby Bridge. Hertzog agreed and
told al-Khatib that from the morning of Sunday, 11 June, buses
would be waiting near the Damascus Gate to transport any Arab
wishing to depart to Jordan, on condition that each departing Arab
signed a statement to the effect that he was leaving voluntarily.
Hertzog also revealed that Shlomo Lahat, then the commander of
Jerusalem and the mayor of Tel Aviv from 1974 until 1993, was put
in charge of implementing the operation, and that 'no contrary
order was given by [Defence Minister] Moshe Dayan at any stage
[to halt the operation]'.[68]

Moreover, the superior Commanding General of Hertzog and
Lahat, the aforementioned Commanding General of the Central
Command 'Uzi Narkiss, in fact told an interviewer in October 1988
that he himself had supervised the implementation of the transfer
operation in 1967, which, according to the interviewer, had resulted
in the total 'transfer of 100,000 [Palestinians to Jordan] without
anybody saying a single word'. Narkiss told the same interviewer in
October 1988:

> I placed several buses in Jerusalem and in other cities [of the West Bank],
> written on them: 'To Amman – Free of Charge'. The bus used to carry
> them to the [partly] destroyed Allenby Bridge and then they would cross
> it [to Jordan]. I spread the news about these buses through individuals
> with wide contacts with the inhabitants, such as members of trade
> unions and chambers of commerce . . . In this [bus] operation between
> 20 and 25 thousand people got out.[69]

One of the extraordinary revelations made by Narkiss in connection with his transfer operation was the daily telephone calls he used

to receive after the war from the dovish Finance Minister Pinhas Sapir:

> Pinhas Sapir used to phone me twice a day, to ask: how many [Arabs] got out today? Is the number of the inhabitants of the West Bank diminishing? The number [of those being transported by the buses?] began with 600 and 700 persons a day, and then it began to decline until it reached a few scores, and after two or three months the [bus?] operation stopped.[70]

The statement of the President's office elicited wide publicity in Israel in November 1991 and surprised Israeli historians. Hertzog's claim that Anwar al-Khatib was a partner in such an organized operation of mass 'transfer' was denied by the latter, who promptly convened a press conference at which he said that he had only asked Hertzog at their Ambassador Hotel meeting for the release of the consuls of Egypt, Syria, Lebanon, Iraq, and Saudi Arabia, all of whom had been detained by the Israeli army, and had asked Hertzog to permit 15 Jordanian officials, who had worked in Jerusalem, to reunite with their families living in Jordan. Al-Khatib added that he had been surprised, a few days after his meeting with Hertzog, to find out that the military administration had organized buses and trucks for mass transportation of Arabs to the Allenby Bridge.[71]

A former Israeli soldier described the 'voluntary' and 'humane' aspects of this operation in a November 1991 interview with *Kol Ha'ir*:

> My job was to take their [each Palestinian's] thumb and immerse its edge in ink and fingerprint them on the departure statement . . . Every day tens of buses arrived. There were days on which it seemed to me that thousands were departing . . . Although there were those departees who were leaving voluntarily, . . . there were also not a few people who were simply expelled . . . We forced them to sign. I will tell you how exactly this was conducted: [for instance] a bus [carrying men] was arriving and only men were getting off, I emphasise – only men, aged 20 to 70, accompanied by border guards. We were told that these were saboteurs, fedayeen, and it would be better that they would be outside the state. They [the Arab men] did not want to leave, and were dragged from the

buses while being kicked and hit by revolver butts. By the time they arrived to my [signing] stall, they were usually already completely blurred [as a result of beatings] at this stage and did not care much about the signing. It seemed to them part of the process. In many cases the violence used against them was producing desirable results from our point of view. The distance between the border point and the [Allenby] Bridge was about 100 metres and out of fear they were crossing to the other side running; the border guards and the paratroopers were all the time in the vicinity. When someone refused to give me his hand [for finger printing] they came and beat him badly. Then I was forcibly taking his thumb, immersing it in ink and finger printing him. This way the refuseniks were removed . . . I have no doubt that tens of thousands of men were removed against their will.[72]

It is also worth noting the reactions of two Israeli historians to the 1991 revelations surrounding the 'transfer' operation of Hertzog and Lahat. Uri Milstein had this to say:

I remember that 5 days after the Six-Day War I was in Jericho. It was empty there and we were told that the [refugees] fled. It is more likely that they [the Israeli army] drove them away. In the War of Independence [the 1948 war] there was no organized transfer, people [Israeli commanders] volunteered to carry it out on their own initiative. In the Six-Day War there were similar situations. Many thought that we had not completed the job in the War of Independence. It is known that there was a plan to conquer Qalqilyah [town] and destroy it. There was also a plan to carry out transfer in Hebron as a revenge for the massacre [of Jews] in [19]29. I have not read about the evacuation of 200 thousand refugees in buses and I am not aware that this has been published anywhere.

Meir Pa'il stated:

This story is new to me, but this does not mean that it is incorrect, particularly in the light of the fact that the refugee camps in Jericho ['Ayn Sultan, Nu'aymah and 'Aqbat Jabir] were emptied of their residents in one–two weeks after the Six-Day War. The travel route of the buses, which operated as described here, from the Damascus Gate to the Allenby Bridge, had to pass via the Jericho valley and the large refugee camps that were there and this is another confirmation of the story. If one of the four men: President Hertzog, Shlomo Lahat, his deputy Shmuel Albak, or 'Uzi Narkiss, confirms this thing, then this story is true and genuine.[73]

Hundreds of thousands of Palestinians fled or were expelled from the occupied territories during and after the June 1967 war. In their book *River Without Bridges*, Peter Dodd and Halim Barakat study the 1967 exodus of the Palestinian refugees and attempt to answer the question: Why did this exodus take place? The answer, according to them, is that:

> the exodus was a response to the severe situational pressures existing at the time. The situational pressures were generated by the aerial attacks upon a defenceless country, including the extensive use of napalm, the occupation of the West Bank villages by the Israeli army, and the actions of the occupying forces. Certainly the most drastic of these actions was the eviction of civilians and the deliberate destruction of a number of villages ['Imwas, Yalu, Bayt Nuba, Bayt Marsam, Bayt 'Awa, Habla, and Jifliq]. Other actions, such as threats and the mass detention of male civilians, also created situational pressures.[74]

Dodd and Barakat (who were not aware of the 'transfer' operation of Herzog and Lahat), added that there were other indirect reasons: the Palestinian villagers were not equipped and ill-prepared to resist and cope with these situational pressures; they were ill-informed and unfamiliar with the terrifying nature of the aerial attacks. To this the social structure of Arab society should be added: the family-centred social structure diminished attachment to community and nation and some Palestinians left to protect their family, particularly the honour of their womenfolk.

In his detailed investigation of the 1967 exodus, William Wilson Harris (who also made no mention of the 'transfer' activities of Hertzog and Lahat) estimated that of a pre-war population of approximately 1.4 million, about 430,000 left the territories occupied in the war (including the Golan Heights and Sinai) between June and December 1967. Most of these refugees left in June 1967. He pointed out that the 1967 refugee exodus varied from one region to another: over 90,000 people (almost 90 per cent of the population) fled the Golan Heights, while the Gaza Strip lost less than 20 per cent of its 400,000 residents. There were also local variations in the West Bank. The high population losses in some regions were the result of a 'psychological legacy of pre-war events, a legacy of assorted fears', for instance, in the Hebron district, in the region surrounding the village of Qibya in the West Bank, where the Israeli army had carried out a large and infamous massacre in October 1953, in which 66 villagers were killed.[75] Another example was in the Latrun salient where the 10,000 residents of Yalu, 'Imwas, and Bayt Nuba were ordered to leave their villages by the Israeli army and the chain-reaction effect of their movement across the West Bank can be traced in the higher losses from other villages on the Latrun-Ramallah-Jerusalem highway.[76]

Encouragement of Arab departure by the Israeli authorities was also reported in the foreign press. *The New York Times* of 26 August 1967 reported that each day for the last two weeks some 500 residents had left the Gaza Strip, adding that 'Any reduction in Gaza area's population is a benefit to everyone in Israel's view.' Several months later, *The Observer* (London) reported on 17 December 1967:

> The opportunity of reprisals on security grounds has been taken to hasten the departure of more people from the West Bank and the Gaza Strip and to prevent the return of those who had fled. The Israeli author-ities believe that whatever the eventual political status of the Gaza Strip, the refugees there should be moved elsewhere.

The Observer of 28 January 1968 also reported: 'It is estimated that between 30,000 and 35,000 people have left the [Gaza] Strip as a result of the measures taken by the Israeli authorities.' *The Guardian* Middle East correspondent Michael Adams wrote: 'No Israeli when he deals frankly with you (and many do) will deny that he would prefer to accept "the dowry without the bride", meaning that, from Israel's point of view, the ideal solution to the problem of the occupied territories would be their absorption by Israel but without their Arab population.'[77]

In addition to the active encouragement of Arab departure, the Israeli army took tough measures to prevent the return of those who had fled during the war or shortly after it. Even after the war, Israeli troops on the Jordan River apparently routinely shot civilians trying to slip back to homes on the West Bank.[78] A statement made by an anonymous soldier, who had served in the 5th Reserve Division on the Jordan River, and was issued from the Tel Aviv office of Hebrew magazine *Ha'olam Hazeh* on 10 September 1967, read:

> we fired such shots every night on men, women and children. Even during moonlit nights when we could identify the people, that is – distinguish between men, women and children. In the mornings we searched the area and, by explicit order from the officer on the spot, shot the living, including those who hid, or were wounded (again: including the women and children).[79]

General 'Uzi Narkiss, the Commanding General of the Central Command, 1965–68, also told an interviewer in October 1988 that after the 1967 war the Israeli troops on the Jordan River killed civilians trying to slip home to the West Bank.[80]

Moshe Dayan's Secret Scheme, June 1967–1970

General Moshe Dayan was appointed Defence Minister on the eve of the 1967 war and retained this powerful post until 1974. He was the most famous and typical exponent of Israeli post-1967 expansionism and the *de facto* integration of the occupied territories into Israel. In essence, Dayan professed the same drive and vision of Gahal-Herut (and later he was to become Foreign Minister in the Begin Cabinet), although his style was more subtle, more politic, and above all, more pragmatic than Zionist Revisionism. For instance on 21 August 1981 Dayan told an interviewer that in principle he favoured [Ariel] Sharon's idea of Jordan as the Palestinian state but 'the more we push such a situation, the more resistance we will create. As formulated I accept it. But certainly no one need be surprised that Hussein [*sic*] is not enthusiastic about handing over his regime to Yasser [*sic*] Arafat.'[81] Dayan instituted a policy of 'creeping annexation', a process by which Israeli administration, jurisdiction, and law gradually, incrementally, and draconianly were imposed on the West Bank and the Gaza Strip, in ever expanding areas, yet without a comprehensive act of legal annexation. That process, also described as *de facto* annexation, is generally seen in the actual transformation of the demographic and physical realities of these areas.

The Israeli government, the Dayan-headed Defence Ministry, and the Mossad (the Israeli external secret service) resorted, by and large, to discreet transfer activities in the aftermath of the war. This method of secret transfer activities, as well as transfer discussions at cabinet level, have been gradually revealed by Israeli journalists and researchers as well as politicians. Examples of these revelations are the research of Meir Avidan, published in *Davar* on 2, 5, and 19 June 1987, and the articles published by two Israeli journalists, Yossi Melman and Dan Raviv, who published an article in *The Washington Post* on 7 February 1988 entitled 'Expelling Palestinians'. The same article appeared in *The Guardian Weekly* (London) two weeks later under the title 'A Final Solution of the Palestinian Problem?' and was similar to an article in the Hebrew daily *Davar* by the authors, which appeared around the same time and was entitled 'This is the History of Transfer'.[82]

Avidan, Melman, and Raviv reveal that less than two weeks after the Israeli victory in the war of June 1967, the Eshkol cabinet convened for a number of secret meetings, held between 15 and 19 June 1967, to discuss a major issue: What to do about the 'demographic problem' – the fact that the bulk of the Arab population of the territories – contrary to 1948 – remain *in situ*. The official transcript of the meeting remains secret. However, according to private diaries kept and notes taken by Ya'acov Hertzog – brother of Haim Hertzog, President of Israel from 1983 to 1993 – who was at the time director-general of the Prime Minister's office, both the Finance Minister Pinhas Sapir and the Foreign Minister Abba Eban called for settling the Palestinian refugees in neighbouring countries.[83] Relying on Avidan's research, Melman and Raviv point out that at these meetings 'sentiment seemed to favour Deputy Prime Minister Yigal Allon's proposal that Palestinian refugees be transported to the Sinai Desert and that Palestinians should be persuaded to move abroad'.[84] According to Hertzog's notes, Allon complained at the meeting of 15 June: 'We do not do enough among the Arabs to encourage emigration.'[85] At the same meeting Menahem Begin, then minister without portfolio, recommended the demolition of the refugee camps and the transfer of their residents to El Arish in Sinai, which had been captured from Egypt.[86] Begin's proposal was supported by the Labour leader and Minister of Transport Moshe Carmel at these discussions.[87]

Avidan also reveals that the Ministerial Committee for Defence decided on 15 June 1967 that: 'Israel will demand from the Arab countries and the Super powers to start preparing an elementary plan to solve the refugee problem. This would include the settlement of refugees in Iraq, Syria, (Egypt?), Algeria, Morocco, Jordan, and other countries (in the presentation of this demand emphasis would be laid on the fact of population exchange)' – that is, that the settlement of the refugees would be in the place of Jews who left Arab countries.[88] Apparently a ministerial committee was set up to look into ways of 'solving the refugee problem'.[89] A few weeks after the June discussions, Dayan went even further, publicly declaring that the resettlement of the refugees must be carried out in the Jordanian kingdom across the river.[90] In the following year, while reviewing the political situation at a meeting of the Rafi[91] Secretariat, Dayan talked about 'encouraging the transfer of the Gaza Strip refugees to Jordan'.[92] In the 1970s Dayan's views on this subject were little changed; Israel should tell the Palestinian refugees in the West Bank and Gaza Strip that

> we have no solution, that you shall continue to live like dogs, and whoever wants to can leave – and we will see where this process leads . . . In five years we may have 200,000 less people – and that is a matter of enormous importance.[93]

In 1974, MK Dayan, in a speech before the Knesset in which he urged the Rabin government to encourage Jewish settlement freely in the occupied territories and maintain military control over them, went on to say that as far as the Palestinian refugees in the West Bank and Gaza were concerned, 'the Arab states now have land and water and also funds and Arab nationhood, and with all of this they can solve the refugee problem in their lands'.[94]

Three years later, in 1978, Dayan wrote in his book *Living with the Bible* that 'all the proposals put forward by Israel to transfer them to other countries and rehabilitate them there, were rejected by their Arab leaders'.[95]

The product of the June discussions was not a total relocation of the refugee camps' residents to the Sinai desert but rather a 'voluntary' transfer plan, designed to 'thin out' the population of the West Bank and Gaza, which later became known as the Moshe Dayan plan, and was revealed publicly for the first time by the son of Yosef Weitz, Ra'anan Weitz[96] – who for many years headed the rural settlement department of the Jewish Agency with responsibility for settling certain areas on the West Bank – at a meeting of the executive of the International Centre for Peace in the Middle East dated 1 June 1985. It is not known whether Ra'anan Weitz himself had anything to do with the Moshe Dayan plan. However, Weitz – a Labour Party man with close connections to government ministers and senior officials – had been appointed secretly by Prime Minister Eshkol in July 1967 to head a team of 120 advisers, 'Arabists', and 'experts' (including three senior professors from the Hebrew University of Jerusalem: the economist Dan Patenkin, the demographer Roberto Bachi, and the sociologist Shmuel Eisenstadt), who were entrusted with the task of suggesting solutions to the problem of Palestinian refugees residing in the West Bank and Gaza Strip.[97] Moreover, in 1969 Weitz himself had worked out a detailed plan for the transfer of 50,000 Palestinian refugees from the Gaza Strip and their resettlement in El Arish – a plan that he had submitted to government ministers and the Labour Party leadership for consideration. However, this plan, which was designed to contribute to the policy of thinning out the teeming refugee camps of Gaza, never reached the stage of implementation, possibly because of the difficulties the Israeli authorities had encountered in their previous attempts to relocate a substantial number of refugees from Gaza to Sinai.[98] According to Ra'anan Weitz, after the June 1967 War Moshe Dayan consolidated a plan for encouraging Arab emigration from the West Bank to South America. Subsequently Israeli 'experts developed a plan for Palestinian settlement in South America and each family in Judea and Samaria which agreed received sums ranging from 3,000 to 5,000 dollars'. Weitz added that some tens of Arab families accepted the proposal and emigrated but none of them remained in South America and after a certain period returned to their houses on the West Bank.[99]

The same scheme was also referred to in public by the Likud Minister of Industry and Trade Ariel Sharon in November 1987, when advocating Arab transfer.[100] The scheme began with the formation of a secret unit charged with 'encouraging' the departure of the Palestinians for foreign shores. The secret unit was composed of representatives of the Prime Minister's office, the Defence Ministry and the Israel Defence Forces. This secret unit is the same one later referred to as the Eshkol unit. This unit, according to Weitz, operated also in the West Bank. General Rehava'am Zeevi refers to the same unit. Zeevi himself was General Commanding Officer, Central Command (with a certain responsibility for the West Bank) between 1968 and 1973. The secret unit functioned quietly for three years from the office of the Israeli military governor in Gaza on 'Omar al-Mukhtar Street, one of the main streets in the city. The unit provided the 'transferees' with one-way tickets to various South American countries, mainly Paraguay, through a Tel Aviv travel agency, and promised to give further financial assistance to get them established once they had arrived.[101] In fact, concern about mass Arab emigration was voiced at the time by member of Knesset Uri Avnery, who – although unaware of the Moshe Dayan plan – noted in his weekly *Ha'olam Hazeh* that the tourist agency Patra, subsidized by the Israeli government, was giving away almost free one-way tickets to Brazil, to stimulate Arab emigration. According to Avnery, it was openly admitted that the aim of the Tel Aviv-based agency was to 'empty' out the Gaza Strip.[102] The Israeli authorities worked intensively to find individual Arabs who were disappointed with their lot and might be candidates for the secret programme.

The clandestine unit, according to Melman and Raviv, purchased land through intermediaries in Paraguay, Brazil, and even pre-Qadhafi Libya for carrying out the scheme.

According to Melman and Raviv, the unit managed, secretly, to 'transfer' a total of about one thousand Palestinians during the three years the plan continued. However, it ended as a result of an unexpected development. In desperation a 'transferee' in Paraguay from the Jabaliya refugee camp (Gaza Strip), who had been promised financial assistance and received none, went to the Israeli consulate in Asunción in May 1970 and demanded to see the ambassador. When his request was denied he pulled a pistol and shot the ambassador's secretary dead.[103] Some patchy revelations about the same secret scheme were also made by General 'Uzi Narkiss, Commanding General of the Central Command until 1968 – with responsibility for the West Bank – who told an interviewer in October 1988 that after the June 1967 war

> some of the Mossad men came to me . . . and then they offered some [Arab] individuals sums [of money] in exchange for them leaving their property [in the Old City of Jerusalem and the West Bank] . . . These sums were part of the government allocations for this matter. Some agreed, but the experiment failed; it succeeded only with several score, until one of our daughters was killed – as a revenge – in our embassy in Paraguay, then the operation was stopped.[104]

The discovery of the Dayan plan led to its collapse. However, there is no reason to assume that 'transfer' activities instigated and promoted by the Israeli authorities as part of their plan 'for solving the Palestinian problem' ended in 1970. In fact other, not so gentle, 'transfer' activities of the Israeli army, under Dayan, in and around the Gaza Strip continued well into 1972. The most important of these was the forcible eviction of 6,000 to 20,000 Bedouin farmers from the Rafah salient, south-west of the Gaza Strip, between 1969 and 1972.[105] This case is also associated closely with Ariel Sharon, the IDF Commander of the Southern Front (end of 1969–71). 'Based on . . . a tacit understanding with Dayan, Sharon . . . undertook a programme to evict the Bedouins who had settled in northern

Sinai, south-west of the Gaza Strip. As the two men flew over the area one day, Dayan casually remarked that it would hardly be a tragedy if there were no Arabs living there,' writes Sharon's biographer, 'Uzi Benziman.[106] 'Sharon understood that Dayan preferred to be circumspect', for political reasons. Dayan had once told Sharon in the mid-1950s, shortly before Sharon had taken over command of the paratroop corps: 'Do you know why you're the one who does all the operations? Because you never ask for written orders. Everyone else wants explicit clarifications. But you never need it in writing. You just do it.'[107] Sharon wrote in his autobiography that Dayan told him in 1970: 'You can start.' Sharon added: 'Anyone other than Dayan would have carefully formulated an order describing what should be done and defining the parameters of the intended action. But from him there was only a signal, the nod of a head.'[108] One of the objectives, according to Benziman, was to fence off the area, creating a 'security belt' around the heavily populated Gaza Strip. 'Sharon's plan called for the isolation of the Gaza Strip from the Sinai peninsula, severing the continuity of the Palestinian population within Gaza by introducing Jewish settlements in its midst, and thinning out the population of the refugee camps. Sharon began by forcibly evacuating thousands of Bedouins from northern Sinai and encouraging the establishment of new [Jewish] settlements in their place,' Benziman explains. While justifying his action on grounds of 'national security', Sharon 'vigorously supported plans for Jewish settlements in the Gaza Strip, to blur the unequivocally Palestinian character of the area'. Years later, Sharon boasted that under the cloak of war against 'Arab terrorism' he had effectively extended the Israeli frontier into northern Sinai.[109]

When a special cabinet committee arrived in Gaza for a briefing from Sharon on his 'anti-terrorist effort' in the Strip and in northern Sinai, Sharon recommended, *inter alia*, the establishment of Jewish settlement there and the elimination of the refugee camps and transfer of their residents. Sharon reveals in his autobiography:

I put a third proposal in front of them, essentially the same proposal I had made in person to Levi Eshkol after the Six-Day War – which he had rejected. I told them – Yigal Allon, Israel Galili and the others – just as I had told Eshkol, that I believed it was time to solve the Palestinian refugee problem and that I was prepared to do it. The essence of my plan was to get rid of the Palestinian refugee camps altogether . . . these places still bred the most serious problems for us and always would. It would be to our great advantage to eliminate them once and for all, and in my view such a thing was quite feasible.

According to this plan, some of the refugees would be settled in Gaza, some others would be settled in the towns of the West Bank, and the remainder would be encouraged by financial incentives to depart. 'I believed we could agree to pay the legitimate claims of Arab refugee families once they had permanently settled in other countries. I had no doubt whatsoever that we could establish a long-term fund for this purpose, that however large a sum we would need for this could be raised from a variety of sources, including the immensely supportive overseas Jewish communities . . . it was the obligation of the Arab world to absorb the Arab refugees . . . The elimination of the camps would be neither easy nor quick; it would take, as I envisioned it, ten years or so,' Sharon wrote.[110]

Sharon complained that he had not been able to persuade Golda Meir's ministers in 1971 to accept his plan for total elimination of the refugee camps. The cabinet ministers, however, 'approved wholeheartedly' his proposals 'to widen the camps streets' – thinning out the population? – and the establishment of Jewish settlements.[111]

The army's eviction of the Bedouin communities from the Rafah area with 'vigorousness, violence and brutality' – on Sharon's order and based on the tacit policy of Dayan and the Golda Meir government – stirred many liberal Israelis and some left-wing kibbutzim, particularly those in the Negev, to protest.[112] Sharon reacted to this public uproar by going on the offensive against his liberal detractors, visiting a number of kibbutzim in the Negev to explain that he was implementing national policy and that the eviction of the Bedouins was perfectly in accordance with the government programme to settle northern Sinai. He also accused the kibbutzim of sheer hypocrisy and reminded them that they themselves were occupying land that had been abandoned by Arab refugees in 1948. Prime Minister Meir also came to the defence of the army's eviction of the Bedouin living between Gaza and northern Sinai. She addressed a gathering at a kibbutz in the Negev: 'My conscience is clear regarding the fact that the minings and murders are worse than the eviction of innocent people.'[113]

In fact, the resistance to Israeli occupation in the late 1960s and early 1970s originated not from the forcibly evacuated, sedentary Bedouin south-west of the Gaza Strip, but from the city of Rafah and the Palestinians of the refugee camps in Gaza. The Israeli army ironically had hired hundreds of those Bedouin for all sorts of jobs, including guard duty.[114] The Bedouin appealed to the Israeli Supreme Court in August 1972 to stop their eviction by the army and allow them to return to their land, but the court rejected the appeal on 23 May 1973 and accepted the government's case, basing its decision on the grounds – the government's arguments – of 'national security'.[115]

Against the background of the public controversy surrounding the Rafah evictions in 1972, a leading Israeli journalist and publicist, Yesha'ayahu Ben-Porat, wrote in justification of these evictions in *Yedi'ot Aharonot*:

> it is the duty of the [Israeli] leadership to explain to the public a number of truths. One truth is that there is no Zionism, no settlement, and no Jewish state without evacuating Arabs, and without expropriating lands and their fencing off.[116]

Ben-Porat pointed out that neither of the two investigations into these evictions suggested a return of the Bedouin to their lands, and that not even the ministers of the Mapam party, a junior partner in the Labour government, were calling for the return of the evictees to their lands.[117] Interestingly, the settlements set up on the lands of the Bedouin farmers in the Rafah salient had to be dismantled less than ten years later as part of the return of Sinai to Egypt under the 1979 Israeli–Egyptian peace treaty.

During the period in which the evictions of the Bedouin farmers of the Rafah salient took place, several hundred Palestinian refugees were forcibly relocated from the Gaza Strip to north Sinai as part of Israel's policy of thinning out the crowded refugee camps, in particular, and the Gaza Strip, in general. As late as 1995 there were 3,000 relocated refugees in Gaza whose plight had not been resolved. In addition to these, there are also members of the Mallahah Bedouin tribe (about one thousand persons), who were first made refugees (from the Beersheba region) in 1948, and who maintain that they were forced to leave their grazing land in the Gaza Strip two months before Israel withdrew from Egyptian territory in 1982. Altogether there were in 1995 about 4,000 Palestinians, who were relocated forcibly from the Gaza Strip to Sinai before 1982, and were left stranded in Sinai after Israel withdrew in 1982.[118]

The forcible eviction of the peaceful, farming Bedouin communities from their fertile land in the Rafah salient, and their replacement by Jewish settlers, represented one example of the ideology of force, which reached its apogee between the 1967 War and the October War of 1973. Both Dayan – who virtually dominated the Labour government's policies in the occupied territories until 1974 – and Sharon – until his retirement from the army in 1971 – in their different style, represented that ideology of force, inherited from Ben-Gurion, which was based on the conviction that the defence of Israel depended exclusively on its own strength. The ideology of force, which helped to reawaken thoughts of transfer after 1967, is rooted in the pre-state Yishuv and the events that led to the establishment of the State of Israel and the consequent Palestinian exodus of 1948. This ideology of force is predicated on a number of premises: a) that Palestinians of the occupied territories would resign themselves to their fate, either being kept down or transferred if they dared to oppose Israel; b) the Arabs only understand the language of force; c) the Arab world is very divided and Israel can create *fait accompli*; and d) it does not matter what the Gentiles say, but what the Jews do – a well-known saying of Ben-Gurion.[119]

Both Dayan and his protégé Sharon felt it was necessary to remind their compatriots, including those who were opposed to Jewish settlements in the Rafah area and the West Bank, of what some of them, the younger generation, never knew. Dayan had this to say in a 1969 speech at the Technion in Haifa:

> We came here to this country, which was settled by Arabs, and we are building a Jewish State . . . Jewish villages arose in the place of Arab villages. You do not even know the names [of these villages], and I do not blame you, because those geography books no longer exist. Not only do the books not exist, the Arab villages are not there either. Nahlal [Dayan's own settlement] arose in the place of Mahlul, Gvat [a kibbutz] in the place of Jibta, Sarid [another kibbutz] in the place of Haneifis, and Kfar-Yehoshu'a in the place of Tal-Shaman. There is not one single place built in this country that did not have a former Arab population.[120]

Given this unflinching perception of uprooting and dispossession of Arab communities in the pre-state period combined with the fact that the Zionist objectives had always proceeded against the wishes of the local population, and given the emergence of the ideology of force and its occupation of the centre ground in Israeli policies toward the Palestinians, from there to the massive settlement of Greater Israel movements – and their transfer schemes – which will be discussed in the following chapters – was only a short step.

Notes to Chapter 2

1. The Arab citizens of Israel numbered just below 400,000 in 1967. In his study of the 1967 Arab refugee exodus, W.W. Harris found that the Arab population of the West Bank immediately prior to the 1967 war was approximately 840,000. The refugee migration reduced this population by between 200,000 and 250,000. However, by 1977, through a very high natural increase, the number of the West Bankers had recovered to over 820,000. See W.W. Harris, *Taking Root: Israeli Settlement in the West Bank, the Golan and Gaza-Sinai 1967–1980* (Chichester: Research Studies Press, 1980), p. 7. The Gaza Strip inhabitants were about 400,000 in 1967. Therefore after June 1967 there were about one million Palestinians in the occupied territories, and altogether within the new cease-fire lines (including the Arab citizens of Israel) there were just below one million four hundred thousand Arabs.

2. A speech delivered at a meeting of the French Zionist Federation, Paris, 28 March 1914, in Barnet Litvinoff (ed.), *The Letters and Papers of Chaim Weizmann,* vol. I, Series B (Jerusalem: Israel Universities Press, 1983), paper 24, pp. 115–16.

3. See protocol of Ruppin's statement at the Jewish Agency Executive's meeting, 20 May 1936, in Yosef Heller, *Bamavak Lemedinah: Hamediniyut Hatziyonit Bashanim 1936–48* [The Struggle for the State: The Zionist Policy 1936–48] (Jerusalem, 1984), p. 140.

4. Israel Zangwill, *The Voice of Jerusalem* (London: William Heinemann, 1920), p. 104.

5. Yehuda Gurvitz and Shmuel Navon (eds.), *What Story Will I Tell My Children?* (Tel Aviv: Amihah, 1953), pp. 128, 132, 134, cited in Fouzi El-Asmar, 'The Portrayal of Arabs in Hebrew Children's Literature', *Journal of Palestine Studies* 16, no. 1 (Autumn 1986), p. 83.

6. Dan Ben-Amotz, *Seporei Abu-Nimr* [The Stories of Abu-Nimr] (Tel Aviv: Zmora-Bitan, 1982), p. 155.

7. In October 1991 Prime Minister Yitzhak Shamir, in his address to the Madrid Peace Conference, resorted to quoting from *The Innocents Abroad* by Mark Twain (who visited Palestine in 1867 and whose description of its natives was either marked by invective or humorously pejorative), to prove that Palestine was an empty territory, a kind of civilizational barrenness that (in Shamir's words) 'no one wanted'; 'A desolate country which sits in sackcloth and ashes – a silent, mournful expanse which not even imagination can grace with

the pomp of life.' For excerpts of Shamir's address, see *Journal of Palestine Studies* 21, no. 2 (Winter 1992), pp. 128–31. The axiom of 'desolate country' was used by Shamir to justify Zionist colonization of Palestine and the obliviousness to the fate of its native inhabitants. Also the current Israeli Prime Minister, Binyamin Netanyahu, resorted to the axiom of 'ruined'/'desolate'/'empty' country by quoting Twain's *The Innocents Abroad* to justify Zionist colonization of Palestine. See Benjamin Netanyahu, *A Place Among the Nations* (London: Bantam Press, 1993), pp. 39–40.

8. Amos 'Oz, 'The Meaning of Homeland', *New Outlook* 31, no. 1 (January 1988), p. 22. 'Oz's article was originally published in *Davar* in 1967.

9. Ibid., p. 21.

10. Cited from the back cover of 'Jerusalem of Gold', Fontana Records, SRF, 67572, MGF 27572.

11. See *Ma'ariv*, 11 June 1967.

12. The Shofar is a horn used on Jewish high holidays to commemorate events of major significance.

13. Translated from Hebrew, Fontana Records, in Uri Davis and Norton Mezvinsky (eds.), *Documents from Israel 1967–1973* (London: Ithaca Press, 1975), p. 220.

14. 'Oz, 'The Meaning of Homeland'.

15. Har-Tzion became a national hero after serving in 'Unit 101', which, under the command of Ariel Sharon, carried out 'retaliatory' operations against Arab targets in the 1950s. The unit was responsible for the attack on the Arab village of Qibya, to the south-west of Hebron, in 1953 in which 63 villagers were slaughtered, and also carried out the expulsion of the al-'Azazmeh tribe from the Negev to Sinai.

16. *Ma'ariv*, supplement, 22 January 1979, p. 6; cited also in Meir Kahane, *Lesikim Be'enekhem* [They shall be Strings in Your Eyes] (Jerusalem: Hamakhon Lara'ayon Hayehudi, 1980/81), p. 230. Har-Tzion believes that the minimal Israeli borders should be: in the north the Litani river, in the east the River Jordan, and in the south half of Sinai should be included.

17. *Davar*, 9 February 1979, p. 17.

18. Quoted in Zeev Schiff and Eitan Haber (eds.), *Leksikon Levitahon Yisrael* [added title: Israel, Army and Defence: A Dictionary] (Tel Aviv: Zmora, Bitan, Modan, 1976), p. 178. In his book *Heroes of Israel*, Haim Hertzog (President of Israel from 1983 to 1993) quotes Ariel Sharon's

description of Har-Tzion as 'The fighting symbol not only of the paratroops, but of the entire Israel Defence Forces.' Chaim Herzog, *Heroes of Israel: Profiles of Jewish Courage* (London: Weidenfeld and Nicolson, 1989), p. 271.

19. See *Ma'ariv*, 6 December 1974, p. 22; cited also in Yair Kotler, *Heil Kahane* (New York: Adama Books, 1986), pp. 89–90.

20. Quoted in Tzvi Shiloah, *Ashmat Yerushalayim* [The Guilt of Jerusalem] (Tel Aviv: Karni Press, 1989), p. 45.

21. Quoted in Aharon Ben-'Ami (ed.), *Sefer Eretz-Yisrael Hashlemah* [The Book of the Whole Land of Israel] (Tel Aviv: Friedman Press, 1977), pp. 20–21.

22. Cited by Ephraim Urbach (a professor of Talmud and Midrash at the Hebrew University of Jerusalem), in *Midstream* (a monthly Jewish review), April 1968, p. 15. Urbach thought that 'this sort of thing is very harmful and not at all edifying'.

23. Cited in Ben-'Ami (ed.), *Sefer Eretz-Yisrael Hashlemah* [The Book of the Whole Land of Israel], pp. 20–21.

24. Cited in Mordechai Nisan, *Hamedinah Hayehudit Vehabe'ayah Ha'arvit* [The Jewish State and the Arab Problem] (Tel Aviv: Hadar, 1986), pp. 119, 200.

25. Tzvi Shiloah, *Ashmat Yerushalayim* [The Guilt of Jerusalem], p. 8. For more details about Shiloah's ideas see below.

26. Moshe Shamir, *Hamakom Hayarok* [The Green Place] (Tel Aviv: Dvir Publishing House, 1991), pp. 95–99.

27. See Eli'ezer Livneh, in *Moznayim* (July 1967).

28. See for instance, Shim'on Ballas in *Haumah*, no. 2 (November 1967), p. 217.

29. Haim Yahil, 'Demography and Israel's Uniqueness', in Ben-'Ami (ed.), *Sefer Eretz-Yisrael Hashlemah*, pp. 312–13; and Haim Yahil, *Hazon Umaavak: Mivhar Ketavim* [Vision and Struggle: Selected Writings, 1965–74] (Tel Aviv: Karni Press, 1977), p. 105.

30. Tzvi Shiloah, *Ashmat Yerushalayim*, p. 24.

31. Tzvi Shiloah, *Eretz Gdolah Le'am Gadol* [A Great Land for a Great People] (Tel Aviv: Otpaz, 1970), pp. 107–108.

32. Tzvi Shiloah, *Eretz Gdolah Le'am Gadol*, p. 102. Exactly the same Katznelson polemics with Hashomer Hatza'ir were cited above by Natan Alterman in justification of the transfer concept in the post-1967 period.

33. Shiloah, *Eretz Gdolah Le'am Gadol*, p. 104; Shiloah, *Ashmat Yerushalayim*, p. 8.

34. Shiloah, *Eretz Gdolah Le'am Gadol*, p. 105.
35. See Tzvi Shiloah in *Moledet*, no. 12 (October 1989), p. 11. In 1973 Shiloah left the Labour Party and joined the La'Am-Likud bloc until 1977. Later he became a Tehiya member of the Knesset and in 1988 was a founding member of the Rehava'am Zeevi-led Moledet, a single-issue transfer party.
36. Ben-'Ami, *Sefer Eretz-Yisrael Hashlemah*, pp. 349–50.
37. See *Haumah*, no. 88 (Autumn 1987), pp. 20–26.
38. Ibid., p. 21.
39. Ibid., p. 26.
40. See Weitz's memorandum: 'The Problem: The Refugees', dated 17 September 1967, in Weitz's papers, The Institute for Settlement Studies, Rehovot; *Davar*, 29 September 1967.
41. This quote is found in the manuscript of Weitz's Diary in the Central Zionist Archives (Jerusalem) A246/7, entry for 20 December 1940, pp. 1090–91. The quote in the article in *Davar* is a slightly edited version of the entry in the diary. The *Davar* article is entitled: 'A Solution to the Refugee Problem: An Israeli State with a Small Arab Minority'.
42. Katznelson was the founder and the leading ideologue of Mapai, the hard-core political component of the ruling Labour Party.
43. Volcani was for many years a director of the Jewish National Fund and a member of the Executive Committee of the Histadrut.
44. Ussishkin was a key leader of the Zionist movement and the Jewish National Fund Board of Directors, the Chairmanship of the latter resting in his hands for nearly twenty years (1923–41).
45. Weitz hints here at the Jewish Agency Transfer Committees and schemes before 1948 and his own investigations in preparation for carrying out the transfer solution.
46. In fact the figure 15 per cent was referred to for the first time in 1948 in the recommendations of the Israeli Government Transfer Committee, of which Weitz was a member, submitted to the Prime Minister Ben-Gurion, on 26 October 1948. According to these recommendations the Arabs should not exceed 15 per cent of the population of the mixed cities such as Haifa.
47. The number of refugees on the West Bank registered with the United Nations Relief and Works Agency (UNRWA) in 1984 was 357,000. In the same year there were 20 refugee camps on the West Bank housing 91,000 people. The other 266,000 refugees resided in the villages and towns. In the Gaza Strip an estimated two-thirds of the 650,000 inhabitants are refugees.

48. The Memorandum was not designed for publication but drafted for Ben-Gurion by the then Transfer Committee.

49. *Davar*, 29 September 1967.

50. Israeli Institute of Applied Social Research, A'si, 'Israeli and Palestinian public opinion', p. 154, cited in David McDowall, *Palestine and Israel* (London: I.B. Tauris, 1989), p. 197. Dr Ya'acov Cohen of the Hebrew University's Hillel institution wrote in an article in *Davar* on 4 October 1967 (p. 14) about the 'dangerous nationalistic atmosphere' which has been created in the wake of the 1967 War and asked 'isn't it a fact that many Jews in Israel would welcome the emigration of the Israeli Arabs to Arab countries?'

51. David Hirst, *The Gun and the Olive Branch* (London: Faber and Faber, 1984), p. 225.

52. See Gide'on Levi, 'Transfer of 100,000 Without Anybody Saying a Single Word', *Haaretz*, 25 October 1988; and Yossi Melman and Dan Raviv in *Davar*, 19 February 1988, pp. 10–11.

53. For further details see Rashid Khalidi, 'The Future of Arab Jerusalem', *British Journal of Middle Eastern Studies* 19, no. 2 (1992), pp. 139–40.

54. See Geoffrey Aronson, *Israel, Palestinians and the Intifada* (London: Kegan Paul International, 1990), p. 19.

55. Melman and Raviv in *Davar*, 19 February 1988, pp. 10–11.

56. See Gide'on Levi, 'Transfer of 100,000 Without Anybody Saying a Single Word', *Haaretz*, 25 October 1988; and Melman and Raviv in *Davar*, 19 February 1988, pp. 10–11.

57. Cited by *Israel Imperial News*, London, March 1968.

58. See Gide'on Levi, 'Transfer of 100,000 Without Anybody Saying a Single Word', *Haaretz*, 25 October 1988.

59. 'Uzi Narkiss, *The Liberation of Jerusalem* (London: Vallentine, Mitchell, 1983), p. 199. Meron Benvenisti, former deputy mayor of Jerusalem, writes:

> At the end of the 1967 war, there were attempts to implement a forced population transfer. Residents of cities and villages in areas near the cease-fire line were expelled from their homes and their communities destroyed; the Israeli authorities offered financial 'incentives' and free transportation to Palestinians willing to leave . . .' (*Intimate Enemies*, London: University of California Press, 1995, p. 191).

60. Aronson, *Israel, Palestinians and the Intifada*, p. 19.

61. Beit-Hallahmi, *Original Sins*, p. 96.

62. Hirst, *The Gun and the Olive Branch*, p. 225.

63. See Yossi Melman and Dan Raviv, 'Expelling Palestinians', *The Washington Post*, outlook, 7 February 1988. See also 'Oded Lifschitz, in *1967–1987: Kovshim 'Atzmam Lada'at* [Added title: A Self-Defeating Conquest] (Tel Aviv: Mapam and 'Al-Hamishmar, 1987), p. 77.

64. Cited in Cossali and Robson, p. 64. See also recollection by the 62-year-old Ibrahim, a construction worker from Gaza, in Lifschitz, *1967–1987*, pp. 77–78.

65. The list of the universities which awarded him honorary doctorates includes: Hebrew University of Jerusalem; Haifa University; Ben-Gurion University of the Negev; Bar Ilan University; the Technion; Weizmann Institute of Science, Rehovot (part of the Hebrew University); Georgetown University (Washington, DC); University of Liberia; Yeshiva University, J.T.S.

66. Cited in Mordechai Nisan, *Hamedinah Hayehudit Vehabe'ayah Ha'arvit* [The Jewish State and the Arab Problem] (Tel Aviv: Hadar, 1986), p. 117.

67. Cited by Shmuel Meiri in *Ha'ir* (Tel Aviv), 8 November 1991, p. 13; *Kol Ha'ir* (Jerusalem), 8 November 1991, p. 19.

68. Ibid.

69. Quoted by Gide'on Levi, 'Transfer of 100,000 Without Anybody Saying a Single Word', *Haaretz*, 25 October 1988. Narkiss also talked about the eviction of the residents of 'four villages in the Latrun area' and the 'flight' of some 60,000 refugees from the three refugee camps near Jericho: 'Ayn Sultan, Nu'aymah, and 'Agbat Jabir.

70. Ibid.

71. Cited in *Kol Ha'ir*, 15 November 1991.

72. Ibid.

73. Cited in *Ha'ir*, 8 November 1991, p. 13.

74. Peter Dodd and Halim Barakat, *River Without Bridges* (Beirut: Institute for Palestine Studies, 1969), p. 54.

75. Harris, *Taking Root*. In October 1953, Unit 101, commanded by Ariel Sharon, attacked the village of Qibya in 'reprisal' for the murder of a mother and two children in an Israeli settlement. Jordan had condemned the Arab perpetrators and offered its co-operation to track them down. UN military observers who arrived at the scene two

hours after Sharon's commandos had completed the operation described what they found:

> Bullet-riddled bodies near the doorways and multiple bullet hits on the doors of the demolished houses indicated that the inhabitants had been forced to remain inside until their homes were blown up over them . . . Witnesses were uniform in describing their experience as a night of horrors, during which Israeli soldiers moved about in their village blowing up buildings, firing into doorways and windows with automatic weapons and throwing hand grenades.

Cited in E.H. Hutchinson, *Violent Truce* (New York: Devin-Adair, 1956), pp. 152–58. Commander Hutchinson was an American UN observer.

76. Harris, *Taking Root*, p. 22.
77. *The Guardian*, 19 February 1968.
78. David McDowall, *Palestine and Israel* (London: I.B. Tauris, 1989), pp. 204 and 302, n. 109.
79. Cited in ibid., p. 302, n. 109.
80. Quoted by Levi, 'Transfer of 100,000', *Haaretz*, 25 October 1988.
81. FBIS, 26 August 1981, quoted in Palumbo, *Imperial Israel*, p. 155.
82. Melman and Raviv, 'Expelling Palestinians'; *The Guardian Weekly* (London), 21 February 1988; *Davar*, 19 February 1988, pp. 10–11.
83. Melman and Raviv, 'Expelling Palestinians', *Davar*, 19 February 1988.
84. Ibid.
85. Ibid.; and Avidan, *Davar*, 2 June 1967.
86. Avidan, *Davar*, 2 June 1967.
87. Ibid.
88. Ibid.
89. See Shim'on Ballas in *Haumah*, no. 2, November 1967, p. 216.
90. Ibid.
91. Rafi – 'Reshimat Po'alei Yisrael' (Israel Workers List). Political party founded in July 1965 by David Ben-Gurion and seven other Knesset members, who seceded from Mapai in consequence of the dissension created by the controversy over the Lavon affair. Subsequently Moshe Dayan joined the new party, which stood to the right of the central tendency in Mapai and, by the late 1960s, had become identified as an advocate of large scale territorial expansion. In the general election of

1965 it obtained 10 seats in the Knesset. Rafi remained in opposition to the Eshkol government until the eve of the June 1967 War, when it entered the National Unity Government, Moshe Dayan becoming Defence Minister. In January 1968 Rafi joined Mapai and Ahdut Ha'avodah to form the Israel Labour Party. By the mid-1970s, however, Rafi's separate identity was largely lost.

92. Cited in Tzvi Shiloah, *Ashmat Yerushalayim* [The Guilt of Jerusalem] (Tel Aviv: Karni Publishing House, 1989), p. 36.

93. Quoted in Noam Chomsky, *Deterring Democracy* (New York: Hill and Wang, 1992), p. 434.

94. *Haaretz*, 24 July 1974, cited in Noam Chomsky, *Towards a New Cold War* (London: Sinclair Browne, 1982), p. 234.

95. Moshe Dayan, *Lihyot 'Im Hatanakh* [Living with the Bible] (Jerusalem: 'Edanim Publishers, 1978), p. 143.

96. Yosef Weitz himself wrote in his diary: 'Instructions were given to experts by the [Eshkol government] to work out a plan' for settling the Gaza refugees in the West and East Bank. However this 'policy' was abandoned later. Weitz, *Yomani*, vol. 6, appendix 21, p. 529.

97. See Yuval Elitzur in *Ma'ariv*, 4 August 1967.

98. See 'Amir Shapira in *'al-Hamishmar*, 12 May 1972, supplement; *Davar*, 25 July 1972; and Danny Tzedoki in *Davar*, 31 August 1972.

99. See *Ma'ariv*, 2 June 1985, p. 2; Mordechai Nisan, *Hamedinah Hayehudit Vehabe'ayah Ha'arvit*, 2nd edition [The Jewish State and the Arab Problem] (Jerusalem: Rubin Mass, 1987), pp. 119 and 200.

100. Melman and Raviv, 'Expelling Palestinians'.

101. Ibid., and Melman and Raviv in *Davar*, 19 February 1988.

102. Cited by Israel Shahak in *Middle East International*, no. 3. (June 1971), p. 22.

103. Melman and Raviv in *Davar*, 19 February 1988.

104. Quoted by Levi, 'Transfer of 100,000', *Haaretz*, 25 October 1988.

105. See Moshe Negbi, *Kevalim Shel Tzedek* [added title: Justice Under Occupation] (Jerusalem: Cana Publishing House, 1981), p. 30.

106. Uzi Benziman, *Sharon: An Israeli Caesar* (London: Robson Books, 1987), p. 119.

107. Ariel Sharon, *Warrior* (London: Macdonald, 1989), p. 250.

108. Ibid., pp. 250–51.

109. Benziman, *Sharon*, p. 119.

110. Sharon, *Warrior*, pp. 258–60.

111. Ibid.

112. Benziman, *Sharon*, pp. 119–21. Early in 1972, in the wake of a public

uproar, David El'azar, the Chief of Staff, appointed General Aharon Yariv to investigate Sharon's actions: Sharon told him: 'I gave the order and I won't deny it.'

113. Ibid., pp. 120–21.
114. Ibid., p. 122.
115. Ibid., p. 121.
116. *Yedi'ot Aharonot*, 14 July 1972.
117. Yesha'ayahu Ben-Porat, 'The Mistake, Naivity, and Hypocrisy', *Yedi'ot Aharonot*, 14 July 1972, weekend supplement, p. 1.
118. See Deborah Pugh in *The Guardian*, 4 January 1993.
119. For further discussion see Amnon Kapeliouk, *Israel: La Fin Des Mythes* (Paris: Editions Albin Michel, 1975), pp. 28 and 183–222.
120. *Haaretz*, 4 April 1969, p. 15.

Chapter 3
Israel's Deportation Policy in the West Bank and Gaza Strip since 1967

From the beginning of the Israeli occupation of the West Bank and Gaza Strip in June 1967, deportations were an integral part of its policies. These policies were based on a set of political decisions that provided for the resurrection and creation of an elaborate structure of military legislation and various administrative methods to acquire the land, stifle any independent political activities and control and thin out the Palestinian population. These practices included administrative detention and town arrest; the demolition of homes and the sealing of shops; the imposition of fines, travel restrictions, prolonged curfews and sometimes virtual siege; the closing of schools and universities; as well as the deportation of political and religious leaders, elected mayors and members of municipal councils, trade unionists, student leaders, academics and professionals. Moreover, throughout the years of occupation the policy of deportation was applied against political activists from all the political groups in the West Bank and Gaza Strip: pro-Jordanian, leading communists and radicals, Fatah activists, supporters of the various Palestinian fronts and factions and Islamic activists. Viewed from this perspective, deportations were also carried out with the aim of eliminating the local political leadership and keeping the native population under control. Needless to say this objective dovetailed with the general aim of thinning out the Palestinian population.

Unlike the mass expulsions of 1948 and 1967, which were carried out largely under cover of armed conflict, Israel has defended its deportation policy since 1967 in the name of security, the standard justification for this practice. The occupation authorities used deportation/banishment/exile as a means of collective punishment and assertion of control as well as a means of removing as many

Palestinians as possible from the 'administered territories' to facilitate their eventual annexation (either wholly or in part) to Israel, as manifested in the expansion of Jewish settlements in these areas.[1]

While all Israeli governments prior to 1993 adhered to the official position that the Palestinians have neither distinct nationality and identity nor national rights in the 'Land of Israel', including the West Bank and Gaza Strip, Israel's deportation policy beginning in 1967 was based on the implicit premise that the very right of the Palestinians to reside in their homeland (a crucial right that technically is reduced by Israeli authorities to the possession of an Israeli identity card) could be questioned. This deportation policy must be viewed within the wider context of Israel's demographic battle against the Palestinians, a battle for acquiring more land and gradually reducing the level of population in the occupied areas.

In June 1967, during the very early days of the Israeli occupation, thousands of Palestinian men, aged 20 to 70, were deported forcibly from the West Bank and Gaza Strip across the Jordan River. This little known operation paved the way for the evolution of Israel's deportation policy. Since 1967, there have been four groups deported and/or banished/exiled within a single deportation policy in the occupied West Bank and Gaza Strip. The first and second categories consisted of residents issued with expulsion orders under Articles 108 and 112 of the British Defence Emergency Regulations of 1945, or Military Order 329 (West Bank) and Military Order 290 (Gaza Strip) of 1969. The first category was of those accused of 'incitement' or membership in 'illegal organizations' and the second group was of those labelled as 'infiltrators', regardless of whether they were born, or had lived most of their lives, in the West Bank and Gaza Strip. Vaguely worded, Article 3(a) of Military Order No. 329 gives the military commander considerable power: 'Any Military Commander may order in writing the deportation of any Infiltrator from the Area, whether charged with an offence under this Order or not, and the deportation order shall constitute a valid legal ground for detaining the said Infiltrator pending his deportation.'[2] The actual selection of deportees, however, was usually done by the Shabak (short for General Security Service), a powerful internal body, which is answerable only to the prime minister.

The third category included those Palestinians who, while in detention for 'security offences', supposedly made a deal with the Israeli authorities under which they were given a reduced prison term in exchange for leaving the occupied territories. The fourth, most common but least publicized, category are those whose effective exile has been carried out on various technical and legal grounds (such as failing to renew their identity cards or not being registered in the 1967 census) that prevented a large number of Palestinians either from remaining in, or returning to, their homes in the West Bank and Gaza Strip. Although this category is not recognized by the Israeli authorities as one of deportees, it may be considered as such, since *de facto* deportation has been the outcome of the legal procedures created by the occupier with the aim of removing people from the West Bank and Gaza Strip.[3]

Under international law there are several human rights conventions which contain provisions relating to the expulsion/deportation/exile of nationals, or to the denial of the right of a national to enter his own country. These provisions include:

I) Article 9 of the 1948 Universal Declaration of Human Rights: 'No one shall be subjected to arbitrary arrest, detention or exile.' In addition, Article 13(2) of the same Declaration: 'Everyone has the right to leave any country, including his own, and to return to his country.'

II) Article 12(4) of the 1966 International Covenant on Civil and Political Rights: 'No one shall be arbitrarily deprived of the right to enter his own country.'

III) Article 3 of Protocol 4 (of 1963) to the European Convention (of 1950) for the Protection of Human Rights and Fundamental Freedoms: 'No one shall be expelled, by means either of an individual or of a collective measure, from the territory of the State of which he is a national.'

IV) Article 22(5) of the 1981 African Charter on Human Rights and Peoples' Rights: 'Every individual shall have the right to leave any country including his own, and to return to his country.'

Israel's policy of individual and mass deportation constituted a clear contravention of international law and conventions, particularly the Fourth Geneva Convention of 1949. Article 49(1) of the Fourth Geneva Convention, which is the fulcrum of the interdiction of deportations from occupied territories, categorically outlaws the expulsion of people from their own country:

> Individual or mass forcible transfers, as well as deportations of protected persons from occupied territory to the territory of the Occupying Power or to that of any other country, occupied or not, are prohibited, regardless of their motive.

This absolute prohibition, for security arguments or military considerations, is reinforced by Article 76, which states that 'protected persons accused of offences shall be detained in the occupied country and, if convicted, they shall serve their sentences therein.' Although Israel signed this convention on 8 December 1949, it consistently claimed that the convention did not apply to the West Bank and Gaza Strip, which it occupied in 1967.[4] Moreover, Israel's policy of expulsion was unanimously condemned by a number of UN Security Council resolutions; for instance, Resolution 607 of 6 January 1988 and Resolution 799 of 18 December 1992. Israel, however, remained largely impervious to international criticism of this practice.

The arbitrariness of this practice is much in evidence; being a form of extra-judicial sanction, deportations were always imposed by administrative orders. The deportees were invariably denied due process: general accusations were usually made against them, but no formal legal charges were ever brought; they never had hearings before a court, and neither they nor their lawyers had access to the evidence on which the decision to deport them was supposedly based. The lack of due process was also exemplified by the absence of an appeal procedure based on the facts of the case. Since 1977, the deportees have been allowed to appeal the deportation order, but what the Israeli Supreme Court has done until now is only to review the expulsion procedure of the Military Commander in order to establish whether the latter acted within the prerogatives granted to him.[5] After 1967 Meir Shamgar,[6] the Israeli Attorney General, became the architect of the Israeli legislation in the occupied West Bank and Gaza Strip. In September 1985, in his capacity as President of the Supreme Court, he referred to the deportation of a Palestinian to Jordan as 'the expulsion of a Jordanian citizen to the Kingdom of Jordan',[7] echoing the denial in official thinking of the existence of a distinct Palestinian identity and nationality and the official claim that the Palestinians of the West Bank were Jordanian citizens, therefore, being alien residents, their deportation to Jordan was (in Shamgar's own words) 'more a kind of return' of 'Jordanian subjects' to their own country. Of course, this was only a cynical argument, since residents of Gaza, who were not Jordanian citizens, were expelled to Jordan, and residents of the West Bank were also deported to Lebanon. Also significant is the fact that since 1977 the Supreme Court has repeatedly underwritten the policy of deportation, a practice which has usually been justified in the name of security.

In 1967 the Israeli authorities decided to reactivate the Defence Emergency Regulations – promulgated by the British Mandatory government in 1945 – with regard to the West Bank and Gaza Strip. Ya'acov Shimshon Shapira, who in 1967 was Justice Minister and in 1948–49 was the first Attorney General for the government of Israel, said about these regulations back in 1946:

> The established order in Palestine since the defence regulations is unparalleled in any civilized country. Even in Nazi Germany there were no such laws and the [Nazi] deeds of Mayadink and other similar things were against the code of laws. Only in an occupied country do you find a system resembling ours. They try to reassure us by saying that these laws apply only to offenders and not to the whole of the population, but the Nazi governor of occupied Oslo also said that no harm would come to those who minded their own business . . .[8]

The level of deportation in each of the four categories described above varied over the years, depending, in part, on changing local and political circumstances. In practice, the policy of deportation was pursued more vigorously under Labour than Likud. For instance, expulsions within the first three categories peaked between 1969 and 1971, when hundreds of Palestinians in the West Bank and Gaza Strip were arrested and immediately deported across the Jordanian or the Lebanese border each year without due process. On a single night in 1970 deportation orders were issued against 300 people. In the same year at least 406 Palestinians were thrown out. In the following year at least 306 residents were expelled. Between 1968 and 1972 over 1,095 people were deported.[9]

During this period, Palestinian political activism and resistance to Israeli policies in the occupied territories was particularly strong, ranging from running a trade union to writing slogans on walls, to taking part in peaceful demonstrations, to organizing protests and strikes, to civil disobedience. In the Gaza Strip the resistance also took the form of armed struggle. The policy of deportation, together with a host of strong-arm tactics, was pursued widely by the then Defence Minister, Moshe Dayan, as a weapon and means of collective sanction against the local population in the Gaza Strip as well as the West Bank.

There are no precise figures on the number of Palestinians deported under successive Labour governments between 1967 and 1977. The official Israeli figures, cited in *The Financial Times* on 9 December 1977, put the number of the deportees at 1,180. A detailed investigation carried out by Ann Lesch for the American Friends Service Committee, found that at least 1,156 Palestinian men and women were deported by the end of 1978 (including nine people expelled by the Likud government in 1978). In addition, two Bedouin tribes, comprising some 350 people, were driven *en masse* from the Jordan Valley in December 1967 and May 1969.[10] This put the total number of the deportees until 1977 at about 1,500. One Israeli source has suggested that at least 1,342 Palestinians of the West Bank and the Gaza Strip were deported by Labour governments during the first decade of occupation.[11] It is possible, however, that the real number was even higher; Danny Rubinstein, who for many years covered the occupied territories for the daily *Davar*, estimated that the real figure until the advent of the Likud was close to 2,000, including those exiled within the third category of deportation: Palestinians who supposedly made a deal with the authorities to depart in exchange for a reduced prison term.[12] Until 1978, less than one per cent of the total number of deportees was allowed to return home.[13]

The estimate of 2,000 deportees until 1977, however, does not take into account those cases in which spouses and dependent children left to rejoin deportees in Jordan. Whatever the exact figure of those expelled between 1967 and 1977 may have been, these evidently included a major portion of local leaders and professionals. A close examination of the list of deportees compiled by Lesch prompted Jordanian journalist Rami Khouri to remark:

> [S]everal hundred of the deportees were in natural 'leadership' roles in their communities, such as municipal officials, teachers or labour union activists, and that at least 100 deportees stand out as hard-core, active leaders in an organized manner, such as presidents of professional associations, editors of newspapers, mayors and municipal council members, heads of students' or women's groups, university presidents and school principals, judges, religious leaders (both Moslem and Christian), lawyers, doctors, village mukhtars, tribal leaders, and heads of social, welfare or charitable organizations.[14]

By eliminating local leaders and professionals, Israeli authorities hoped to provide a further incentive for other residents to depart voluntarily.

Until November 1969 the main routes of deportation were the Allenby and Damiyah bridges across the Jordan River. Following protests by the Amman-based Committee of Expelled Palestinians, the Jordanian authorities in October 1969 were nudged into acting against the use of these bridges for expulsions. Israel, however, shifted its deportation routes to the south, across the hostile and dangerous terrain of the Wadi Araba desert between the Dead Sea and the Gulf of Aqaba, exploiting the unmarked and loosely controlled border between the two countries for that purpose. From November 1969 until the end of 1973, over 800 Palestinians were expelled across the isolated and deserted border in the Wadi Araba desert. After 1974 the deportees were dropped in south Lebanon as well as expelled to Jordan across Wadi Araba.[15] One summary expulsion across the Wadi Araba desert was described by deportee Yusuf 'Abdullah 'Udwan from Irtah, in the West Bank:

There were twelve of us. On 1 July 1970 we were taken to the Beer Sheba [sic] prison. The guards told us that this was the first stage of our release. When we arrived in Beer Sheba[,] we were told it was banishment. Next morning at six o'clock we were handcuffed and blindfolded and our feet were chained. In reply to our questions we were told that we were going home. They put us in a truck and we travelled for about four hours. When the truck stopped we were taken to another vehicle and travelled for about three hours more. We didn't know where we had been taken to. When the vehicle stopped[,] the cloth was taken off our eyes. We saw then that we were in an armoured car. We were surrounded by other armoured cars loaded with armed soldiers. We were on the road, and around us extended the desert. An officer came and ordered us in a threatening voice: 'Now you walk towards the East [sic]', and he pointed at the dunes of the endless desert. 'Anyone coming back will be shot. Anyone coming back in a month, a year, or any other time must know that only death awaits him here.' To the East [sic] the burning sands of the desert were waiting for us. It was midday in July. Our heads had no cover; our shoes were plastic slippers. We each had a water bottle with lukewarm water and a bag with sand-covered food. We started walking in the terrible heat of noon without knowing where our steps would take us. We were afraid of getting lost in the desert. We remembered the Egyptian soldiers who died in the Sinai sands after suffering hunger, thirst and sun stroke. We walked for more than two hours until suddenly we met a first-line post of the Jordanian army. They thought we were spies and started shooting at us. By a real miracle none of us were wounded, and finally we succeeded in convincing them, and we were taken to Amman. As you know, the Jordanian authorities refused to accept people deported across the bridges. So the Israeli authorities wanted to confront them with facts. I think they expected the Jordanians to kill us. We were told later that we had been banished near the Al-Dahl region, in Wadi Arabah [sic]. Our feet were inflamed when we arrived in Amman. The skin of my shaved head had peeled off because of the sun. The desert was a nightmare.[16]

117

In the early years of the occupation those expelled had a diverse political background. However, until the civil war in Jordan (1970–1971), prominent among the deportees were public figures with pro-Jordanian views. During this period, the expelled included Rouhi al-Khatib, the mayor of East Jerusalem who was deported on 7 March 1968, Nadim al-Zaru, the mayor of Ramallah, deported on 6 October 1969, Shaykh 'Abdul-Hamid al-Sayih, President of the Muslim Religious Council, who was deported across the Jordan River on 23 September 1967 and subsequently was appointed minister in the Jordanian government. Both al-Khatib and al-Sayih had taken part in the protest activities against Israel's annexationist policies in Arab East Jerusalem. Mayor al-Khatib described his deportation as follows:

> A number of armed Israeli soldiers dashed into my house after midnight . . . on March 7, 1968, and instructed me to dress myself and to accompany them for interrogations at the headquarters in Jerusalem. I did and then, instead of taking me to such an office, they drove me directly to Jericho and kept me in an office until six o'clock in the morning. By that time the assistant Israeli military governor of Jericho appeared and gave me the order of deportation, issued by the Minister of Defence of the Israeli forces. No trial, no accusations, and no self-defence. Immediately they put me into one of the cars, drove directly to the bridge, and told me to go to the east side of the Jordan and to Amman . . . My family was kept in the dark until midday, when they heard of my deportation on the radio.[17]

Also prominent among the pro-Jordanian and East Jerusalemite deportees were Anton 'Atallah, the Director of the Arab Land Bank, who was deported on 26 December 1967, and Dr Nabih Mu'ammar, the Director of the East Jerusalem al-Maqasid hospital, who was deported on 16 April 1969. Also in the early years, radical and communist leaders were targeted; the communist leader Faiq Warrad was expelled on 7 December 1967, and the trade union leader Michel Sindaha was deported on 28 April 1970. In the first three years of occupation, deportations from the West Bank had a devastating effect on the pro-Jordanian elite and the radical leaders.[18] The targeting of various local leaders and political activists continued in the early and mid-1970s, singling out the leaders of the banned Palestinian National Front; the radical leader Sulayman al-Najjab of al-Birah was deported on 28 February 1975. At one point in the early and mid-1970s the main target became the activists of the Palestine Liberation Organization and its various factions in the West Bank and Gaza Strip.[19]

The two thousand deportees fall under the first three categories described above, but do not include the large fourth group who were effectively exiled. The number of these residents throughout the occupation was estimated to be particularly large, although no actual figures have been given. Hundreds of husbands and wives who wanted to live normal lives in the West Bank and Gaza Strip found themselves without residency status and were forced at gun point to cross the Jordan River. The expulsion of these husbands and wives, which continued until 1990 and was executed bureaucratically under the pretext of improper residency, falls under the fourth category of deportation and is an integral part of Israel's demographic battle with the Palestinian people.[20]

Under the first and second Likud governments (1977-1984), deportation as a weapon of punishment did not cease, but was used sparingly. For instance, there were nine deportations in 1978; in May 1980 the mayor of Hebron, Fahd al-Qawasmeh; the mayor of Halhoul, Muhammad Milhem; and the Islamic Sharia judge of Hebron, Shaykh Rajab al-Tamimi, were expelled to Lebanon. The decline in deportations occurred possibly as a result of mounting international pressure on Israel and the strong international condemnation of the Likud settlement policies in the West Bank and Gaza Strip. However, the return of Labour to power, following the formation of the National Unity government of both Likud and Labour with Yitzhak Rabin at the head of the Defence Ministry, brought about not only a diminution of the international condemnation of Israeli practices but also a sharp rise in administrative deportations, under what came to be known as Rabin's 'iron fist' policy. Rabin and the 'security' establishment followed in the footsteps of their mentor Moshe Dayan, an early proponent of the expulsion weapon as an effective and deterrent punishment. On 17

February 1985 'Abdul-'Aziz 'Ali Shahin, a prominent leader in the Gaza Strip, was deported across the northern border into Lebanon.

According to *The Jerusalem Post* of 5 August 1985, the National Unity government decided at a cabinet meeting to reactivate the use of 'administrative detention, deportation' and other measures, 'to clamp down on terrorism and incitement in the administered areas . . . Persons constituting a security risk' as well as 'West Bank Arabs in student, professional and municipal groups, ranging from trade unionists to lawyers, to members of student union executives' would be singled out for expulsion.[21] The 'revival' of this administrative practice was conceived as an integral part of Rabin's self-declared 'iron fist' policy, which was not the result of an upsurge in Palestinian resistance activities as much as of pressures from various forces within the Israeli establishment and the Gush Emunim settlers to act against the Palestinians.[22] Between August 1985 and the end of 1986, thirty-seven Palestinians from the West Bank and Gaza Strip were expelled on the grounds of not having valid identity cards, or designated as 'infiltrators' and accused of 'incitement' or being leaders of 'illegal organizations'. From August 1985 to mid-January 1988, forty-six residents of the occupied territories were deported on the same grounds, while eight others were appealing their expulsion orders. Of the forty-six deportees, twenty-one were residents who earlier (20 May 1985) had been released together with 1,150 other Palestinians from Israeli jails as a result of an agreement exchanging prisoners between Israel and Ahmad Jibril's Popular Front for the Liberation of Palestine-General Command. In fact, those deportees accused of 'incitement' and of being leaders of 'illegal organizations' included a deposed member of the municipal council of al-Birah, the editor of the daily *Al-Sha'ab*, Akram Haniyyah (deported on 28 December 1986), a journalist, trade unionists, student leaders and other residents.[23]

While many mainstream Palestinian political activists were targeted after the revival of the deportation policy in August 1986, beginning early in 1988 Islamic activists became prominent among the deportees.[24] The 'co-ordinator of activities in the territories', Shmuel Goren, declared on Israel Television on 29 August 1988 that Israel will continue to deport or try to deport those who 'engage in incitement, in calling for civil uprising and attacks against us', if they cannot be tried for whatever reason.[25] The exile of the local leadership that chooses to protest against or resist the occupation remained a preferred option of the Israeli authorities during the middle and late 1980s.

The forty-six deportees mentioned above, however, were not the only residents effectively exiled during this period. Many more fell into the third group and were compelled to leave following the expiry of their prison term. At the time of their trial they had supposedly made a deal with the authorities to leave the occupied territories in exchange for a reduced prison term. Deportees in the fourth group were residents of the West Bank and Gaza Strip who were not allowed to return on the pretext that they were not in the area at a certain time following a stay abroad; or were forced to limit their visit to their families in the occupied areas to three months or less on the grounds of not having proper residency permits. An elaborate system of laws and regulations was created to force the Palestinians to leave, or to prevent them from returning. Joost Hiltermann, a researcher with Al-Haq (Law in the Service of Man), the Ramallah-based human rights organization, explained:

> Few Palestinians have any doubt that these practices are part of an overall Israeli policy to remove as many Palestinians as possible, and to keep out those who left or were forced to leave.[26]

The Israeli response to the popular Palestinian *intifada* that broke out in December 1987 was similar to previous answers to Palestinian resistance to the occupier's policies since 1967, only this time the scale of the repressive measures undertaken by the Israeli army was much greater. To crush the Palestinian *intifada*, the military authorities, under the direction of Defence Minister Rabin, imposed collective sanctions on an unprecedented scale. These included mass arrests and detentions, 'limb breaking', beatings, and opening fire on unarmed protesters, which resulted in the death of 1,418 persons up to July 1995, the wounding of tens of thousands of others and prolonged curfews and house demolitions as well as administrative deportations. The 1,418 Palestinians who died as a result of Israeli repression included 260 persons under the age of sixteen. In comparison, during the same period (1987–1995) 297 Israelis died as a result of Palestinian attacks.[27] In the first year of the *intifada* the number of Palestinians expelled from the West Bank and Gaza Strip, within the first and second categories of deportation, doubled in comparison with the previous two-and-a-half years. On a single day, on 17 August 1988, twenty-five residents were served with expulsion orders.[28] From the eruption of the *intifada* until the end of 1989, sixty-four Palestinians were deported by the National Unity government. Again in 1991 eight Palestinians were expelled by the Shamir government.[29]

Rabin's tenure of office as Defence Minister (1984–90), was characterized by the 'iron fist' policy and, during the opening phase of the *intifada*, he reportedly gave the widely known 'break their bones' order.[30] However, there was another, less publicized aspect of his policies that had more to do with actual 'transfer' activities. The Palestinians were being 'spirited across the border', but not even surreptitiously as Herzl recommended in 1895. In March 1990, the Israeli English-language monthly *New Outlook* published an article under the headline '"Creeping Transfer" Hits the West Bank', which explained:

> Since the end of May 1989, Israeli functionaries accompanied by machine-gun-toting soldiers have been swooping down on villages, barging into targeted homes, rousing the startled occupants, and within minutes hustling frantic wives and children into commandeered taxis which are ordered to take them to the Jordan River border crossing. At the border, they are forced over the bridge into uncertain exile in Jordan, while back in the villages stunned husbands and fathers begin the mournful ordeal of coming to grips with their sudden loss. Some 250 Palestinian families have been affected to date.[31]

The targets of this new kind of expulsion, according to *New Outlook*, 'have been mainly men, women and children whose lives, by and large, have been anonymous and politically passive. Most often they are villagers with no record of trouble-making whose only defect has been a specific vulnerability to Israeli legalism.'[32]

According to Israel's regulations these deportees did not have legal residency, which was given to Palestinians who were present in their villages and towns during the Israeli census shortly after the 1967 war. The occupier's law denied residency to those people who left the territories during the hostilities or shortly after and to those people who were working, studying or even visiting relatives in other countries. In the first two years of the occupation some family reunions were allowed to take place but subsequently the applications of thousands of young couples (often relatives) were systematically turned down without explanation. As a result, many husbands and wives who chose to try to live a normal life together in the West Bank or Gaza found themselves without residency status, and, under the intensified crackdown on the *intifada* ordered by Rabin, they found themselves being forced at gunpoint across the Jordan River. According to *New Outlook*, in the second half of 1989, 200 persons were expelled this way.[33] On 6 December 1989, the Hebrew daily *Hadashot* published an article headlined 'And What's New in Rabin's Transfer'. *Hadashot* revealed that in the previous week the Shin Bet had arrived in the village of Bayt Kahel, near Hebron, and picked up six women and nine children – tearing apart six families – and deported them. They belonged to the category of 'without valid papers'. *Hadashot* also called the deportees victims 'of the transfer of women and children under orders from Defence Minister Yitzhak Rabin'.

On 16 December 1992, the Rabin government set a new record for the number of Palestinians served with expulsion orders on a single day when an unprecedented 413 such orders were issued against the alleged activists and leaders of Hamas (Islamic Resistance Movement). The majority of these deportees (about 250) came from the West Bank and the rest from the Gaza Strip. In terms of localities, the largest group came from the city of Gaza and the second largest from the city of Hebron. The deportees included about 30 lecturers, mainly from the Islamic universities of Gaza and Hebron, about 20 doctors and five engineers. Also among the expellees were *imam*s of mosques, clerks of the religious courts, administrators of the Muslim holy places as well as employees of educational, health and welfare institutions: schools, kindergartens, clinics, kitchens for the needy and aid organizations for the disabled, orphans and prisoners' families.[34] Evidently the deportees were overwhelmingly clerics, professionals, and intellectuals. Dr 'Abdul-'Aziz Rantisi, well-known as a Hamas spokesperson in Gaza and one of the deportees, representing the beleaguered group in South Lebanon, said that 108 of the men were *imams*, 10 were doctors, 18 engineers, 18 had university doctorates, 25 were lecturers at the Islamic University in Gaza and 250 held bachelor degrees.[35]

Since 1967 nothing has unified Palestinians more than deportations. The Palestinian national struggle is based more on resistance to expulsion and insistence on the right to return than on any other particular ideological doctrine. To Palestinians, who were traumatized by the mass displacements of 1948 and 1967, the large-scale deportations of 1992 were seen as a signal that the threat of 'transfer' from the West Bank and Gaza had not diminished under the new centre-left coalition of Prime Minister Rabin. Thus, in the weeks following the deportations, there was an unusual degree of unity among the Palestinians. This unity, however, masked major political divisions and discords over the peace talks with Israel – divisions that were soon exposed and even deepened following the Declaration of Principles signed between Israel and the PLO in September 1993. Almost certainly the deportations have contributed to the dramatic rise in Hamas's popularity in the occupied territories and the decline in the popularity of the pro-negotiation camp of the PLO.

In any event, both the deportations and the Oslo agreements have contributed to the emergence of a new and complex political situation in the West Bank and Gaza: armed resistance against the Israelis has been carried out largely by radical and popular Islamic organizations such as Hamas and the Islamic Jihad, while the mainstream pro-negotiation camp in charge of the new Palestinian National Authority (PNA) has been making strenuous efforts to curb this armed resistance.

Mass expulsion was described by some of its Israeli critics as a 'mini transfer'.[36] Israeli novelist A.B. Yehoshu'a, in a 1993 interview, warned the Palestinians that, if after the establishment of a

Palestinian state in the West Bank and Gaza, they still did not behave themselves, they would be expelled to Jordan. Yehoshu'a had this to say:

> I cannot be certain that my solution [a Palestinian state in the West Bank and Gaza] would not be ruined by the Palestinians; that after we return Judea and Samaria, even in stages and in accordance with agreements, including demilitarization and inspection, and anyhow a day might come when they would start sending Katyushas towards us or doing something similar . . . if that day arrives, when they would violate the agreements we concluded with them, I then, as a dove and left-wing man, I will say: we would then act against them in the most drastic and severe manner, that is to say: we would evacuate them. I would say to them: if after I had given you the possibility of establishing your own state, be independent, and run your own life, and you were not up to it – then get out of here. We would take them and transfer them across the Jordan [River] in an orderly manner . . . Transfer. I am saying explicitly: if they were not capable, after they were given independence, to live in good neighbourliness – then they should get out of here. If it becomes clear that after all you have done they are not able to control themselves and the destructive forces among them, we would then transfer them across the Jordan [River], and let them be there.[37]

The mass deportation of December 1992, carried out in flagrant violation of Lebanon's sovereignty by dumping the expelled Palestinians on its territory, represented a new dimension for Israel's deportation policy and set a precedent in Israel's ongoing demographic battle with the Palestinians, a battle for more land and less people. While security, a standard Israeli justification for deportation, was invoked, this 'mini transfer' had more to do with the desire to remove as many Palestinians as possible from the West Bank and Gaza Strip. The mass expulsion was completely out of proportion; about 1,600 Palestinians were rounded up, and over 400 of them were handcuffed, blindfolded, transported to the Lebanese border in the middle of the night and told to walk, while soldiers fired shots over their heads. This was carried out in the middle of a harsh winter, without charge or due process, in retaliation for the killing of four Israeli soldiers. Prime Minister Rabin (who also held the Defence portfolio), a veteran of 'transfer', having taken part in the expulsion of over 60,000 residents of the twin towns of Lydda and Ramle in July 1948, bragged to a BBC reporter on 8 February 1993:

> We knew we were making an unprecedented move. Which government in the past 20 years was prepared to expel or remove temporarily 25, not to mention 400 people? I felt at the time a need to level an immediate, tough blow against Hamas that went beyond everything done previously. I achieved that aim, whether it involved 300 or 400.[38]

Typically, the same Rabin once boasted in a Knesset debate that he had broken more Palestinian 'bones', demolished more houses in the West Bank and Gaza Strip, and expelled more Palestinian 'inciters' than his Likud detractors.[39] Rabin's politics have always borne the stamp of military thinking and his personal political philosophy has its roots in the ideology of the more hard-line 'activist' elements in the Zionist Labour movement, going back to Ben-Gurion and the pre-state Palmah strike force.

Rabin's statements also highlight the 'psychological' dimension behind the re-introduction of this mass expulsion policy. As an unidentified 'senior political source' told the daily *Yedi'ot Aharonot*, the mass expulsion had been intended 'to shock psychologically the Palestinian masses'. According to the same 'source', this aim had been achieved because 'they are now afraid that Israel may proceed to another mass expulsion as soon as tomorrow'.[40] Rabin's 'psychological' reasons were predicated on a presumed 'nature of the Arabs', who, according to his doctrine, respected and feared Israel only because of its power, toughness, high handedness and resolve.[41] Elaborating further on the historical and psychological reasons behind the expulsions, the former deputy mayor of Jerusalem, Meron Benvenisti, wrote in *Haaretz* on 4 February 1993:

> Israeli attitudes (towards the Palestinians) have always rested on power. Israelis have always believed that they could blot out Palestinian hostility by displays of resolve. They have always believed that the Palestinians

could be forced to accept the status quo by the use of naked power. Now, however, against all that logic, the Palestinian community refused to submit to brute force. By so doing, Palestinians dashed Israeli hopes that Israeli power alone could guarantee order on Israeli terms . . . But a democratic society finds it difficult to reconcile itself with arbitrary use of naked power alone. Hence, it searches for excuses and self-justifications. At later stages of the expulsion affair, a number of apo-logias were proffered in a confused manner, of the same sort which throughout the history of Zionism have been regularly invoked to appease guilt. First, the use of force was said to be justified in self-defence against the threats to one's very survival. Second, the use of force was said to be justified in order to bring the enemy to his senses . . . Third, the use of force was said to be justified when it 'conforms to the law'. Fourth, anyone not sharing in the experience of the formation of the Israeli Jewish society was said to be incapable of understanding the situation . . . All such apologias share something in common: they all seek to prove that the new status quo resulting from the expulsion needs to be treated in isolation and requires separate solutions.

Such apologias have been instrumental in shaping Israeli policies in the wake of the expulsion. First, it was imperative to make it axiomatic that the expulsion could not be reversed.[42]

On the face of it, the introduction of mass expulsions at short notice in December 1992 appeared to be a revenge response to the killing of four Israeli soldiers, including Sergeant Nissim Toledano, who had been kidnapped and murdered by Palestinian militants earlier in the month. There is, however, evidence to suggest that this mass expulsion, and the way in which it was executed, had been discussed at length by the 'security' establishment in the early days of the *intifada* four years previously. According to the Hebrew daily *Yedi'ot Aharonot*, one of the proposals put forward then by the former Chief of Staff, Lieutenant Geneneral Ehud Barak[43] (then Deputy Chief of Staff), was mass deportations for a 'fixed period'. General Barak had submitted his proposal again at a session of the influential Knesset Foreign Affairs and Defence Committee, held several months before the December 1992 expulsion, which had been devoted to discussing the 'security situation' in the West Bank and

Gaza Strip.[44] It is worth noting that General Barak was 'reported to have Rabin's ear on a variety of issues and is considered to be his protégé'.[45] In August 1995, Prime Minister Rabin appointed Barak as Minister of the Interior. Several months later, in the aftermath of Rabin's assassination, Barak became Foreign Minister in Shim'on Peres's cabinet.

Large scale deportations were also hinted at by Zeev Schiff, a military commentator for the daily *Haaretz* with close links to the military establishment, on 16 December 1992, shortly before the Rabin cabinet decided on the extensive deportations, possibly reflecting prevalent views within the politico-military establishment.[46] Another journalist, Onn Levi, revealed in the daily *Davar* that officers and officials of the 'security' establishment, the public prosecution system and the Justice Ministry had long been discussing the introduction of a new legal mechanism that would enable the authorities to execute deportations more speedily, and that the kidnapping and murder of Sergeant Toledano were merely a catalyst for the mass expulsion of the Hamas activists and sympathizers. The 'security system', according to Levi, had no intention of confining itself to the expulsion of the 413 men.[47] All this points to the existence of ongoing secret discussions within the politico-military establishment on the use of large scale deportation, discussions that also formed the background for the policy decision by the Rabin cabinet in December 1992.

Although the mass deportations of December 1992 were condemned by some liberal Israelis, they were found 'legal' by the Israeli Supreme Court. They also enjoyed the mass support of the Israeli Jewish public and were endorsed by almost the entire Zionist political spectrum, including all the dovish ministers in the Labour-Meretz cabinet. All members of the cabinet voted for the deportations except Justice Minister David Libai, who shortly after the event stated that

> in effect, the authorities have given themselves the possibility to put people . . . on buses or a boat and deport them without giving them any right to be heard to prove they are the right people or to prove whether suspicions against them have any basis or not.[48]

Conclusion

Between 1967 and 1992 Israel's deportation policy in the occupied West Bank and Gaza Strip obtained the seal of approval of the Israeli Supreme Court, in clear contravention of international law and conventions. As already pointed out, there may have been some link between the extent of international pressure on Israel to halt its deportation policy and the actual level of deportation. After both the 1984 and 1992 elections, with Labour returning to power, the international pressure on Israel diminished; in June 1992 there was even international euphoria at the success of Labour in the election. Perhaps because of the fading international condemnation of Israeli practices, the Labour leadership may have judged that it would be easier to embark on higher levels of deportation. The previous Likud governments, being internationally isolated and censored and domestically criticized by Israeli liberals, found it much more difficult to carry out large scale deportation. Moreover, in an attempt to divert attention from the mass deportation of the 413 people in December 1992, and following the almost unanimous and strong international condemnation of its action, Israel decided in late April 1993 to allow thirty exiles, deported between 1967 and the outbreak of the *intifada* in December 1987 (mostly elderly men and women, including the 80-year-old Rouhi al-Khatib), to return to their homes.[49] Notwithstanding this 'peace' token, made at the time of the resumption of the ninth round of the Middle East peace talks, these returnees represented only a tiny fraction of those exiled between 1967 and 1992.

Since the Oslo Accords were signed in September 1993, Israel has reluctantly announced its willingness to process 2,000 applicants for family reunion annually. However, the number of those awaiting family reunion – wives and children unable to live with their husbands and fathers – is estimated at 120,000. There are another estimated 100,000 persons who have been denied re-entry into the West Bank and Gaza on grounds of having stayed abroad for periods longer than permitted by the Israeli authorities.[50] There is also the question of the previously discussed 300,000 people displaced by the 1967 war or expelled shortly after, and their descendants.

129

Although consideration of their case for return is allowed for in Article 12 of the Declaration of Principles, no progress had been made on this issue as of the middle of 1996.

Notes to Chapter 3

1. See Joost R. Hiltermann, 'Israel's Deportation Policy in the Occupied West Bank and Gaza', *The Palestine Yearbook of International Law*, vol. III (1986), p. 156. This paper was first published by Al-Haq (Law in the Service of Man), the Ramallah-based human rights organization, in 1986 as Occasional Paper No. 2. It was reprinted in part with certain changes in *The Palestine Yearbook of International Law*. A second edition of Occasional Paper No. 2 was published by Al-Haq in August 1988.

2. For the full text of this order and the similar Military Order No. 290, see *The Palestine Yearbook of International Law*, Vol. III (1986), pp. 146–149.

3. See *Punishing a Nation* (Ramallah, West Bank: Al-Haq, December 1988), p. 160, note 3.

4. See Joost R. Hiltermann, *Israel's Deportation Policy in the Occupied West Bank and Gaza* (Ramallah, West Bank: Al-Haq, Second Edition, August 1988), pp. 36-37.

5. Hiltermann, 'Israel's Deportation Policy', p. 156.

6. The legal-cum-military career of Meir Shamgar is of some importance here: President of the Supreme Court since 1983; Justice of the Supreme Court, 1975–83; Attorney General, 1968–75; served in various legal capacities in the Israel Defence Force (IDF), ending up with the rank of Brigadier General; served as Military Advocate General until 1968 and legal adviser to the Ministry of Defence. Curiously, Shamgar is also a member of the Strasburg-based Council of International Society on Law of War.

7. Cited in Hiltermann, *Israel's Deportation Policy*, p. 39. The judgement is also excerpted in English in *Israel Yearbook on Human Rights* 16 (1986), pp. 329–330. This so-called legal argument was originally advanced by Shamgar in a publication in 1971 (at a time when he was serving as Attorney General). See Meir Shamgar, 'The Observance of International Law in the Administered Territories', *Israel Yearbook on Human Rights* 1 (1971), pp. 262–282. Shamgar wrote (p. 274): 'Deportation of a person to Jordan is . . . neither deportation to the territory of the occupying power nor to the territory of another country. It is more a kind of return or exchange of a prisoner to the power which sent him and gave him its blessing and orders to act.' Shamgar's proposition about the 'legality' of deporting Palestinians from 'Judea and Samaria' to Jordan was endorsed by Yoram Dinstein, a prominent professor of International Law and currently President of

Tel Aviv University. See Y. Dinstein, 'Expulsion of Mayors from Judea', *Tel Aviv University Law Review*, no. 158 (1981)(Hebrew); Y. Dinstein, 'The Israel Supreme Court and the Law of Belligerent Occupation: Deportations', *Israel Yearbook on Human Rights* 23 (1993), p. 23.

8. Quoted in Sabri Jiryis, *The Arabs in Israel* (New York: Monthly Review Press, 1976), p. 12.

9. See Ann M. Lesch, 'Israeli Deportation of Palestinians from the West Bank and the Gaza Strip, 1967–1978', part I, *Journal of Palestine Studies* 8, no. 2 (Winter 1979), p. 103, Table 1; Yoel Marcus in *Haaretz*, 18 December 1992; Roni Shaked and Danny Sadeh in *Yedi'ot Aharonot*, 18 December 1992, p. 4; and *Punishing a Nation*, p. 143. Palestinian historian 'Arif al-'Arif compiled a list of 1,480 names of Palestinians deported and exiled from the West Bank and Gaza Strip to Jordan between 23 September 1967 and 8 June 1972. For the list of names, see M.R. Mehdi, *A Palestine Chronicle* (London: Alpha Publishing Co., n.d. but possibly 1973), pp. 37–84.

10. See Lesch, 'Israeli Deportation of Palestinians', part I, pp. 101–31; and part II, in *Journal of Palestine Studies* 8, no. 3 (Spring 1979), pp. 81–112; Rami G. Khouri, 'Potential Leaders Expelled: Israel's Deportation Policy', *Merip Reports* 8, no. 65 (March 1978), p. 23.

11. See *Yedi'ot Aharonot*, 18 December 1992, p. 4.

12. See Danny Rubinstein in *Davar*, 19 February 1988, p. 16.

13. Lesch, 'Israeli Deportation of Palestinians', part I, p. 106.

14. Khouri, 'Potential Leaders Expelled', p. 24.

15. See Lesch, 'Israeli Deportation of Palestinians', part I, pp. 107–108.

16. Quoted in Felicia Langer, *With My Own Eyes* (London: Ithaca Press, 1975), pp. 62–63.

17. Quoted in Lesch, 'Israeli Deportation of Palestinians', part I, p. 109, note 17. In his book *Jerusalem: The Torn City* (Jerusalem: Isratypeset, 1976), pp. 209–10, Meron Benvenisti, a former deputy mayor of Jewish Jerusalem, claims that the expulsion of al-Sayih and al-Khatib temporarily 'paralysed' the Palestinian protest activities in Arab East Jerusalem.

18. See Lesch, op. cit., pp. 108–109, citing a paper by Elie Rekhess and Asher Susser of the Shiloah Institute, Tel Aviv University.

19. Danny Rubinstein in *Davar*, 19 February 1988, p. 16.

20. Hiltermann, *Israel's Deportation Policy*, p. 2.

21. *The Jerusalem Post*, 5 August 1985.

22. Hiltermann, *Israel's Deportation Policy*, p. 86.

23. Hiltermann, 'Israel's Deportation Policy', p. 156, note 2, p. 157 and for the list of the 37 deportees, see pp. 186–87; Hiltermann, *Israel's Deportation Policy*, p. 1.

24. Danny Rubinstein in *Davar*, 19 February 1988, p. 16.

25. Quoted in *The Jerusalem Post*, 30 August 1988, p. 17.

26. Hiltermann, 'Israel's Deportation Policy', pp. 184 and 186.

27. Cited in Avishai Margalit, 'The Terror Master', *The New York Review of Books*, 5 October 1995, pp. 18–19.

28. See *The Jerusalem Post*, 18 August 1988; *Punishing a Nation*, p. 143. Not all Israeli politicians were content with these deportations. For instance, Reserve General Raphael Eitan, a former Chief of Staff – and currently Minister of Agriculture and Environment in the Israeli cabinet – told an interviewer in November 1989 that Israel should lift all legal restrictions to enable the security forces to expel all Palestinians in Israeli detention centres – over 12,000 persons at the height of the *intifada* – by transporting them in 'air-conditioned buses' across the border. See Gide'on Reicher in *Yedi'ot Aharonot*, 16 November 1989.

29. See *Yedi'ot Aharonot*, 18 December 1992. According to the estimate of Al-Haq (Law in the Service of Man), during the second year of the *intifada* (December 1988–December 1989), no less than 1,600 curfews were imposed in the West Bank and Gaza. Some 1,000,000, about 60 per cent of the total population of the occupied territories, were placed under prolonged curfew at some point during that year.

30. See Chaim Bermant in *The Observer* (London), 21 June 1992, p. 13.

31. Jerry Levin, '"Creeping Transfer" Hits the West Bank', *New Outlook* (March 1990), p. 28.

32. Ibid., p. 28.

33. Ibid., p. 29.

34. See Danny Rubinstein in *New Outlook*, January–February 1993, p. 14.

35. See *Middle East Economic Digest (MEED)*, London, 8 January 1993, p. 6.

36. 'They Did a Mini-Transfer', interview with A.B. Yehoshu'a, *Ma'ariv*, 22 December 1992.

37. 'The Proposal of A.B. Yehoshu'a: A Conditional Transfer': interview with A.B. Yehoshu'a, *Zman Tel Aviv* supplement to *Ma'ariv*, 16 April 1993.

38. Quoted by Naseer Aruri in *Middle East International*, No. 445, 5 March 1993, p. 17.

39. Cited by Hami Shalev in *Davar*, 18 December 1992.

40. Nahum Barne'a in *Yedi'ot Aharonot*, quoted in Israel Shahak, 'The Deeper Significance of the Mass Expulsions', *Middle East Policy* 2, no. 1 (1993), p. 70.

41. Shahak, 'The Deeper Significance of the Mass Expulsions'.

42. Quoted in ibid., pp. 70–71.

43. Barak was the army Chief of Staff from 1991 until 1995. He joined the Labour Party and in August 1995 was appointed Minister of the Interior in the Rabin government. Many Israelis believe that Rabin was grooming Barak as his successor to the Labour leadership. Two prominent Israeli commentators, Nahum Barne'a and Simon Shiffer, claimed in *Yedi'ot Aharonot* of 17 June 1994 that under Rabin the entire structure of the Israeli cabinet was being ignored, with generals taking its place.

44. Danny Sadeh in *Yedi'ot Aharonot*, 18 December 1992, p. 4. See also Yossi Torpestein in *Haaretz*, 18 December 1992, p. 3a.

45. Myron J. Aronoff, 'Labor in the Second Rabin Era: The First Year of Leadership', in Robert O. Freedman (ed.), *Israel Under Rabin* (Boulder, CO: Westview Press, 1995), p. 137. See also Motti Basok in *Davar*, 19 June 1994; *Ma'ariv*, 18 August 1995, weekend supplement, p. 5.

46. See Zeev Schiff in *Haaretz*, 16 December 1992, p. 1.

47. *Davar*, 18 December 1992.

48. Quoted in Lynn Welchman, 'The Illegality of Expulsion', *Palestine Solidarity* (January–February 1993), p. 4.

49. See Derek Brown in *The Guardian*, 30 April 1993, p. 11.

50. David McDowall, *The Palestinians: The Road to Nationhood* (London: Minority Rights Publications, 1994), pp. 148, 192, n. 3.

Chapter 4
Post-1967 Pressures on 'Israeli' Arabs

Farming the land was the backbone of the Palestinian economy before 1948. For Palestinians who remained in Israel, their attachment to the land of their ancestors can hardly be over-emphasized. As natives of Palestine, the land for them was a means of livelihood, a symbol of identity, survival and security in the face of the 1948 exodus and dispersal of their compatriots. The question of land use and development has always been crucially important for the survival of the Palestinian Arab minority in Israel. Land expropriation is probably the most significant aspect of the policy of deprivation pursued by Israel against this minority. Predicated on the Zionist premise of more land for the would-be Jewish newcomers and settlers, Israel's policy of land confiscation destroyed the livelihood of many Israeli Arabs, severely curtailed the development of Arab localities and threatened to undermine the very survival of a territorially-based Arab national minority in Israel.

The outcome of the 1948 war and the cease-fire agreements between Israel and Arab countries left Israel in control of over five million acres of Palestinian land. After 1948, the Israeli state took over the land of the 750,000 Palestinian refugees, who were barred from returning, while the remaining Palestinian Arab minority was subjected to laws and regulations that effectively deprived it of most of its land. The history of expropriation began immediately after 1948. The entire massive drive to take over Arab land has been conducted according to strict legality. Since 1948 Israel has enacted some thirty statutes that transferred land from private Arab to state ownership.[1] In 1955, the then Arab affairs editor for the Hebrew daily *Haaretz*, Moshe Keren, described this process as 'wholesale robbery in legal guise. Hundreds of thousands of dunams [*sic*] were taken away from the Arab minority.'[2]

135

In 1948, each Arab village had on average approximately 2,280 acres of arable land; by 1974 this was reduced to 500 acres.[3] Between 1948 and 1990 the Israeli Arabs lost close to one million acres of land.[4] As a result of this massive land seizure and the state's land use policies within the Green Line, over 90 per cent of the land is owned by the state and the Jewish National Fund. These lands are owned in perpetuity by the 'Jewish people', not the citizens of Israel, excluding the Arab citizens from ownership. By self-definition, these lands are utilized almost exclusively for the fulfilment of the Zionist goals of Jewish settlement and population dispersion. Inevitably, this land use policy has resulted in the massive dispossession of the Arab minority.[5] According to Reverend Riah Abu al-'Assal of Nazareth:

> In 1948, 16.5 dunams were allowed per capita for the Arab minority. Today about 0.5 dunam is allowed. We have no more space to bury our dead . . . I am not exaggerating. I live in a town called Nazareth which has become the most crowded town in the country . . . In the Greek Orthodox Cemetery in Nazareth – and the Greek Orthodox community numbers over 11,000 people – they dig up the graves of those who died ten years ago to bury the newly dead.[6]

The land was expropriated by the authority of laws passed by the Israeli parliament, and transferred to Jewish control and ownership. Consequently, Palestinian Arabs in Israel, who in 1948 were largely peasants and farmers, had been transformed into day labourers by 1980, when over 75 per cent of adult males were working in Jewish factories and Jewish towns. These workers returned each evening to their localities, which, being left largely neglected and under-developed, have become virtually hostels.

When the Arab citizens held a general strike and demonstrated peacefully against a wave of land confiscation on 30 March 1976 (subsequently commemorated annually as Land Day), six young people were shot dead by the army. The then Rabin government refused to set up a commission to investigate the killings. Land seizure continued after 1976, mainly in the Negev. A survey conducted by Sammy Smooha of Haifa University in 1988 found that

58 per cent of all the Arabs in Israel and 75 per cent of all land-owning Arabs in Israel reported having lands expropriated by the Israeli state.[7] Moreover, the Arab proportion reporting land take-over had risen sharply from 57 per cent in 1976 to 75 per cent in 1988.[8] This reported rise was due to two main reasons: first, the massive expropriation of lands of the Negev Arabs, in the name of building new military airfields as a result of the withdrawal from Sinai in 1982; and second, the setting up in the Galilee of Jewish Regional Councils with jurisdiction over large tracts of Arab-owned land. In the case of Galilee, these land tracts were technically not expropriated, but taken out of the jurisdiction of Arab localities and annexed to neighbouring Jewish settlements; they lost much of their value for their Arab owners and deprived the Arab localities of potential use and development.[9]

The setting up of the Misgav Regional Council in October 1982, ostensibly with the aim of providing services for 25 Jewish settlements in the heart of Galilee, with jurisdiction over tens of thousands of dunums of Arab-owned land, has had an adverse effect on the development of 23 Arab villages in the region (with a total population of 129,872 according to the 1983 census). By removing the development of these Arab-owned lands from the control of Arab localities and placing them under the control of Jewish settlers the villages have been prevented from developing. The policy has generated strong protests from the Galilee Palestinians, who detected yet another subtle tactic linked to the ongoing strategy of de-Arabizing the Galilee and deterritorializing its Palestinian population.[10]

The plans for evacuating the Negev Arabs from their lands and concentrating them in semi-urban townships in the Negev began many years before the signing of the Israeli-Egyptian peace treaty. As early as 1964, Yitzhak 'Oded, a leading authority on Israel's land policies toward the Arab minority, wrote:

> The transfer has a triple purpose: 1. to redress the [demographic] ratio between Jews and Arabs in underpopulated areas; 2. to provide land for [Jewish] settlement and development projects; 3. to release more Bedouin manpower for labor in the Jewish economy.[11]

The Israeli land take-over policy was linked closely in official think-ing with the aim of establishing a large majority of Jewish over Arab inhabitants in both regions, the Negev and the Galilee. Thus, the longstanding state objective in Galilee has been referred to as the 'Judaization of Galilee' policy, and later has been disguised as the 'Development of Galilee' or the 'Populating of Galilee' project. It is also important to note that all Zionist parties in Israel, left, right, and centre, have consistently supported the objective of establishing new Jewish settlements in the Galilee and the Negev in order to create a large majority of Jews over Arabs and to contain Arab demography in both regions. Even the left-wing Zionist party Mapam, which has opposed the establishment of Jewish settlements in the West Bank and Gaza, has sponsored some of the new kibbutzim built in the Galilee, amid several large Arab villages in areas densely popu-lated by Arabs, within the framework of the 'Judaization of Galilee' project.

The 'Judaization of Galilee' policy, undertaken by the Jewish Agency in co-operation with the Jewish National Fund and various government ministries, is also part and parcel of the institutionalized ethnic and national discrimination against the Palestinian citizens of Israel. Referring critically to this policy, Professor Assa Kasher of Tel Aviv University said:

> The government's policy of Judaization of Galilee is . . . a discriminatory policy. It would be exactly as if the American government promoted the Christianization of New York. The Jewish Agency, which is an organism elected by the Jewish people, has the right to encourage Jews to settle in Galilee. But the Israeli government, which should represent all citizens of the Israeli state, does not have this right. The problem resides in the fact that the activities of the Jewish Agency are completely scrambled with those of the government. This scrambling is intentional, and is designed to serve a policy of discrimination. This is reprehensible and must be prohibited.[12]

However, according to Israeli political geographer Oren Yiftachel, 'no organized Jewish objection ever challenged the Judaization of Galilee concept'.[13] Regarding the Negev Arabs, Yitzhak 'Oded also wrote in 1964:

powerful elements in [the Labour government] are anxious to remove the Bedouin from the Negev ... Four years ago Mr Moshe Dayan, perhaps the most determined backer of transfer of the Bedouin to the north and Minister of Agriculture at the time, sponsored a plan to move them to the centre of the country [in the vicinity of Ramle].[14]

Dayan had left the army in 1957 to enter politics and had become active in the ruling Mapai party. He had been a close associate of Prime Minister Ben-Gurion, who had appointed him Minister of Agriculture in 1959, a position Dayan had held until 1964. It is likely that the Dayan plan to evacuate the Arabs from their lands in the Negev had been connected closely with Ben-Gurion's obsessional dream of populating the Negev with many Jews. Ultimately, the Dayan scheme was shelved because the Negev Arabs refused to co-operate. However, according to 'Oded,

When Mr Dayan first openly broached the plan to transfer the Bedouin of the Negev, everyone was assured that any implementation of transfer would be strictly voluntary. The increasing tendency to apply pressure that may be noted since then shows that stress is beginning to be laid on coercion, in one way or another.[15]

In the event, the Negev Arabs were not relocated to the centre of the country, but rather were evacuated from most of their lands in subsequent years under pressure to new, semi-urban townships in the Negev itself.

By the end of 1976, the Israeli authorities had removed thirty-one Bedouin settlements, and were planning to evacuate fifty-four additional settlements.[16] Three years later, in 1979, a decree was issued by Agriculture Minister Ariel Sharon declaring the entire area of the Negev south of the 50-degree line of latitude (a line beginning below the Dead Sea) as a protected nature reserve in which the Bedouin were forbidden to graze their black goats. Consequently an area constituting almost half of the country was put out of bounds to Bedouin herders who would not be able to live off the desert south of the 50-degree line.[17]

In an effort to hasten the evacuation of the Negev Bedouin from their lands and their forced sedentarization, a special armed unit, known as the Green Patrol, was set up in 1976 to 'locate and rapidly evacuate' people who were deemed to be trespassing on state lands, that is to say, outside the areas permitted for the Negev Bedouin. The Green Patrol was set up as an arm of the Ministry of Agriculture's Nature Reserve Authority and of the Israel Land Administration. Its activities against the Negev Bedouin were stepped up in the late 1970s and early 1980s, partly as a reflection of the hard-line and militarist attitudes of Agriculture Minister Sharon and of Reserve General Avraham Yoffe, head of the Nature Reserve Authority, who was also an ideological comrade-in-arms of Sharon.[18] Yoffe, who was also a member of the Knesset (Likud) from 1974 to 1977, believed that the extension of Israeli sovereignty over 'Judea' and Samaria and Gaza would cause 'part [of the Arab inhabitants] to emigrate from here and the other part to remain as loyal citizens of the state of Israel'.[19] The activities of the Green Patrol were described by Dov Coller of the Civil Rights Association in Israel as follows:

> What they do in fact is to remove beduin [sic] families from the land of the Negev and direct them towards the six projected towns. The Green Patrol confiscates animals, beats up women and children, and destroys homes. It also puts pressure on Jews in adjacent areas to cooperate in removing beduin from their lands.[20]

Other civil rights activists thought that members of the Green Patrol were 'paranoid' about the Bedouin and sought to rid the central Negev of every last one of them 'by hook or by crook'.[21]

Dozens of Bedouin families were made homeless, after their metal houses or tents were bulldozed or burnt, often with the occupants' belongings inside; herds were either confiscated or scattered; shots were fired and smoke bombs were used to get people out of their houses; dams were demolished; fruit and olive trees were uprooted and crops were ploughed over. The Hebrew press was full of eyewitness accounts of these forceful evictions throughout the late 1970s and the 1980s. Shmuel Toledano, a former prime ministerial adviser on Arab affairs, recalled hearing 'tens of horror stories recorded on tape' from people who were harassed, beaten up and brutally evacuated by the patrol, without due process.[22] The Israeli government policy of forcing the Negev Bedouin to move from their lands into planned townships continued into the early 1990s. The policy goals have been to restrict the Bedouin to as little land as possible; moving to the townships has been the only legal option open to them. In 1990 members of the 'Azazmeh Bedouin tribe were evicted from their lands by the Israeli authorities on the pretext that the area was required for military purposes. Within three months, the land was handed over to a Jewish agricultural settlement. Fiona McKay, a British lawyer working for a human rights organization in Israel, wrote in March 1995:

> Since 1990, this part of the tribe had been living under hazardous environmental conditions close to a chemical factory at Ramat Havav [in the Negev] which emitted foul-smelling fumes and caused respiratory and skin problems, particularly among children.[23]

In the summer of 1994 the evictees from the 'Azazmeh tribe demonstrated in front of the Israeli Knesset, after failing to persuade the Labour government to find a solution for their plight. On 11 December 1994, 800 members of the same tribe, in a direct challenge to Israeli government policy, decamped 30 kilometres south to the lands traditionally owned by the tribe. And a month later the Rabin government agreed in principle to allow the tribe to establish an 'agricultural' settlement. This was the first time such a concession has been made by an Israeli government to a Negev Bedouin tribe. Although the Bedouin make up 22 per cent of the population of the Beersheba district, they have not one single agricultural settlement. The Jewish population of the same district has 134 settlements.[24]

The above activities took place many years after the military government was abolished in 1966. The victims were not the noncitizen Palestinians of the occupied territories, but rather Palestinian citizens of Israel. Some Israeli politicians were not satisfied with the policy of coercively concentrating the Negev Arabs in a few semiurban settlements in Israel. The idea of moving the Negev Arabs completely out of Israel continued to percolate even in Labour Party circles. For instance, in September 1982 a Labour-Alignment Member of the Knesset, Uri Sabag, suggested that the Negev Arabs, who by then numbered over 40,000 people, should be evacuated to, and resettled in, the West Bank, outside the Green Line. Sabag's proposal would have resulted in depriving the Negev Arabs of their Israeli citizenship and transferring them across the border of the state. Not surprisingly, the proposal was rejected strongly by Negev Arab leaders, who 'consider[ed] the Sabag proposals tantamount to eviction and dispossession'.[25]

The mass immigration of Jews from the former Soviet Union in 1990–1991 reinforced fears among the Israeli Arabs of further land losses in the 1990s.[26] Many of these Russian newcomers have been directed to the Galilee within the renewed efforts to 'Judaize the Galilee' and reduce the so-called Arab 'demographic threat' there and in the Little Triangle, and the Negev. The mass Soviet immigration has been considered by Israeli policy makers as a national asset that can be used to change radically the demographic and geographic structures in Israel to establish a firm Jewish majority in the Galilee, the Little Triangle, and the Negev. For the Palestinians, including those living in Israel, it has increased their fear of displacement and expulsion from their homeland.[27] The fear of losing the remainder of their land to the Jews, as well as of being further marginalized in consequence of the large scale Jewish immigration, provided perhaps the two key issues in the opposition by Israel's Palestinians to this large Jewish immigration. In the December 1990/January 1991 issue of *New Outlook*, two researchers at the Institute of Arab Studies of Giva'at Haviva showed that the 'Palestinian Arab citizens of Israel are gravely concerned by the mass Soviet Jewish immigration and what it portends for their future status in Israel':

On the personal level, fears have been expressed about the possible loss of jobs and future job opportunities, and in fact there have already been newspaper reports of Israeli Arabs being fired from jobs they held for years to make way for new immigrants. There is also widespread anxiety and ferment that private Arab land will be expropriated on a large scale in order to implement government plans to create several settlements for the immigrants in the Galilee and Wadi Ara areas, currently dense Arab population centres – and this at a time when Arab villages suffer from a severe shortage of housing for young couples and land reserves for building.[28]

On the civil level, there was fear that discrimination and inequality would increase. Between 1990 and 1992 several cases were reported in which Arab physicians in Israeli hospitals were replaced by new Russian immigrants.[29] Israeli Arab reaction on the political and national levels was, according to the Giva'at Haviva report, that

> the new immigration has far-reaching significance for the Arabs. First, it reiterates the lack of symmetry between Israel's 'Law of Return', which applies to Jews, and the as yet unrealized 'Right of Return' of the Palestinians. Secondly, the controversy about settling new immigrants in the territories is detrimental to any peace process, which in the opinion of most [Israeli] Arabs should lead to a Palestinian state beside Israel. Israel's Arab citizens are also anxious about the possibility of a 'transfer' of Palestinians from the occupied territories, and in the future, perhaps even from inside Israel proper . . . to make room for new Jewish settlements.[30]

When Abna al-Balad (Sons of the Homeland), a secular nationalist movement with a network of local Arab groups in many Arab villages in the Galilee and Little Triangle, published a manifesto entitled 'The Soviet Jewish Immigration is a Threat to Our Right to Remain in Our Homeland' and issued a petition to the Soviet leaders requesting that they stop the immigration of Soviet Jews to Israel – a petition that apparently was signed by several hundred Israeli Arabs – Minister of Religious Affairs Zvulun Hammer (who is currently Minister of Education in the Binyamin Netanyahu cabinet) reacted furiously, proposing openly that the Israeli citizenship of the petition's authors and distributors be revoked.[31] The same December 1990/January 1991 issue of *New Outlook* reported that Minister of Housing 'Ariel Sharon has announced a plan to settle hundreds of thousands of immigrants in a string of new settlements to be established along (and within) the Green Line, exploiting his position as minister of housing to "Judaize" Arab-populated areas inside Israel.'[32]

Containing the Arab 'Demographic Threat'

In mid-1949 the Palestinian minority in Israel was estimated at 150,000, approximately 17 per cent of the total population. By 1951 the Arabs were down to 11 per cent, due to mass Jewish immigration. However, by mid-1953, the Arab population, which traditionally enjoyed a very high birth rate, had risen to 180,000, and by the mid-1950s it was about 200,000. It has been shown that the phenomenal and rapid natural increase of the Palestinian minority in Israel was a major cause of fear for Prime Minister Golda Meir. Already in 1949, many leaders of the ruling Mapai had echoed the same sentiment that 'too many Arabs' had been allowed to remain in Israel and had been given Israeli citizenship, and with their high birth rate these Arabs, Mapai MKs warned, were bound to increase very rapidly. The same concern prompted Prime Minister Ben-Gurion himself to initiate in the same year an award given by the state to every mother giving birth to a tenth child. However, ten years later Ben-Gurion, still Prime Minister, abolished it, after realizing that contrary to his pronatal policies regarding Jewish women, many Arab women got the award.[33] To circumvent the dilemma surrounding his pronatal policies, Ben-Gurion proposed that responsibility in this area be transferred from the state to the Jewish Agency.[34]

Israel's Ambassador to the United States Avraham Harman wrote to Prime Minister Ben-Gurion on 11 May 1961, expressing the same demographic concerns that were preoccupying senior Israeli government officials. Harman had this to say:

> It ought to be taken into consideration that even if peace were to prevail between us and the Arabs, it would not be desirable that the Arab minority in Israel becomes too large, and it is already . . . close to 15% of the total population.[35]

A month later, Harman's boss, Foreign Minister Golda Meir, had this to say at a meeting at the Foreign Ministry on 5 June 1961: 'The question is what percentage of Arabs in the state we can allow ourselves [to accept]?' In response, Shmuel Divon, a senior adviser on Arab affairs, said:

> It should be understood that a solution to the [Arab] refugee problem does not necessarily mean peace or getting closer to peace. Perhaps yes, and perhaps it would be the contrary: because of the increase in the percentage of Arabs in the state . . . 25% of Arabs in the state they could [in the future] dictate the course of the political life.[36]

A year later, in April 1962, Ben-Gurion appointed a committee headed by the government statistician and prominent demography professor Roberto Bachi to investigate the population trends and present recommendations on policies in this regard. Publicly the committee's recommendations, which were presented four years later, avoided making suggestions regarding the politically sensitive issue of the high birth rate among Arab citizens. However, the committee concluded that 'some aspects and problems in the demographic trend in Israel are causing concern' and that 'a high rate of [Jewish] population growth seems most desirable from the standpoint of political and national security factors'.[37] According to Roberto Bachi, in 1968 the government of Levi Eshkol 'endorsed the recommendations of a Committee for the problems of natality . . . This committee indicated the dangers implied in the decrease of Jewish natality in Israel and in the Diaspora.'[38] At the same time the Eshkol government also established the Demographic Centre, an official unit (first located in the Prime Minister's Office, and later in the Ministry of Labour and Welfare) 'which has been active since then in various fields such as: giving advice to Government offices in fields related to the conditions [of Israeli Jewish?] mothers and children, increasing further awareness for demographic problems, sex and family education, research in demographic fields, etc.'[39] Bachi had investigated the Arab and Jewish population trends in Palestine as early as 1944 and had submitted a confidential report to the Haganah and the Jewish Agency, then chaired by Ben-Gurion, on 16 October of that year, in which he had concluded that because of the high Arab birth rate the Jews would remain a minority even if one million Jews were to immigrate to the projected Jewish state. One of the political solutions suggested by Bachi was Arab transfer:

> If in the achievement of [Jewish] majority we see one of the major roles of Zionism, then an important aim of our movement should be to create economic and political conditions which would enable the transfer, by peaceful means, of a large part of the Arab population to other countries and to cause a demographic movement of the Arabs of the Land of Israel in the direction of the east [towards Syria and Iraq].[40]

Of course this opinion had been formulated before the Palestinian exodus of 1948, when the native inhabitants of Palestine were still an overwhelming majority, and obviously the situation of the Arab minority in Israel in the 1960s was markedly different. However, the public recommendations made by Bachi's committee in the 1960s demonstrated once more the Zionist demographic fear.

The net immigration average of Jews to Israel had declined from 53,000 in 1963, to 46,000 in 1964, to 23,000 in 1965. Gross immigration further declined to 13,000 in 1966, while emigration from Israel was of the same order. Consequently, following the Bachi committee's recommendations, measures needed to be taken to raise the birth rate of the Jewish population. An inter-ministerial committee was established in 1966 to look into the birth rate issue, as well as a Centre for Demography.[41] This centre is operated by the Israeli government and is attached to the Welfare Ministry. In addition to collecting data on Jewish birth rates in Israel and abroad, the Centre initiates pronatal policies among Israeli Jews, supporting larger Jewish families and higher birth rates.[42]

Until 1967, the Shabak, which had played a major role in enforcing the system of control and exclusionary domination imposed on the Arab minority in the post-1948 period, was also concerned with the high birth rate among Israel's Arabs. Shabak put forward various proposals designed to bring about a reduction in Arab natural growth including 'plans for encouraging [Arab] emigration'. According to Benziman and Mansour, these emigration plans were not put into effect. However, one of the suggestions made by Shabak, which later became a government policy line, was the demarcation of jurisdiction boundaries, and the formulation of building plans, for the Arab villages in a way that would force the villagers to abandon their agricultural and territorial space (including their agricultural lands) and especially their rural building methods. The assumption behind this deterritorialization and forced urbanization process was that the reduced space involved in urban housing methods would cause a reduction in the Arab birth rate.[43]

Since the occupation of the West Bank and Gaza Strip, with their solid Palestinian population, demography has obsessed leaders in Israel. After June 1967 there was a slight rise in net immigration and in 1990–1991 there was a mass immigration of Jews from the former Soviet Union. Yet the demographic concern remained an ever present subject in public debates and political speeches. Some Israelis openly proposed a blunt discriminatory approach on demography and Arab birth control: encouragement of large Jewish families, birth-control measures for the Palestinians in Israel and the Occupied Territories, as well as the adoption of an open policy of encouraging Arabs to emigrate to countries overseas. In an editorial of *Ma'ariv*, Israel's largest circulation newspaper, Shmuel Schnitzer, who was in favour of annexing the newly acquired territories to Israel, stated on 29 September 1967: 'a high [Palestinian Arab] birth rate is not a decree from Heaven. It is a danger against which society must defend itself [by all means].' Viewing the matter in long-range terms, Schnitzer suggested that Israel should 'fight' against the Palestinian 'population explosion' both in Israel and the West Bank and Gaza Strip 'by all the legislative, information and preventive means' at its disposal. In addition to the encouragement of high birth rate among Israeli Jews, Schnitzer proposed:

> we must make it clear to the Arab minority that it is not free to maintain in this small and poor country the highest birth rate in the world. [We should] also persuade the superpowers that one of the solutions to the problem of refugees [residing in the Occupied Territories] is in the

departure of Arabs for the classical countries of immigration, with international financing; we would also give the Arabs who would want to leave the country the possibility of taking with them an amount [of money] that would fully compensate them for their property and would [give them] a good chance to begin a new life in [an]other country.

The same concern over the high Palestinian birth rate was voiced in the influential American Zionist monthly periodical, *Commentary*: 'There are more little Arabs born every year than there are Jews living in the whole world.'[44] In their book *The Threat Within: Israel and Population Policy*, Singerman et al., reflecting the same worry as many Israeli leaders, suggested that the Israeli government should pursue an 'anti-natalistic' policy of encouraging the adoption of birth control by Israeli Arab women as a way of reducing the natural Arab growth and preventing what they saw as an eventual Arab majority inside the Green Line within a century.[45]

The so-called Arab 'demographic problem' has also been raised by Professor Arnon Sofer, a prominent political geographer from Haifa University, who is widely known to have close connections with the Israeli establishment and who has been involved in various official plans within the 'Judaization of Galilee' project. In a 1991 article Sofer wrote: 'in my view the demographic problem constitutes the paramount danger to the foundations of the Jewish-Zionist state. As such, it demands bold and difficult decisions in order to meet the threat before it is too late.'[46] Sofer explained that he was in favour of withdrawing from most of the West Bank and Gaza Strip in order to preempt the creation of a binational state and get rid of the Arab 'demographic threat' as well as in order to concentrate on populating the Galilee with more Jews and deal with the 'Arab problem' in Israel proper.

'Israel's Arabs constitute a real problem for Israel's Jews', he wrote. He explained further:

Inside Israel proper (the Green Line) the [Jewish : Arab] ratio will be 78 : 22 [by the year 2000]. Thus in the year 2000 the situation within the Green Line will be substantially different from that in Eretz-Israel as a whole, with a minority population of only about one fifth. While this ratio does not constitute a demographic threat, I would suggest that we should not make light even of a majority:minority ratio of 78:22. On the other hand, the modernization processes currently being experienced by the Arabs in Israel make it likely that their natural growth rate will continue to decline. Moreover, the Arabs' growing propensity to acquire higher education leads to an increase in emigration in search of greater personal satisfaction and the fulfilment of employment expectations.[47]

In the spring of 1995, Sofer, in a clear reference to the so-called Arab 'demographic problem' in Israel proper, provoked a storm of protest from Israeli Arabs when he stated publicly that the 'wombs' of Israeli Arab women were the most serious threat Israel was facing. The heads of the Arab Local Councils in Israel (effectively the leadership of Israel's Arabs) called on Education Minister Amnon Rubinstein to sack Sofer from his position at Haifa University, where nearly a quarter of the students are Arabs. Rubinstein, however, refused to act against him declaring that Israeli universities were independent institutions.

Israeli policy makers and leaders continue to view the natural increase of the Arab minority as an obstacle to Jewish immigration, and to the settlement and dispersion of a Jewish population throughout the country, and consequently as a threat to the Zionist-Jewish character of the state. The declining Jewish birth rate is often contrasted with the high natural growth among the Arab citizens. The proportion of Muslims in Israel rose from 7.5 per cent in 1951 to 13.7 per cent at the end of 1986 due both to their strong natural increase and to the incorporation of East Jerusalem after 1967. Until the 1960s the Muslim population of Israel had an exceptionally high fertility (over nine children per woman), exceeding that of other Middle Eastern Muslim populations. In 1988, Muslim fertility remained comparatively high: while the Jewish population of Israel increased in that year by 1.6 per cent, the Muslim population rose by 3.3 per cent (which is the result only of natural increase). Although in 1951, the percentage of Jews in Israel was 89 per cent, since 1964 it has tended to decline, decreasing to 82 per cent at the end of 1987. The Arab proportion rose during the same period from 11 per cent to 18 per cent. 'This has come about inasmuch as the natural increase of the Jews is much lower than that of non-Jews and because of the drop in their net migratory increase.'[48]

Throughout the 1980s demography was a major topic of debate in the Hebrew media and in political speeches. A very 'worrying' problem for Zionism, declared Michael Dekel (who was Deputy Defence Minister in the Likud government in the 1980s) in October 1982, is the 'frightening natural growth of the Israeli Arabs within the Green Line, which is among the highest in the world'.[49] The journalist Ora Shem-Ur, a well-known, open campaigner for Arab expulsion, claims that in October 1985 Minister of Trade and Industry Ariel Sharon 'had shown great interest' in the subject of her book *Greater Israel* (1985) – which dwells largely on the 'Arab demographic threat' and the transfer solution – 'and he [Sharon] was interested in reading the book as quickly as possible, in order to prepare the demographic subject for discussion at a cabinet session'.[50] In 1993 the leader of the Likud party and Israel's current Prime Minister, Binyamin Netanyahu, wrote: 'if the statistics suggest any demographic "threat" at all, it comes not from the Arabs of the territories but from the Arabs of pre-1967 Israel [i.e. the "Israeli" Arabs]'.[51]

In May 1986 the Israeli cabinet and the Knesset held open discussions on Jewish and Arab birth rates.[52] On 11 May 1986, the Israeli government devoted a special session to the 'demographic problems' of Jews in Israel. Shortly after, the government established a working group formed by representatives of various ministries and the Jewish Agency and co-ordinated by the Demographic Centre to prepare a programme for demographic policies.[53] Moreover, in all the proposals that successive prime ministerial advisers on Arab affairs put forward in recent years, with the aim of formulating policies towards Israel's Arab minority, this minority is perceived as constituting a 'demographic danger'.[54]

The most explicit connection between the so-called Arab 'demographic threat' and the desire to encourage Israeli Arabs to emigrate was made in 1976 in an internal memorandum by a very senior Israeli official, Yisrael Koenig, the Northern District Commissioner of the Interior Ministry. In addition to Koenig, the memo was prepared by three leading Jewish public figures in the northern district: Tzvi Alderoty, the mayor of the Jewish town of Migdal Ha'emek in the Galilee (Alderoty was subsequently tipped for the post of head of the Labour Party's Arab Department), the mayor of 'Afula town, Shim'on Shehori, and the secretary of Upper Nazareth's Labour Council, Menahem Ariav.[55] With the exception of Koenig, all three local leaders were members of the Labour Party. The memo was submitted to Prime Minister Rabin's office in early March 1976 as a secret document. Since its publication in *'Al-Hamishmar*, the newspaper of the Mapam party, on 7 September 1976, this document has come to be known as the Koenig Report. It was written primarily by Koenig, who held the powerful post of the Interior Ministry's representative in the northern district, controlling the allocation of budgets for Arab local councils, in a region where some 60 per cent of the Israeli Palestinians resided. Out of concern that the Arab population in the northern district would exceed the Jews there and of growing politicization and Palestinization among Israeli Arab youth, Koenig urged the government to adopt a policy of actively encouraging young Arabs to go abroad for study and not to return, to reduce the number of Arab employees in Jewish enterprises, to tighten control further on political activities and to increase surveillance over Israeli Arabs. The Koenig Report consisted of two sections, the first of which was signed on 1 March 1976, one month before the general strike of the Land Day. In this section, under the heading 'The Demographic Problem and the Manifestations of Arab Nationalism', the author stated that the Arab minority had increased from 150,000 in 1948 to over 450,000 in 1975 (excluding the Arab residents of the unilaterally annexed East Jerusalem):

> The natural increase of the Arab population in Israel is 5.9 per cent annually against a natural increase of 1.5 per cent annually among the Jewish population.
>
> This problem is particularly acute in the northern district where there is a large Arab population. In mid-1975 the Arab population of the northern district was 250,000 while the Jewish population was 289,000.

A regional examination shows that in western Galilee the Arab population constitutes 67 per cent of the total; in the region of Yizre'el the Arab population constitutes 48 per cent of the total population. In 1974 only 759 Jews were added to the population of the northern district while the Arab population increased by 9,035.

According to this rate of increase, by 1978 Arabs will constitute over 51 per cent of the total population of the district.[56]

Koenig went on to argue that since 1967 the Israeli Arabs had become 'nationalistic' as a result of their contact with the Palestinians of the West Bank and Gaza:

I do [feel] in regard to the Arab population – that the Arabs' increase in the Galilee will endanger our control of that area and will create possibilities for military forces from the north to infiltrate into the area in proportion to the acceleration of the nationalistic process among Israeli Arabs.[57]

He also suggested, *inter alia*, adoption of a more aggressive policy aimed at encouraging Israeli Arabs, particularly the youth, to emigrate. The government should make 'trips abroad for studies easier, while making the return and employment more difficult – this policy is apt to encourage their emigration'.[58] This particular proposal echoed Rabbi Meir Kahane's plan of encouraging the Israeli Arabs to emigrate.

According to a very conservative estimate, around 5 per cent of Israel's Arabs, mostly educated people, had left the country between 1948 and 1974 and had not returned.[59] A memorandum written by Israel's internal security service in the early 1950s claimed that until July 1951, 2,000 Israeli Arabs had emigrated voluntarily through the Absorption Ministry (which was in charge of absorbing Jewish immigrants in Israel), and that more than 2,000 other Israeli Arabs had left the country unofficially by crossing the borders into Arab countries.[60] Koenig emphatically suggested that it would be the educated youth who, in the face of strictly restricted educational and job opportunities, would be forced to emigrate. Therefore, by adopting a more aggressive policy the government would be able to engineer Arab emigration to contain and control Arab demography.

The leak of the secret memo provoked wide condemnation among liberal Israelis, and Israeli Arab leaders called for Koenig's dismissal. Commentators in the Hebrew press were divided, with most expressing objection to some of the measures suggested by Koenig, but lending support to some of his goals such as of the Judaization of Galilee and the 'containment of Arab radicalism'.[61] Many prominent Jews in the Galilee, however, expressed support for Koenig's proposals. More importantly, Prime Minister Rabin refused to condemn the memo. His government refused to sack Koenig or even to dissociate itself from his proposals. Koenig himself was defended strongly by Interior Minister Yosef Burg[62] as well as by heads of Jewish local authorities and rabbis in the Galilee, who held public meetings in support of the Northern District Commissioner. There were also some functionaries of the Mapam Party in the north who expressed backing for Koenig.[63] Did Koenig's memo reflect the official position of the Rabin government, which at the same time was also intensifying its 'Judaization of Galilee' policy? Although a definitive answer must await the opening of the official records, Shmuel Toledano, former prime ministerial adviser on Arab affairs, revealed in an interview in August 1989 that during the 1970s 'tendencies and wishes to encourage the emigration of [Israeli] Arabs through the extension of assistance to them so that they would leave the state, but not against their wishes', prevailed among the Jewish establishment dealing with the Arab minority in Israel.[64] Another point is also evident: Koenig had held his key post since 1964, serving several Labour administrations.[65]

The military government was abolished in 1966, only to be replaced by a more subtle and less intrusive, but equally effective, system of bureaucratic and administrative control. Therefore, the institutionalized policies of domination and control remained essentially unchanged in their basic assumptions and goals, although their means have been slightly modernized. Control over the Arab minority was transferred from the army to the police. The latter's role and presence in Arab villages and towns was even expanded during the 1980s.[66] The internal secret service, the Shabak, also continued to play an important part in this system of domination and control, although after 1967 much of its efforts were directed against the Palestinians of the West Bank and Gaza Strip. Moreover, the abolition of the military government did not bring an end to the frequent use of the sweeping administrative powers of the 1945 Defence Emergency Regulations. For instance, on 1 December 1980 the Begin government used these regulations to ban the holding of the Congress of Arab Masses, a forum which aimed at establishing an all-Arab citizens' representative body. On 12 April 1981 the same government outlawed the National Co-ordinating Committee, an umbrella organization representing nine political groups. During the 1980s the standard 'security' reason was used repeatedly to close Arabic newspapers and publications. For instance *al-Raya*, of the Sons of the Homeland movement, was outlawed in 1989 and *Sawt al-Haq Wa-al-Huriyyah*, of the Islamic movement, was banned for three months in 1990.[67] The frequent resort to these regulations enabled the authorities to invoke the usual accusations of incitement and subversion without allowing due process. Even 30 years after the military government had been abolished, it was still possible in accordance with these regulations (and the 1979 amendments) to detain Arab citizens without trial, to demolish houses of Israeli Arabs, to close off Arab localities, to impose a curfew on a village and to institute other administrative measures without due process.

The use of these regulations against Arab citizens intensified after the outbreak of the *intifada* in the occupied territories in late 1987, prompted by the increasing sympathies expressed by Israel's Palestinians for their brethren in the West Bank and Gaza. After the one-day strike of Israel's Arabs on 21 December 1987 in solidarity with the occupied territories, Likud MK Haim Kaufman (deputy finance minister in the early 1980s, and between 1984 and 1988 chairman of the Likud Knesset faction and of the coalition) put forward a proposal for the reimposition of the military government on areas of concentrated Arab population in the Galilee and the Little Triangle.[68] A year later the Minister of Science and Energy, Yuval Neeman, in a speech before the Tehiya Party's council, threatened the same Arab citizens that their solidarity with the *intifada* could lead to their transfer from Israel. The continuation of the *intifada*, Neeman warned darkly, also could result in the expulsion of the Palestinians of the West Bank and Gaza Strip.[69]

Equally significant is the fact that the abolition of the military government did not end the policies of exclusion and discrimination against the Arab citizens. The reason for that is simple: discrimination against the Arab citizens basically stems from the Zionist ideology and official self-definition of the state, which defines itself as the 'state of the Jewish people' (including those Jews who are not its citizens), and not the state of all its citizens, let alone the Arab citizens. (The term 'Jewish' in Israel is a political-national, legal-administrative and religious concept.) On the basis of this analysis, anyone among the Arabs of Israel who opposes the Law of Return (1950), which accords any Jew the automatic right to settle in Israel – contrasting with the denial of any return for the country's Palestinian refugees exiled since 1948 – could be accused directly of disloyalty to the state of Israel and of challenging its existence, and ultimately could be threatened by the revocation or suspension of citizenship. Such a threat in fact was made by the Minister of Religious Affairs, Zvulun Hammer, in the Israeli television programme in Arabic 'Encounter', in early March 1990.[70] The concept of citizenship which lies at the heart of Western liberal democracies is lacking in Zionism and Israel. Consequently, the Arab citizens are treated as foreigners and squatters in their own homeland. Israel does not have a constitution. Instead, it has basic laws dealing with the Knesset, the president of the state and the government. The Knesset election law, which can only be changed by a two-thirds majority, includes a July 1985 amendment that defines Israel as the 'state of the Jewish people'. Although officially most of the Israeli Arabs are allowed to vote in general elections for the Knesset, any party challenging this definition of Israel would be banned from participating in the general election.[71] During the 1985 debate on this amendment, a very large majority in the Knesset rejected a proposal to declare Israel a 'Jewish state and the state of all its citizens', which implicitly would include the Arab citizens. What this Basic Law (the Knesset election law) tells the Palestinians in Israel is that Israel is not their state. Indeed, the usually cautious Arab MK Tawfiq Tubi stated in his criticism of the law:

> To state today in a law that the state of Israel is the state of the Jewish people means to tell 16 per cent of the citizens that they don't have a state at all and to establish that they are residents without a state.[72]

During the 1988 general election two non-Zionist, predominantly Arab lists, the Communist party and the Progressive List for Peace, which both accept the state of Israel but criticize its Zionist character, were forced to issue contradictory statements and disguise their positions in order to be allowed to take part in the election.[73] The same definition of Zionism and the state of Israel ensures that the Arab citizens remain separate and vastly unequal.

In late 1985 and early 1986, shortly after the Knesset law re-affirmed the definition of Israel as 'the State of the Jewish people' – contrasting with the simultaneous and explicit rejection by the Knesset of a proposal to define Israel as 'a Jewish state and the country of all its citizens' – a passionate public debate on the nature of Israeli identity and the Arab citizens therein erupted between Anton Shammas, an Israeli-Arab writer, who in 1986 wrote his now famous novel *Arabesques* in Hebrew, and A.B. Yehoshu'a, one of Israel's foremost authors, who is known for his 'liberal' views and was once described by *The New York Times* as 'a kind of Israeli Faulkner'. Shammas argued that Zionism had completed its mission in 1948 with the establishment of Israel; that the Law of Return, which confers on Jews a favoured status and denies Palestinian aspirations, is blatantly discriminatory and should be replaced by Western-style immigration laws; that Israeli Jews should come to terms with the reality of a multi-cultural and binational Israeli society in which Israeli-Palestinians (who constitute nearly one-fifth of the population) would be accepted as full, equal citizens; and that a single civil identity common to all those living within the borders of the State of Israel should be created.

Yehoshu'a, in contrast, reflecting a liberal and left-wing Zionist opinion that views the Law of Return as the legal embodiment of the Zionist-Jewish character of the state, and for whom Israeli identity is essentially the consummate expression of Jewish identity, rebuked those who did not repudiate Shammas's vision of 'a non-sectarian state for all its citizens':

> The Law of Return is the moral basis of Zionism . . . if you accept the morality of the whole Zionist process in this sense, then with a clear conscience you can come to Anton Shammas and say: You, the Israeli Arab, or the Palestinian with Israeli citizenship, you are a minority here . . . If you want your full identity, if you want to live in a state with an independent Palestinian personality, with an authentic Palestinian culture, get up, take your belongings and move yourself one hundred meters to the east, to the Palestinian state which will be established alongside Israel.[74]

The Palestinian state to which Yehoshu'a suggested Shammas move does not yet exist. There were those Israelis who saw Yehoshu'a's 'get up, take your belongings and move yourself one hundred meters to the east' as a call for the expulsion of the Arabs from Israel, as the commentator for the daily *Haaretz* noted on 17 January 1986: 'Kahane would not have formulated better.'[75] Shammas himself also responded sharply, lumping Yehoshu'a with 'his brothers, the members of the Jewish terror organization'. He also wrote that if and when the Palestinian state is established, 'I do not wish to leave my country and my kindred and my father's house for the land that he, in this case, A.B. Yehoshua, will show me.'[76]

The Arabs in Israel have experienced an improvement in living standards and the level of education since 1948. Many Arabs enjoy the modern services of running water, electricity, high standard of housing, health care, and education. However, the policy based on discriminatory foundations set in place by successive Labour governments in the 1950s and 1960s continued under the Likud after 1977. The Israeli Arabs are treated differently from the Jewish population in every area of government activity and service. In August 1979 Meron Benvenisti, a former deputy mayor of Jerusalem, writing in *Haaretz* observed:

> [Israel's] Arab minority has been discriminated against ever since the

State of Israel has existed. Israel's Arabs live in the shadow of deprivation in almost every sphere of life. The present [Likud] government only changed the style, not the content. Up until now discrimination was justified by 'objective' and 'practical' arguments, such as security . . . now it seems that the government has given up these delicate stylistic [explanations].[77]

Discrimination against the Arab citizens has been blatant and institutionalized. In his book *Arab and Jew: Wounded Spirits in a Promised Land*, the American Jewish journalist David Shipler describes the lack of representation of Israeli Arabs in the state's major economic and political institutions as follows:

The proportion of Arabs in the population as a whole is about 1 in 6, but it is only 1 in 60 in senior government posts, 1 in 300 in university academic positions, and 1 in 16 on the executive committee of the Histadrut federation of labour unions. As of the early 1980s, there was not a single Arab among the 625 senior officials of the prime minister's office, the Bank of Israel, the state's comptroller's office, or the Ministries of Finance, Housing, Health, Industry, and Communications. There were 2 Arabs among the 109 senior officials in the Education Ministry, 1 of 104 in the Agriculture Ministry, 1 of 114 in the Ministry of Labour and Social Affairs, and 1 of 133 in the national police.[78]

Other features of Israel's policy of discrimination against its Arab citizens were described by Shipler in a four-part series in *The New York Times,* 27-30 December 1983:

much of the discrimination is built into law. More generous child welfare payments, subsidized government loans for housing and other benefits are available to those who had at least one family member in the army, thereby excluding all Arabs, who are exempt from the draft.[79]

The Times Higher Education Supplement (London) reported on 18 August 1995 that an Arab judge appeared in 1995, for the first time in Israel's history, at the Supreme Court. In fact Israel's Labour-Meretz government, lasting from June 1992 to May 1996, stressed the importance of promoting full integration of Israel's Palestinians into public life. However, only nine Arab judges have been appointed in Israel out of a total of 256 judges appointed at all levels (excluding the military and religious courts). None of the 14 judges on the Labour Relations Tribunals is an Arab.[80]

The Arab citizens pay taxes like everyone else. Yet the range and quality of services the government provides for them is vastly inferior to those provided for the Jewish population. Prime Minister Shim'on Peres claimed in 1986 that the per capita budget allocation by the government for Israeli Arabs was 30 per cent of that allocated for Jews.[81] The available evidence, however, shows that the official discrimination is much greater. As already demonstrated, the Israeli Arabs are excluded from over 90 per cent of the land. Ninety-nine per cent of the public housing programmes undertaken by the government exclude its Arab citizens. The Education Ministry's per capita allocation for the separate Arab school system is 10 per cent of the Jewish standard.[82] The Jewish municipalities and local councils receive from the government five times more money for development than Arab villages and towns of similar size. Discrimination in water allocation is even greater. Like most of the land, water in Israel is publicly controlled. The average government subsidy to an Arab farmer is 1,500 shekels annually, while a Jewish farmer receives almost ten times more, 14,000 shekels.[83] There is only one Arab among the 4,000 directors on the boards of the 210 government owned companies. There are no Arabs at the top level of the civil service. Even the Department of Muslim Affairs in the Ministry of Religions is headed by a Jew. Similarly, the Muslim Waqf funds are administered by the Israeli government.[84] There are now more than 14,000 Arab graduates of Israeli universities. Data from the universities themselves show that out of 4,700 tenured positions in Israel's universities, only 16 are held by Israeli Arabs, and more than half of the 16 positions are in Haifa. A strongly worded letter of protest at this blatant discrimination, signed by most Israeli Arab academics, was delivered to the Education Minister, Amnon Rubinstein (who belongs to the relatively liberal Meretz Party), in August 1995.[85]

It remains an open question whether the discriminatory policies pursued by successive Israeli governments, combined with the efforts to keep the Arab citizens at the bottom of the socio-economic scale as well as the official and public perception of the need to contain the Arab 'demographic threat', have also had the underlying motive of pushing many Israeli Arabs (especially the educated ones), to emigrate (in line with the Koenig Report recommendations): a more discreet and unstated form of transfer.

Since the late 1970s, several thinly veiled and explicit threats have been made by Israeli ministers and senior officials (from Labour and Likud) to expel Israel's Arabs if they did not mind their manners; something to the effect 'if you don't behave you'll be out'. Calls for expelling Israel's Arab minority were publicly made by Tel Aviv's deputy mayor, David Shikma, in the mid-1970s,[86] Foreign Minister Dayan in January 1979, Defence Minister Rabin in 1988, President Hertzog in 1988, Ariel Sharon in 1980 and 1982, Energy and Science Minister Yuval Neeman in 1990, as well as other Likud ministers and officials. In general these threats were meant to be verbal warnings and a punitive weapon rather than wholesale or active policies.

Dayan's 1979 threat was directed at both Israel's Arab minority and the Palestinians of the West Bank and Gaza Strip after the leadership of Israel's Arabs openly declared its solidarity with the struggle of the Palestinian people for self-determination and the establishment of a Palestinian state in the West Bank and Gaza Strip. The circumstances of Dayan's threat were the following. In January 1979, the 14th session of the Palestine National Council ('parliament in exile') was held in Damascus. At the same time the heads of the Arab Local Councils in Israel held a conference in Nazareth. The Hebrew daily *Yedi'ot Aharonot* reported on 21 January 1979:

> [On 20 January] the conference expressed official and full support for the PLO as the representative of the Palestinian people, and there were voices in support of the legitimate struggle of the Palestinians. Many speakers stated their solidarity with the Palestinians in Judea and Samaria and the Gaza Strip and demanded that they be given independence.[87]

Simultaneously, six Israeli Arab students at the Hebrew University sent an open message of support to the PNC meeting in Damascus. The students, who later vehemently denied having called for armed struggle against Israel, argued that their message to the PNC expressed their political views within the framework of the law. Both official and public reaction in Israel, however, was one of outrage. A Knesset debate was scheduled to discuss the two incidents that showed increasingly open solidarity of Israel's Arab citizens with fellow Palestinians. Israel Television allowed the journalist Ora Shem-Ur to put forward her well-known views in favour of expelling all Arabs from the 'boundaries of the Land of Israel'.[88]

The Israeli (Jewish) Student Union called for drastic action to be taken against the Arab students. *Yedi'ot Aharonot* reported on 22 January 1979:

> The students' unions at all universities appealed to their rectors to expel immediately the Arab students who had signed the message to the PLO [that is, the PNC's 14th session] . . . [on 21 January] the students' union in Haifa called on the government to banish all the students involved in the scandal beyond the boundaries of the state . . . Students at Tel Aviv University demanded the introduction of a special application form on which potential students would have to state whether they supported the PLO. Should the answer be yes, they argued, the application should be rejected.[89]

In fact the six Arab students were not the only Israeli Arabs to send a message of support to the PNC's 14th session in Damascus. On 28 January 1979 the Secretary-General of Rakah (the Israeli Communist Party) and member of Knesset Meir Vilner revealed that he had sent a secret message to the same PNC session in Damascus, urging it to accept the two-state solution: the establishment of an independent Palestinian state in the West Bank and Gaza, based on mutual recognition between Israel and the Palestinians.[90]

The remarks by Foreign Minister Dayan were made on 23 January 1979 against the background of the above-described public uproar in the wake of the two incidents. *Yedi'ot Aharonot* of 24 January 1979 quoted Dayan as threatening the Palestinians in Israel and in the West Bank and Gaza: 'If they are going to follow the line of Islamic fanaticism, they should realize that they will pay very dearly for it, just as they did in 1948.'[91] Dayan's warning was made at a meeting of the State of Israel Bonds Organization (a Zionist fund-raising organization, operating in the United States, Canada, and other Western countries, with an army of volunteers recruited from all branches of the Zionist movement in the West, with the main task of selling Israeli bonds), held at the Jerusalem Hilton Hotel on 23 January. At this meeting Dayan said that if the Palestinians did not want 'to live together with us on equal grounds' (the phrase 'living together in Judea and Samaria' had been repeatedly used by Dayan since June 1967 as a euphemism to express Israel's determination to hold on to the West Bank and Gaza), then:

> like the voices that we are hearing now – even coming from inside the students studying in Hebrew universities – and some Arab circles and leaders here talking about a Palestinian state [Dayan is hinting here at the Nazareth conference and the statement made by the heads of the Arab Local Councils in Israel in support of a Palestinian state in the West Bank and Gaza] . . . if they will not be satisfied and if they don't want to live together with us, then I say they will have to pay for it. They will have to pay for it very dearly, if they will try to materialize what they are talking about now. If they will be carried away with the wave of the fanatic Islamic mood that's going around, then they better would remember and have in mind what happened with the Arab people in 1948, that had the chance to live with us at peace . . . So they find themselves now, some of them, as refugees in Lebanon and that should serve as a lesson.[92]

The Israeli government also responded by imposing restriction orders on the six Arab students involved in the Hebrew University incident, using administrative measures based on the 1945 Defence (Emergency) Regulations. On 27 January 1979 at 3 A.M. the six students were forcibly removed from the Hebrew University and confined to their villages for three months during which period they were ordered to report twice daily to the nearest police station.[93]

Dayan's threat of expulsion was not an isolated one. Less than two years later, on 1 December 1980, Agriculture Minister Ariel Sharon made a similar threat that was specifically directed at Israel's Arab citizens. Sharon, who at the same time was also presiding over the ongoing 'Judaization of Galilee' policy, said at a conference of the Likud's municipal division in Kiryat Gat:

> We have no inclination of dispossessing Arab citizens in the Galilee. But I would advise the Arab citizens in the region not to radicalize their attitudes in order not to bring about another tragedy like the one that befell the Palestinian people in 1948. Even if we do not want it, it may recur.[94]

This threat was made on 1 December 1980, when the Begin government imposed a ban on the attempted general congress of Israel's Arabs in Nazareth. The National Committee of the Local Arab Authorities, established in 1974 to campaign for municipal equality between Arab and Jewish citizens of Israel, attempted to hold the general gathering in Nazareth in December 1980. One of the main aims of the attempted congress was to protest against the intensification of Israel's 'Judaization of Galilee' policy, since some 60 per cent of Israel's Arabs live there. In an interview with the daily *Ma'ariv* in September 1977, Sharon referred to Israel's Arab citizens as 'foreigners' and 'aliens'. Sharon claimed that 'national [that is, state] land is actually robbed by foreigners . . . Although there is talk of the Judaization of Galilee, the region is regressing into a Gentile district . . . I initiated strong action to prevent aliens [Arab citizens] from taking state land.'[95] Sharon's statement as well as other threatening statements made by Likud ministers in the late 1970s and early 1980s aroused deep fears among the Palestinians in Israel, who were deeply concerned about the growing 'Kahanism' of the ruling Likud Party. For instance, attorney Muhammad Mi'ari, a member of the Secretariat of the National Committee for the Defence of Arab Lands (which was created in response to the expropriation of Arab lands in the mid-1970s), remarked shortly after his election to the Eleventh Knesset in July 1984:

> I suppose fear is a possible response. The issue has more dangerous

implications, when we understand that Kahane does not differ essentially from Tehiya and some of the religious parties. Nor is he different from Likud's Sharon and Shamir; the only difference is that Kahane is allegedly unbalanced and lacks political 'sophistication'. He says exactly what he thinks while others, such as Likud or Tehiya members, try to disguise their real positions with more moderate ones.[96]

In the late 1970s and the early 1980s more than 50 new 'Mitzpim' ('look out') settlements were set up all over the Galilee (within the framework of the Judaization of Galilee programme), with the aim of monitoring the behaviour of, and removing, Arab citizens who were accused by the authorities of encroaching on state lands, lands which in fact had been expropriated from Israeli Arabs in the 1950s and 1960s. Evidently, the implementation of these hard-line measures by the Israeli government against the Arab citizens, including the intensification of the Judaization of Galilee policy and the setting up of the 'Green Patrol' (which was entrusted with the task of forcibly evicting Bedouin citizens in the Negev), was accompanied by harsh and threatening declarations by Israeli ministers. In Sharon's view the Arab citizens were 'aliens' and 'foreigners' who had no right to state lands which should be preserved exclusively for Jews. Besides, if Israel's Arabs did not mind their manners, they would be expelled.

In the same context in which the attempted Israeli Arab general congress was banned (in December 1980), another Likud minister, Gide'on Patt, Minister of Industry and Trade, contemptuously proposed at a public meeting, held in Migdal Ha'emek in the Galilee on 2 December 1980, that the state of Israel should keep an open door for any Israeli Arab citizen 'who does not like to live here. He can take a taxi cab . . . to cross the [Jordan River] bridge . . . We will even wave him goodbye.'[97]

Early in the *intifada* when the Arab citizens expressed solidarity with their brothers in the Occupied Territories, Haim Hertzog, Israel's president, warned Israel's Arabs 'against another chapter in the Palestinian tragedy', an implicit threat of expulsion.[98] About the same time, Hertzog's colleague Yitzhak Rabin (then Defence Minister) warned Israeli Arabs: 'you should remain as you have been until now, loyal . . . In the distant past you have known tragedy, and it would be better for you not to return to that tragedy.'[99] Every Palestinian and Israeli Jew understands perfectly what Rabin's and Hertzog's warnings imply. Rabin himself had taken part in carrying out Ben-Gurion's order to expel 60–70,000 Arab residents from the twin towns of Lydda and Ramle in 1948.[100]

At the local government level, the popular mayor of Tel Aviv-Jaffa, Reserve General Shlomo Lahat, was quoted in 1990 as calling for the complete 'Judaization' of Jaffa,[101] a mixed city (which until 1948 was almost entirely Arab) that had only a small Arab minority of about 10,000. It can also be pointed out that the same mayor resisted any attempt to replace Rehava'am Zeevi (the leading advocate of transfer) from his position as Chairman of the Tel Aviv museum. Earlier, in September 1986, Lahat had permitted the displaying of National Circle broadsheets, which called for the transfer of Israel's Arab citizens, on its billboards throughout the city.[102] A movement founded in early 1986 by the well-known journalist Ora Shem-Ur, the National Circle is, like the Kach movement, preoccupied with a single-minded platform of Arab expulsion. Its largely secular, middle-class members probably never exceeded 1,000 persons, and its main activities have concentrated since its foundation on press publicity, lobbying members of the Knesset, and promoting public agitation through billboards and posters.[103] However, the director-general of the Jerusalem municipality (led by Teddy Kollek) – unlike Lahat and his top executives – refused in August 1986 to permit the display of the same posters on the grounds that they were likely to stir up conflict in the mixed city.[104]

Acre, in the north, is another town that was almost entirely Arab until 1948. Now its Arab residents constitute a quarter of the total population, and the local Jewish leadership is still seeking to reduce the Arab population by relocating it to adjacent Arab villages in the Galilee. However, some local Jewish leaders would not be satisfied with internal relocation. During the 1989 election campaign for the Acre municipal council, the Likud candidate publicly espoused the solution of transferring the Arab citizens out of the country.[105] In the neighbouring town of Nahariya, a Likud deputy mayor bragged in 1991 of his efforts to bring about transfer.[106] In the same election campaign of 1989, the winning candidate for the mayor of Nahariya declared his strong opposition to Arab citizens living in the town.[107] To the east of Nahariya, in the Galilee 'development' town of Karmiel – founded in 1964 on 5,000 dunums of land from the three Arab villages of Dayr El-Asad, Bi'ineh, and Nahef, which were expropriated within the then Labour government's effort to 'Judaize the Galilee' under a cynical ruse of the Law for Acquisition of Land in the Public Interest – Mayor 'Adi Eldar, a Labour Party man, decided, according to the September/October 1991 issue of *New Outlook*, not to allow local Arabs, some of them labourers in Karmiel factories, to rent apartments in the town; Karmiel (the population of which had grown to 28,000 by 1991) is a 'pure Jewish town', Eldar pronounced proudly.[108] Several years earlier, when an Arab attempted to purchase a flat in the Jewish neighbourhood of Neve Ya'acov in East Jerusalem, Mordechai Eliahu, Israel's Sephardic Chief Rabbi between 1983 and 1993, pronounced: 'In the Land of Israel it is forbidden to sell apartments to Gentiles.'[109] Evidently, these attitudes expressed by leaders of local councils were very popular among the Jewish public, in general, and the Jewish electorate, in particular. For instance, in an interview in January 1990, Ehud Olmert, a prominent Likud leader and member of the Israeli cabinet in charge of Israel's Arab population from 1988 to 1990 (later to be Health Minister between 1990 and 1992, and subsequently mayor of Jerusalem), remarked (perhaps with only little exaggeration):

> Ninety-nine per cent of the Israelis [Israeli Jews] are saying in the secret of their hearts: if it was possible to pulverize [or dust] them [Israel's Arabs] out of here, it would be preferable. There is an understandable prejudice against the [Israeli] Arabs among the Jewish public, and, in my opinion, this is the most popular feeling.[110]

A few years earlier, Ehud Olmert had pronounced that the Arab 'demographic threat represents a danger to all our forms of life' – but he did not suggest a solution.[111]

In late 1992, several months after the formation of a Labour government, a telephone survey on Israeli attitudes to racism and xenophobia was initiated by Labour member of the Knesset Avraham Burg, in his capacity as chairman of the Knesset's Education Committee. The survey revealed that 28 per cent of Israeli Jews would prefer a 'pure' Jewish state, a state without the Arab citizens, and that a quarter of the interviewees supported pressure aimed at inducing the Arab citizens to leave the country.[112]

Throughout the 1980s there was a noticeable rise in racist attacks against Israeli Arab citizens across the country. For instance, in June 1987 scores of Jewish residents of the Ramat 'Amidar neighbourhood of Ramat Gan stormed a flat rented and occupied by Arab students and beat them up. The Israeli press widely reported the racist statements made by many residents of Ramat 'Amidar, who were objecting to Israeli Arab citizens (including many Arab students studying in the Tel Aviv area) residing in their midst.[113]

The transfer concept was also raised in March 1987 by Professor Arnon Sofer of Haifa University. At the request of 'Amos Gilbo'a, Minister Moshe Arens's adviser on Arab affairs, Sofer prepared a report in which he analysed the theoretical options available to the government of Israel in its dealing with the 'problem' of the Arab minority. The concept of population transfer was among the various options discussed in the document. Sofer concluded that, although it was 'technically' possible to carry out mass expulsion in 1987, such an option was 'impractical', since Israel would be forced 'to pay a very heavy international price' for it. Sofer also suggested that, although he was not in favour of transfer, if there was an intention within the Israeli establishment 'to solve' the problem of the Arab minority through 'population exchange', it would be better to speed up the processes, because it would be preferable to 'exchange' 800,000 Israeli Arabs now than to 'exchange' 1,200,000 people in the year 2000.[114] Sofer concluded that the option of transfer was not a feasible solution to the 'problem' of the Arab minority in Israel. However, it seems that the very idea of raising such a solution, even hypothetically, by Sofer himself (in a document presented to senior government officials in charge of Arab affairs) as well as by leading ministers and officials (from Labour, Likud, and right-wing parties) throughout the late 1970s and 1980s betrays the deep-seated feeling among leading figures in the Israeli establishment that it would be better to be rid of the Arabs in Israel.

Discriminatory policies against the Arabs in Israel, although slightly softened over the years, were still in effect in 1995. After the election of the Labour–Meretz government in June 1992 ministers usually tended to stress in public the importance of promoting full integration of Israel's Palestinians (who are often described by Israeli officials as 'Israeli Arabs', not as 'Israeli-Palestinians') into public life. The same ministers also pronounced themselves in favour of promoting equality in budget allocations among Arabs and Jews. However, this commitment has been largely rhetorical. Although discrimination in budget allocations decreased slightly under the administrations of Rabin and Peres, the latter serving as Prime Minister until May 1996, discriminatory policies against the Arabs in every sphere of public life persist.

Notes to Chapter 4

1. For selected Israeli laws affecting Arab land ownership, see Oren Yiftachel, *Planning a Mixed Region in Israel* (Aldershot, England: Avebury, 1992), appendix 1, p. 313.
2. Quoted in Ian Lustick, *Arabs in the Jewish State* (Austin and London: University of Texas Press, 1980), pp. 175–76.
3. Gilmour, *Dispossessed*, p. 108.
4. Benjamin Beit-Hallahmi, *Original Sins* (London: Pluto Press, 1992), p. 91.
5. Henry Rosenfeld, 'The Class Situation of the Arab National Minority in Israel', *Comparative Studies in Society and History* 20, no. 3 (July 1978), p. 400. Professor 'Uzi Ornan estimates that 95 per cent of the lands within the Green Line are classified as state land. Cited in Noam Chomsky, *Socialist Revolution* 5 (1975), pp. 45–46. For further discussion of land alienation and its effect on Arabs, see Elia Zureik, *The Palestinians in Israel* (London: Routledge & Kegan Paul, 1979), pp. 115–22; Ran Kislev, 'Land Expropriations: History of Oppression', *New Outlook* (September–October 1976), pp. 23–32.
6. Riah Abu Al-Assal, 'Zionism: As It Is in Israel for an Arab', in *Judaism or Zionism?* (London: Zed Books, 1986), p. 172.
7. Sammy Smooha, *Arabs and Jews in Israel*, vol. 2: *Change and Continuity in Mutual Intolerance* (Boulder, San Francisco: Westview Press, 1992), pp. 157–58.
8. Ibid.
9. See ibid., p. 158.
10. See Ghazi Falah, 'Israeli "Judaization" Policy in Galilee', *Journal of Palestine Studies* 20, no. 4 (Summer 1991), pp. 76–80.
11. Yitzhak 'Oded, 'Bedouin Lands Threatened by Takeover', *New Outlook* 7, no. 9 (November–December 1964), p. 45.
12. Quoted in Arie Dayan, 'The Debate over Zionism and Racism: An Israeli View', *Journal of Palestine Studies* 22, no. 3 (Spring 1993), p. 98.
13. Oren Yiftachel, *Planning a Mixed Region in Israel:* (Aldershot: Avebury, 1992), p. 256, n. 10.
14. 'Oded, 'Bedouin Lands', p. 47.
15. Ibid., p. 51.
16. Kurt Goering, 'Israel and the Bedouin of the Negev', *Journal of Palestine Studies* 9, no. 1 (Autumn 1979), p. 15.
17. See Yosef Goell, 'Encounter in the Negev', *The Jerusalem Post*, 18 March 1983, p. 7.

18. Ibid.
19. Cited in Ben-'Ami, *Sefer Eretz-Yisrael Hashlemah*, p. 186.
20. Quoted in Maddrell, *The Beduin of the Negev*, p. 10.
21. Goell, 'Encounter in the Negev', p. 7.
22. Maddrell, *The Beduin of the Negev*, p. 10.
23. Fiona McKay, 'A Pyrrhic Victory for Israel's Bedouin', *Middle East International*, 3 March 1995, p. 18.
24. Ibid., p. 19.
25. Quoted in *The Jerusalem Post*, 15 September 1982, p. 3.
26. Smooha, *Arabs and Jews in Israel*, vol. 2, p. 158.
27. Majid Al-Haj, 'Soviet Immigration as Viewed by Jews and Arabs: Divided Attitudes in a Divided Country', in Calvin Goldscheider (ed.), *Population and Social Change in Israel* (Boulder, CO: Westview Press, 1992), p. 92.
28. Sarah Ozacky-Lazar and Ibrahim Malik, 'Israeli–Arab Anxieties', *New Outlook* (December 1990/January 1991), p. 20.
29. Asa'ad 'Azayzah, 'The Impact of Soviet Immigration on Arab Local Authorities' (Hebrew), paper presented to a Haifa University Symposium in 1992.
30. Ozacky-Lazar and Malik, 'Israeli–Arab Anxieties', p. 20.
31. Ibid., pp. 20–21. Hammer has served in most Israeli cabinets since the mid-1970s: Minister of Welfare from 1975 to 1976; Minister of Education and Culture from June 1977 to 1984; Minister of Religious Affairs from October 1986 to June 1990; Minister of Education and Culture from June 1990 to June 1992; Minister of Education since June 1996.
32. *New Outlook* (December 1990/January 1991), p. 21.
33. Reinhard Wiemer, 'Zionism and the Arabs after the Establishment of the State', in A. Schölch (ed.), *Palestinians Over the Green Line* (London: Ithaca Press, 1983), p. 46. In the early 1950s Ben-Gurion also discussed with senior intelligence officers in the Israeli army the idea of converting Israeli Arabs including Bedouin to Judaism. Cited in Benziman and Mansour, *Dayarei Mishne*, p. 51.
34. Eli Lobel, 'Palestine and the Jews', in Ahmad El Kodsy and Eli Lobel, *The Arab World and Israel* (New York: Monthly Review Press, 1970), p. 85.
35. Quoted in Benziman and Mansour, *Dayarei Mishne*, p. 21. Throughout the 1950s and 1960s Harman was a senior Israeli government official. In July 1948, he was appointed Deputy Director of the Press and Information Department of the Foreign Ministry, a post he held

until the following year, when he became Consul General in Montreal. In 1953 he was appointed Consul General in New York. Two years later he returned to Israel as Assistant Director General of the Foreign Ministry, a position he held until 1956, when he was named head of the Information Department of the Jewish Agency and a member of the Agency's Executive. In 1959 he was appointed Ambassador to the United States, a position he held until 1968, when he resigned his post to become president of the Hebrew University of Jerusalem.

36. Quoted in Benziman and Mansour, *Dayarei Mishne,* p. 23.

37. Cited in Wiemer, 'Zionism and the Arabs', pp. 46–47.

38. See Roberto Bachi, 'Population of Israel', *New Encyclopedia of Zionism and Israel* (London and Toronto: Associated University Presses, 1994), p. 1067.

39. Ibid.

40. Bachi's report is found in the Central Zionist Archives, Jerusalem, 525/8223.

41. Lobel, 'Palestine and the Jews', pp. 85–86.

42. Beit-Hallahmi, *Original Sins,* p. 94.

43. Benziman and Mansour, *Dayarei Mishne,* p. 47.

44. Edward Grossman, 'Journal from Israel', *Commentary* (October 1969), p. 64.

45. Cited in Zureik, *The Palestinians in Israel,* pp. 115 and 224, n. 35.

46. Arnon Sofer, 'Demography in Eretz-Israel: 1988 and the Year 2000', in Natasha Beschorner and St John B. Gould (eds.), *Altered States? Israel, Palestine and the Future* (London: School of Oriental and African Studies, 1991), p. 10.

47. Ibid., p. 15.

48. Bachi, 'Population of Israel', pp. 1059, 1063, 1065.

49. Cited in *Ma'ariv,* 8 October 1982, p. 19.

50. Shem-Ur, *Te'ud Politi,* p. 100; and Ora Shem-Ur, *Yisrael Rabati* [Greater Israel] (Tel Aviv: Nogah Press, 1985).

51. Benjamin Netanyahu, *A Place Among the Nations* (London: Bantam Press, 1993), p.303.

52. Beit-Hallahmi, *Original Sins,* p. 94.

53. Bachi, 'Population of Israel', p. 1068.

54. Benziman and Mansour, *Dayarei Mishne,* p. 98.

55. *Ma'ariv,* 8 September 1976.

56. See the text of the Koenig Report in *Journal of Palestine Studies* 6, no. 1 (Autumn 1976), pp. 191–200.

57. Ibid., p. 191.

58. Ibid., p. 196.

59. Cited in Zureik, *The Palestinians in Israel*, p. 108.

60. Cited in Benziman and Mansour, *Dayarei Mishne*, pp. 57–58.

61. Yiftachel, *Planning a Mixed Region in Israel*, pp. 192–93, n. 4.

62. Yosef Burg's career as Cabinet Minister spanned four decades and he held more cabinet posts than any other politician in Israel. He was a Member of Knesset from 1949 to 1988 and served as Deputy Speaker in the First Knesset; Minister of Health from 1951 to 1952; Minister of Posts from 1953 to 1958; and Minister of Social Welfare from 1959 to 1970. He was minister of the Interior, Police, and Religious Affairs from 1970 to 1984, and was Minister of Religious Affairs from 1984 to 1986. Since 1989 he has been Chairman of Yad Vashem, the official Holocaust remembrance authority of Israel for the commemoration of Jews who were murdered during the Holocaust.

63. See *Ma'ariv*, 8 and 9 September 1976. Two Likud MKs, Yigal Cohen and 'Akiva Noff, also publicly welcomed the preparation and publication of the Koenig Report. Noff even demanded the convening of the Knesset's Foreign Affairs and Defence Committee to discuss the 'ethnic demographic problems in the northern region'. See also *'Al-Hamishmar*, 8 and 10 September 1976.

64. Cited in Benziman and Mansour, *Dayarei Mishne*, pp. 59–60.

65. He remained in the same job until resigning in 1986, after serving in the Likud administrations of Menahem Begin and Yitzhak Shamir and the National Unity government headed by Shim'on Peres. See also David K. Shipler, *Arab and Jew: Wounded Spirits in a Promised Land* (London: Bloomsbury, 1987), pp. 442–43.

66. Sammy Smooha, *Arabs and Jews in Israel,* vol. 2, p. 255.

67. Ibid., p. 253.

68. Cited in *The Jerusalem Post,* 25 December 1987, p. 8.

69. Cited in *Haaretz,* 9 December 1990, p. 3a.

70. Said Zeedani, 'Democratic Citizenship and the Arabs in Israel', in Nur Masalha (ed.), *The Palestinians in Israel* (Haifa: the Galilee Centre for Social Research, 1993), pp. 72, 81, n. 5; *Al-Midan* (Nazareth), 23 March 1990; Qassim Zayd and Yoram Bar, in *'al-Hamishmar*, 3 March 1990; and Ozacky-Lazar and Malik, 'Israeli–Arab Anxieties', p. 21.

71. See Beit-Hallahmi, *Original Sins*, pp. 86–89.

72. Quoted by Nadim Rouhana, 'Accentuated Identities in Protracted

Conflicts: The Collective Identity of the Palestinian Citizens in Israel', *Asian and African Studies* 27 (1993), p. 122, citing Knesset proceeding of 31 July 1985.

73. Smooha, *Arabs and Jews in Israel*, vol. 2, p. 175, n. 1.

74. *Politikah* no. 4 (December 1985), cited in Joel Beinin, 'Israel at Forty: The Political Economy/Political Culture of Constant Conflict', in Ian Lustick (ed.), *Arab–Israeli Relations*, vol. 7 (New York and London: Garland Publishing, 1994), pp. 82, 90.

75. Ibid.; and David Grossman, *Sleeping on a Wire: Conversations with Palestinians in Israel* (London: Jonathan Cape, 1993), p. 251.

76. Grossman, *Sleeping on a Wire*, p. 250.

77. *Haaretz*, 15 August 1979, p. 9.

78. Shipler, *Arab and Jew*, pp. 439–40.

79. Quoted in Elia Zureik, 'Crime, Justice, and Underdevelopment: The Palestinians Under Israeli Control', *International Journal of Middle East Studies*, 20 (1988), p. 415.

80. Zureik, 'Crime, Justice, and Underdevelopment', pp. 416–17.

81. Beit-Hallahmi, *Original Sins*, p. 90. See also Ghazi Falah, 'Pluralism and Resource Allocation among Arab and Jewish Citizens of Israel', in Masalha (ed.) *The Palestinians in Israel*.

82. Beit-Hallahmi, *Original Sins*, p. 90.

83. Amos Elon, 'The Jews' Jews', p. 14, citing David Grossman's *Sleeping on a Wire: Conversations with Palestinians in Israel*.

84. Ibid. The situation in the Ministry of Education is particularly revealing. Although the Arab pupils constitute about 20 per cent of the total body of pupils in Israel, only 3 per cent of the high-ranking positions in the Ministry of Education are held by Arabs. Among the directors and deputy directors of the six regions of the Ministry of Education, there is not a single Arab. Even the Division for Arab Education in the Ministry was for forty years headed by a Jew. In 1987 an Arab was appointed to this post, and then only after it had been emptied of any real authority in decision making and resource allocation. Majid Al-Haj, *Education, Empowerment, and Control: The Case of the Arabs in Israel* (New York: State University of New York Press, 1995), p. 208.

85. See Paul Jeffrey, *The Times Higher Education Supplement*, 18 August 1995, p. 36. See also Al-Haj, *Education, Empowerment, and Control*, p. 208.

86. Gilmour, *Dispossessed*, p. 109, citing *Israel and Palestine*, no. 51 (August 1976), p. 3.

87. Quoted in *Middle East International,* 2 February 1979, p. 11.

88. Cited by Aharon Bakhar, in *Yedi'ot Aharonot,* 26 January 1979, p. 17.
Another right-wing figure, lawyer Yedidya Beeri (a member of the
Knesset, 1974–78; member of the Central Committee of the Likud
Party; member of the Foreign Relations Committee of Israel Bar
Association; and Chairman of the Board of the Public Council for the
Prevention of Noise and Air Pollution), wrote that Prime Minister
and Defence Minister Begin should use the 1945 Defence
(Emergency) Regulations to expel both the six Arab students and the
heads of the Arab Local Councils from Israel. See *Yedi'ot Aharonot,* 21
January 1979, pp. 11 and 34.

89. Quoted in *Middle East International,* 2 February 1979, p. 12.

90. Cited in *Summary of World Broadcasts (SWB), Part 4: The Middle East
and Africa* (Reading, BBC), 30 January 1979.

91. *Yedi'ot Aharonot,* 24 January 1979, p. 3.

92. Dayan's speech is quoted in *Summary of World Broadcasts (SWB), Part 4:
The Middle East and Africa* (Reading, BBC), 25 January 1979.

93. See *Davar,* 28 January 1979.

94. Quoted in *Haaretz* editorial, 4 December 1980; Sammy Smooha,
'Existing and Alternative Policy towards the Arabs in Israel', *Ethnic and
Racial Studies* 5, no. 1 (January 1982), p. 87. See also Bernard Avishai,
The Tragedy of Zionism (New York: Farrar Straus Giroux, 1985), p. 298;
Yossi Melman and Dan Raviv, 'A Final Solution to the Palestinian
Problem', *Guardian Weekly,* 21 February 1988.

95. Quoted in Smooha, 'Existing and Alternative Policy', p. 87; see
Sharon's interview by Dov Goldstein in *Ma'ariv,* 9 September 1977,
p. 24.

96. See Mi'ari's interview in *Journal of Palestine Studies* 14, no. 1 (Autumn
1984), p. 44.

97. Cited in *Haaretz* editorial, 4 December 1980. See also Yossi Melman
and Dan Raviv, 'Expelling Palestinians', *The Washington Post,*
7 February 1988. Patt has been MK since 1970; Minister of Housing,
1977–1979; Minister of Industry and Trade, 1979–1984; Minister of
Science and Development, 1984–1988; Minister of Tourism, 1990–
1992.

98. See *Jerusalem Post International,* 23 January 1988.

99. Quoted from the Hebrew press in David McDowall, *Palestine and Israel*
(London: I.B. Tauris, 1989), pp. 259–60.

100. On Rabin's role in this widely documented episode, see e.g., Benny
Morris, 'Operation Danny and the Palestinian Exodus from Lydda

and Ramle', *The Middle East Journal*, 40, no. 1 (Winter 1986), pp. 82–109.

101. See *Yedi'ot Aharonot,* 12 and 17 July 1990.

102. See *Ha'ir,* 19 September 1986.

103. Shem-Ur, *Te'ud Politi,* pp. 127, 133.

104. See *The Jerusalem Post,* 9 September 1986.

105. Cited in Smooha, *Arabs and Jews in Israel,* vol. 2, p. 245.

106. Ibid., citing an article by 'Atallah Mansour in *Haaretz,* 20 March 1991.

107. *Davar,* 18 May 1989; *Haaretz,* 19 May 1989, cited in Smooha, *Arabs and Jews in Israel,* vol. 2, p. 245.

108. See Dan Leon in *New Outlook* (September/October 1991), p. 48. A similar pronouncement was made in 1977 by the then chairman of the local council of Karmiel, Baruch Wenger. *Haaretz,* 20 July 1977. See also Lustick, *Arabs in the Jewish State,* p. 177; and Jiryis, *The Arabs in Israel,* p. 109.

109. Cited in *Haaretz,* 17 January 1986.

110. Quoted in Benziman and Mansour, *Dayarei Mishne,* p. 95.

111. Cited by Sh. Z. Abramov, *Haaretz,* 23 July 1988.

112. Cited by Peretz Kidron, *Middle East International,* no. 440, 18 December 1992, p. 4.

113. Smooha, *Arabs and Jews in Israel,* vol. 2, pp. 244–45. Also in the early and mid-1980s the Israeli press widely reported the activities of MENA (an acronym for the 'Defenders of Natzrat 'Illit'), a racist local organization formed in Upper Nazareth, in the Galilee, to pressurize Arab residents to move out of the town. MENA, although composed of local residents of Upper Nazareth, formed close ties with the Kach movement, and publicly advocated the transfer of Israel's Arab minority out of the country. Also in the mid-1980s a number of anti-Arab racist incidents related to the issue of Kiyoso Street in Jaffa were covered widely in the Hebrew press.

114. Benziman and Mansour, *Dayarei Mishne,* p. 60.

Chapter 5
Palestinian Transfer and Israeli Settlements

Labour's Proposals

The Moshe Dayan transfer plan, described earlier, shows that the Labour governments of Levi Eshkol and Golda Meir had pursued an undeclared, secret, 'voluntary' transfer plan from 1967 to 1970, although these governments neither advocated outright annexation of the West Bank and Gaza nor explicitly or publicly supported the demands of the Whole Land of Israel movement. However, the concept of transfer has never been the exclusive property of the Right but rather has been advocated by mainstream Labour Zionism. Exponents of transfer still permeate the Labour Party. For example, the revelations of the 1980s that it was Labour's leaders and military commanders (David Ben-Gurion, Yisrael Galili, Yigal Allon, Moshe Carmel, Yitzhak Rabin, Moshe Dayan, and others) who oversaw the expulsions of 1948, and that for some Labour leaders it remained, evidently, an open option for consideration after 1967. The views of Rabin, who became Prime Minister in 1992, are revealing of these attitudes. For example, in February 1973, as ambassador to the United States, Rabin stated in a discussion organized by the mass-circulation daily *Ma'ariv*:

> The problem of the Gaza [Strip] refugees should not be solved in Gaza and not in El Arish, but in the East Bank [that is, Jordan], mainly. I would make efforts to reach a minimum [number of] refugees on the West Bank . . . In my opinion it is possible to bring about population shift on a basis other than the use of force. I want to create in the course of the next 10 to 20 years conditions which would cause natural migration of population to the East Bank . . .[1]

In the following year, after becoming prime minister, Rabin repeated the same statements in interviews with two foreign newspapers. 'I would like to create in the course of the next 10 to 20 years conditions which would attract natural and voluntary migration of the refugees from the Gaza Strip and the West Bank to Jordan . . . To achieve this we have to come to an agreement with King Hussein and not with Yasser Arafat.'[2] In an interview with the Italian weekly *Epoca* he added: 'there is a need for a place to which it would be possible to transfer a quarter of a million refugees, who are residing in crowded conditions in the Gaza Strip. Such a place can only be Jordan.'[3]

Labour Zionism has traditionally been consistent in regarding the King of Jordan (and formerly the Amir of Transjordan) as the partner for negotiation, not the local, indigenous population of Palestine. Rabin was breaking no ground in this respect, nor in connection with the Labour government's pursuit of transfer schemes as has been illustrated by the Dayan scheme of the immediate post-1967 period. Moreover, Rabin appeared to be echoing the secret decision taken by the Eshkol cabinet Ministerial Committee for Defence on 15 June 1967 demanding the transfer of the refugees to Arab countries. Labour Zionism's justification for these schemes has always been predicated on the assumption that the Palestinians should have no difficulty in regarding Jordan, (Syria or Iraq) as their homeland and that the Palestinians, including the peasantry, had no strong attachment to their homes and lands and could easily be relocated to some other neighbouring country.[4]

Rabin's statements show clearly that he believed in what might be termed 'creeping transfer', that is, the creation of conditions that would cause the residents of the occupied territories to leave. In 1984, he was back in charge of the occupied territories as Minister of Defence in the National Unity coalition of Labour and Likud. His six-year tenure of office was characterized by the 'iron fist' policy and, during the opening phase of the *intifada*, he reportedly gave the widely known 'break their bones' order.[5]

The notion of 'voluntary' transfer also finds echoes in the thinking of some supporters of pragmatic Zionism including senior army officers. Shlomo Gazit[6] warned in a lecture at the Hebrew

University in December 1981 against 'evacuating any part of historic Land of Israel' which must 'remain entirely under Jewish control' as 'a basically Jewish state'. It is therefore necessary to face 'the problems of the Arabs of the historic Land of Israel'. He argued that 'Israel regards this as a humanitarian problem and not a political problem, and it therefore follows that the solution for them must be found outside the territories of the historic Land of Israel.'[7] Since then, however, Gazit has expressed contradictory statements. In a 1988 article in *Haaretz*, he described the transfer solution as an 'entirely false messianism', while simultaneously explaining the reasons why he had agreed to attend a conference organized by the open transfer campaigner Reserve General Rehava'am Zeevi in Tel Aviv in February 1988 and pronouncing himself in favour of mass Arab 'voluntary' and 'agreed' 'transfer'. Although Gazit opposed the idea of outright expulsion (not on moral grounds: 'I find it difficult to understand the negative connotations involved in the term "transfer"') as a dangerous solution leading to further escalation, he saw nothing wrong in

> the second form which talks about voluntary transfer. Within a comprehensive Israeli–Arab peace agreement, the Arab states, on the one hand, and the Palestinian leadership, on the other, would agree to a plan for transferring the Arab population existing within the boundaries of the Land of Israel and its resettlement in the territories of Arab states. The expression 'voluntary', of course, does not mean that each and every one of the would-be transferees would have a free, personal choice (and this did not happen in the Sudeten region, between Turkey and Greece or between India and Pakistan). Yet the political leadership agreed to this plan out of an awareness and understanding that such transfer was the political option [best] chosen vis-à-vis other alternatives. This is a painful surgical operation, yet an operation that has a real solution to the problem . . . such agreement if it will be achievable and practicable, should not, of course, be rejected out of hand.[8]

Prior to 1977 all Labour cabinets were guided by the Allon Plan which envisaged the annexation of 40 per cent of the West Bank and the Gaza Strip. The plan was conceived by the late Deputy Prime Minister Yigal Allon, although it was never formally approved. Nevertheless, it was rendered operational in 1970 and constituted a guideline for the establishment of Jewish settlements in the West Bank. Allon's disappointment at the 'demographic' outcome of the 1967 war, which unlike the 1948 war did not bring about the evacuation of most of the Arab inhabitants of the newly acquired territories, was expressed at a meeting with a delegation of the Whole Land of Israel movement, apparently in November 1967:[9] 'Is this the way to occupy Hebron? A couple of artillery bombardments on Hebron and not a single 'Hebronite' would have remained there. Is this the way to occupy Jerusalem [without driving the Arabs out]?'[10]

Clearly Allon believed that the emigration and relocation of the Arab refugees from the Gaza Strip and the West Bank would contribute to neutralizing Israel's 'demographic' problem. It is against this preoccupation with Israel's 'demographic problem' that his plan must be viewed. Although the above-mentioned transfer plan of Dayan was a direct outcome of the cabinet discussions of June 1967, the Allon plan was, almost certainly, informed and inspired by these same transfer 'sentiments' and 'proposals'. The Allon Plan envisaged expanding Israel's borders on the West Bank – these borders must be based on the River Jordan – the Gaza Strip and the Golan Heights through establishing new Jewish settlements there which must be under Israeli sovereignty and which would constitute facts the Arabs would have no choice but to accept during peace negotiations.[11]

The basic thinking behind the Allon Plan of assuring the maximum land and the minimum number of Arabs – or an overwhelmingly Jewish state from the demographic point of view[12] – remains essentially the fundamental position of the Labour Party. In 1984, Yitzhak Navon, the relatively moderate ex-president of Israel and a leading Labour politician, declared during the general election campaign: 'The very point of Labor's Zionist program is to have as much land as possible and as few Arabs as possible!'[13] Navon's statement seemed to confirm the belief that the Labour Party wanted to annex *de facto* as much as possible of the West Bank and thin out as many as possible of its Palestinian residents. Such statements have not only obfuscated the differences between Labour and the annexationist Likud but have also reinforced the recurring theme in the 'demographic' debate that a large Arab population could not be integrated into the Israeli state and consequently have contributed to the increasing Israeli public support for transfer ideas. Labour politicians have warned about the 'demographic threat', implying that annexation of the densely populated areas of the West Bank and Gaza would mean the end of the Jewish state.[14] Yet Labour 'demographic threat' arguments only reinforced the notion that an integral Jewish state without Arabs was, and remains, Zionism's basic aim, and that the cardinal problem of annexation was that it might bring more Arabs into the Jews' midst. These arguments only exacerbated the alienation of Palestinian citizens of Israel. Moreover, Labour demographic criteria not only made the values of secularism and democracy irrelevant but also contributed to the fact that the Israeli public's comprehension of this racist notion leads it to favour transfer rather than a compromise and withdrawal from the territories.

Labour's position on the occupied territories was altered as a result of the decision by Prime Minister Rabin to have direct negotiations with the Palestine Liberation Organization (PLO). However, even after signing the 1993 Declaration of Principles, the Labour government remained opposed to the establishment of a Palestinian state in the West Bank; against Israel's return to the pre-1967 borders; and for retaining most of the Jewish settlements in the occupied territories. Indeed, in the spring of 1995 the Rabin government took a decision to build eight thousand new housing units in the Israeli settlement of Ma'ale Adumim, located at the centre of the West Bank and half way between Jerusalem and Jericho. This decision to double the size of Ma'ale Adumim is also linked to Labour's strategy of annexing greater Jerusalem to Israel and some kind of partition of the West Bank between Israel and Jordan-Palestine. According to Labour's plans, most of Gaza and fragments of the West Bank, which will be administered by the Palestinian National Authority, will be federated with Jordan. This scenario falls within the traditional Labour axiom of 'maximum land and minimum Arabs'. Of course, it is still too early to judge the long-term historical consequences of the Israel–PLO agreements.

Until 1993 there was a convergence between Likud and Labour on the Palestinian question. Both parties, when in power, preferred to deal with the rulers of Arab states rather than with Palestinian representatives. Until 1993 both parties strongly opposed negotiations with the PLO. The Declaration of Principles signed between Israel and the PLO marked an abrupt departure from the long-standing bipartisan (Likud–Labour) position of refusing to talk with the PLO. However, the Labour government recognized the PLO, but without recognizing its goals of ending the occupation, liberating the Palestinians, and decolonizing the West Bank and Gaza Strip. Moreover, Labour and Likud still strongly oppose the establishment of an independent Palestinian state. Perhaps the long-term hope that somehow the Palestinian refugees in the West Bank and Gaza will move away is one factor in the Rabin government's refusal to contemplate a Palestinian state in the West Bank and Gaza. A mini state could not absorb the refugees of Gaza along with refugees from elsewhere. A Jordan–Palestine 'state' might well absorb the Palestinians of most of the West Bank and Gaza, under the guise of settlement in their former homeland, leaving parts of the West Bank effectively under Israeli control.

It is true that Labour Zionism has always been more sensitive to Western public opinion, and its style has been more subtle, more politic and above all more pragmatic than Likud's Zionist Revisionism. In essence, however, both major groupings have taken the position that Jordan is a Palestinian state – the 'Jordanian Palestinian Arab state', in the official parlance of both the Likud and the Labour parties.[15] According to Labour's 'Jordanian option', some densely populated Arab sections of the West Bank – these are not contiguous but made up of three sections totalling about 60 per cent of the West Bank territories – are to be returned to Jordanian control[16] and that would take the bulk of the Palestinian population out of the Jewish state. Labour has always ruled out withdrawing from occupied East Jerusalem and the Jordan Valley and has backed 'security settlement' in the Jordan Valley and elsewhere in the West Bank.

After the accords between Israel and the PLO were signed, Prime

Minister Rabin did his utmost to preserve, and even strengthen, all the Jewish settlements in the occupied territories. The security of Jewish settlers became central to the current Israel–PLO negotiations. The Rabin government allocated $330 million for the completion of bypass roads connecting Jewish settlements to each other and to Israel proper. This ambitious project, with its huge budgetary allocation, together with the construction of settlements and infrastructure in and around Jerusalem, is expected to 'annex' more than 35 per cent of the West Bank to Israel. Israeli journalist Haim Baram, reporting from West Jerusalem in *Middle East International* of 23 June 1995, wrote:

> The first year after Oslo was euphoric, but then the ugly reality began to emerge: it has become absolutely clear that the Rabin government has no intention of dismantling the settlements; the process of releasing Palestinian political prisoners is agonisingly slow and certainly behind schedule; Israel plans to annex a great amount of land around Jerusalem and to create irreversible facts which amount to actually taking over at least 35 per cent of the occupied West Bank; the repression in the occupied territories continues unabated, including the official and semi-official use of torture and the fascist-style operation of the death squads. This was the case before Oslo, but the illusion that a new era has dawned has been dashed.[17]

Likud's Proposals

Between 1977 and 1992, the Likud government moved fast toward settling and extending Israeli sovereignty over 'Judea', 'Samaria', and Gaza and unilaterally annexed the Golan Heights. During Begin's premiership, the Knesset passed a law prohibiting the evacuation of any Jewish settlement from the West Bank and Gaza, which was tantamount to *de facto* annexation.[18] This move was in line with the Likud Party manifesto:

> The right of the Jewish people to Eretz Yisrael is eternal and indisputable, and linked to our right to security and peace. The State of Israel has a right and a claim to sovereignty over Judea, Samaria, and the Gaza

Strip. In time, Israel will invoke this claim and strive to realize it. Any plan involving the handover of parts of western Eretz Yisrael to foreign rule, as proposed by the Labour Alignment, denies our right to this country.[19]

Prime Minister Yitzhak Shamir (1983–84, 1986–92), restating the Likud policy at a meeting of the Knesset's Foreign Affairs and Defence Committee in June 1991, declared: 'We think that Judea, Samaria, and Gaza are an inseparable part of the State of Israel, and will fight to put that thought into practice.'[20]

In fact, the Likud governments under both Menahem Begin (1977–83) and Yitzhak Shamir did not call for legal comprehensive annexation of the West Bank and Gaza. An extension of the Israeli sovereignty formula of *de facto,* creeping integration, however, which would enable Israel to settle the land while restricting the Palestinian inhabitants to ever shrinking enclaves, and at the same time finding ways to deport the leadership and removing part of the population, was pursued by Likud. Outright, comprehensive legal annexation, on the other hand, would sharply raise the question of citizenship for the residents of the territories, while a *de facto*, creeping annexation appeared to be widely supported in Israel. In any event the logic of the Likud's extensive settlement policies seems to be that the Arab population must be reduced one way or another. Danny Rubinstein, the Israeli journalist who has covered the occupied territories for the daily *Davar*, noted as early as 1979:

Regarding those [people] who on no account want Israeli withdrawal from Judea and Samaria – these [transfer] ideas are very logical. Anyone who aspires to and claims Israeli sovereignty over Judea, Samaria and Gaza – including the Begin government – must understand that there is no way out save the removal of the Arabs from the territories. With over one million Arabs Israeli rule will not be established in Nablus and Hebron, and all the settlement will not help. The supporters of the Likud government know this secretly in their hearts. The Gush Emunim people and the 'Whole Land of Israel's faithful' are talking about this, some privately and some publicly. On the other hand Rabbi Kahane is not interested in the refined tactic. He and his followers bring the principles of the government policy to absurd truth.[21]

It is hardly surprising, therefore, that many important Likud leaders, both openly and privately, have voiced support for Arab transfer. Immediately after the 1967 conquests, at a secret meeting of the Israeli cabinet, Menahem Begin, then minister-without-portfolio, recommended the demolition of the refugee camps of the West Bank and Gaza and the transfer of their residents to the Sinai Desert, which had been captured from Egypt.[22] In the early 1980s, during the negotiations between the Likud and Tehiya over the latter joining Begin's government, Tehiya's Tzvi Shiloah asked Begin whether his 'government is thinking about the transfer of refugee camps in southern Lebanon to northern Lebanon, thus reducing their danger to peace in Galilee?' Begin replied: 'the question of refugees is indeed a serious question. I am about to appeal in a statement to Saudi Arabia, Libya, Iraq and other Arab countries to absorb in their countries the refugees of the camps in Lebanon. What, Iraq has no lands and water and Saudi Arabia and Libya have no oil revenues?'[23]

General Ariel Sharon had been Special Adviser to Prime Minister Yitzhak Rabin between 1975 and 1976. Before becoming Begin's Defence Minister and presiding over the invasion of Lebanon in 1982, Sharon, as Minister of Agriculture and Chairman of the Ministerial Committee on Settlement, was at the heart of Likud's intensive settlement policies in the West Bank.[24] Although the Likud government cited security arguments in defence of its settlement policies, it is clear that the government's position was founded on the abstract, uncompromising ideological claim of the 'Whole Land of Israel' for the 'Jewish people'. To all intents and purposes the settlement policies of the Gush Emunim movement – which will be discussed later – and of the state became one and the same after Begin and Sharon rose to power. Sharon, who had used the 'iron fist' to smash Palestinian resistance in Gaza in 1970 and to evict, ruthlessly, thousands of the Arab inhabitants of the Rafah salient from their homes, believed that the blitzkrieg strategies he had employed on the battlefield could be applied to the political and demographic problems of the West Bank and Gaza. In the opinion of MK and Reserve General Matityahu Peled (1923–95), Sharon (in 1981) would try to thin out the Arab population of the territories 'by a variety of measures which will fall short of forcible deportation or open atrocities'.[25]

The creation of economic distress and economic discrimination against the Arab population of the occupied territories was a deliberate and systematic policy aimed at encouraging voluntary emigration. *The Jerusalem Post* reported in 1982 that more than 100,000 people had emigrated from the West Bank since 1967.[26] According to Dr Bernard Sabella of Bethlehem University, the overall number of Palestinians who emigrated from the West Bank and Gaza Strip between 1967 and 1990 was over 300,000 people, or 18.3 per cent of the Palestinian population in these territories.[27] Economic migration in part has been precipitated by the seizure of Arab land. 'The seizure of Arab land does not increase friction with the Arab population,' Sharon argued, 'it will prevent such friction in the future.'[28] The creation of economic hardship was not the only measure taken to make people leave 'voluntarily'. Israeli journalist Amnon Kapeliouk, writing in the Hebrew daily *'Al-Hamishmar*, described the growth of 'transfer' groups in Israeli society as well as within the Likud government. These ruling circles were proposing a 'final solution' for the Palestinian problem:

> there are also people in official posts who are prepared to create a situation which would force most of the population of the territories to leave their homes and to wander off to Jordan . . . The instrument for creating such a situation is collective punishment. The policy of collective punishment is not new. We saw it in its full glory in the days when Moshe Dayan served as 'the emperor of the territories'. But the difference between the policy pursued then and the one carried out under the Likud government is that now it is done with the clear purpose of making the inhabitants' lives unbearable [and making them want to leave]. The curfew in Hebron, which lasted over two weeks, was not the end of the story. The daily harassment of the inhabitants and the cutting of all the elementary services – such as the cutting of all the telephones

in the town, even those in doctors' clinics – all of these are not designed to deter the inhabitants . . . and not to punish them . . . but to make life unbearable so that the inhabitants will either rise up and be expelled by the instruments that have been prepared for this (as revealed by General Yariv, who condemned these horrific plans), or they will prefer to leave voluntarily.[29]

Throughout the 1980s, Sharon (who is currently Minister of National Infrastructure in the Binyamin Netanyahu cabinet and is back at the heart of the Likud's intensive settlement policies in the West Bank) was among the most powerful 'higher-ups' who promoted public debate on, and support for, the transfer solution. In 1982, Sharon implied, shortly before and perhaps while contemplating his planned invasion of Lebanon, that the Palestinians might have to be expelled, warning that they should 'not forget the lesson of 1948'.[30] 'The hint is clear,' Amnon Kapeliouk commented, citing Sharon's statement.[31] Sharon's threat of a new mass expulsion if the Palestinians did not mind their manners also seemed to be directed toward the Palestinians as a whole (those citizens of Israel as well as the inhabitants of the occupied territories). Upon becoming Defence Minister in 1981, Sharon had initiated the most brutal period of repression in the occupied West Bank and Gaza and set about crushing all opposition to the Israeli occupation. Shortly after Sharon's threat was made, *Middle East International* correspondent Amos Wollin reported from Israel that intensive preparations were continuing in the West Bank and Gaza for much harsher measures to combat Palestinian opposition to the Likud's settlement policies:

Palestinian residents have been warned that resistance to occupation, colonisation, and the civil administration's effort [launched by Sharon] to impose Begin's version of 'autonomy for the Arabs of the land of Israel', or eventual territorial annexation, may easily lead to a repetition of the 1948 tragedy, when the local Arab population was forced into permanent exile in the neighbouring states. In the same way hundreds of thousands of 1948 refugees in the West Bank and Gaza camps would again be required to move eastwards, this time into Transjordan, which Israeli government leaders describe as 'the already existing Palestinian state'. Repeated hints of such a scenario becoming reality (thus also solving demographic and land problems in Israel's interest) may be meant to reduce Palestinian resistance and encourage the 'moderates' to cooperate with the autonomy plan.[32]

Sharon was inspired greatly by Ben-Gurion's and Dayan's thinking and action. In an attempt to legitimize his public advocacy of transfer, Sharon was among the first to reveal, in November 1987, Dayan's transfer plan which operated between 1967 and 1970: 'for several years after the Six-Day War, assistance was given to Arabs who wished to emigrate from here. There was an organization [set up by the Ministry of Defence] which dealt with it.'[33] Sharon is not usually known for his euphemism as to how the Palestinians should be dealt with, and he had no hesitation in describing openly the Palestinian citizens of Israel as 'foreigners'.[34] However, Sharon is fully aware, like other Israeli leaders, of the explosive nature of the transfer issue. In an interview in 1988 he put it more delicately: 'You don't simply bundle people on to trucks and drive them away . . . I prefer to advocate a positive policy, like enhancing the level of technical education in the [occupied] areas – to create, in effect, a condition that in a positive way will induce people to leave.'[35]

After the eruption of the *intifada*, many prominent Likud supporters called for the appointment of Sharon to a key ministerial post with direct responsibility for dealing with and suppressing the popular Palestinian uprising. Among them was Rafi Eitan, a former Adviser to the Prime Minister on combating terrorism (1978–85) and Chairman of the Board of Directors of Israel Chemicals. Eitan urged the government 'to declare all the parts [of the territories] in which the *intifada* is active as zones in which a war situation exists. This would enable me legally to do things that today I cannot do; for instance to transfer population from one place to another in Judea and Samaria, to expel inciters without a prolonged legal process, to confiscate for security needs land and property.'[36] Eitan had urged ten years earlier that 'every Israeli who enters the territories, and even the Old City of Jerusalem, should carry arms and know how to use them. In my judgement more Israeli civilians must be allowed to carry weapons. Some claim that such a state of affairs will be exploited for the worst purposes. My answer: already at this time several thousand weapons are in the hands of the IDF personnel, the police and Israeli civilians.'[37]

Statements made by key Likud politicians in favour of the mass expulsion of Arabs from the West Bank and Gaza began long before the eruption of the *intifada* in December 1987, and these statements were being made increasingly in Knesset debates and by leading Knesset members and ministers. Michael Dekel,[38] who was Deputy Defence Minister in the 1980s, has been among Likud's most ardent public advocates of transfer. A very 'worrying' problem for Zionism, Dekel declared in October 1982, is the 'frightening natural growth of the Israeli Arabs within the Green Line, which is among the highest in the world'. As for the population of the West Bank and Gaza, which the Likud government would never give up, 'there is nothing left to them, apart from looking for their future in [countries] overseas,' Dekel said. With a 'mocking smile', he added that Israel should set up 'schools for construction work for the Arabs of Judea and Samaria in order to encourage them to emigrate to Arab countries while equipped with Israeli certificates'.[39] Five years later, in July 1987, Dekel, then a confidant of Shamir, and Rabin's Deputy Minister of Defence, argued that the United States and the West had a 'moral and political' responsibility to oversee the 'transfer' of the Palestinian population of the West Bank to Jordan.[40] Two months later, in September 1987, Dekel (while still serving as Deputy Defence Minister) said in an interview with the Hebrew daily *Davar*: the West Bank is an integral part of the Land of Israel; 'it is clear that we will never give up the West Bank. [The Jewish] settlements [are] first of all a political measure'; the 'transfer' of the Arabs from the West Bank to their 'homeland' in Jordan could be carried out as part of the process of reaching a political settlement in the Middle East. Recognizing the difficulty of carrying out mass expulsion in time of peace, Dekel said that the transfer solution would neither be carried out immediately, nor in one go, but would be implemented as a gradual process and part of a political settle-ment that would include the 'return' of the Palestinian Arabs to their 'homeland' in Jordan. According to Dekel, there was 'no alter-native' to 'transfer'.[41]

Was Dekel articulating the tacit premises of Likud government policy toward the Arab population of the occupied territories? Since the early 1980s around Dekel congregated a group of Likud Party activists, campaigners and senior figures who openly argued that a mass transfer was 'the only way to solve the Palestinian problem'.[42] It also may be pointed out that Shamir never dissociated himself from the public statements of his protégé. Dekel and his colleagues publicly argue that the West Bank and Gaza can be transformed by a combination of massive Jewish settlement and the mass dispatch of the existing one and a half million plus Arabs across the Jordan River, starting with the residents of the refugee camps.

Another member of the Shamir government who publicly supported the transfer solution was Minister of Science and Development and the Chairman of the Tehiya Party Professor Yuval Neeman. A prominent nuclear physicist and colonel in the reserve, Neeman's credentials include being a member (and formerly Acting Chairman) of the Israel Atomic Energy Committee since 1965; Chairman of Israel Space Agency since 1982; Minister of Science and Development between 1982 and 1984 (in the first Cabinet of Shamir); and Minister of Energy and Science, 1990–92 (in the last Cabinet of Shamir). Neeman also served as Senior Adviser to and Chief Scientist of the Ministry of Defence, 1975–76, during the first government of Yitzhak Rabin. In 1984 Neeman, while a serving minister, expressed a rather transparent position in favour of transfer in his book *The Policy of Sober Vision* (1984), in which he asserted that Israeli citizenship and the right to vote must not be given to the Arabs of the West Bank and Gaza after their legal annexation to Israel – except for those individuals

who would identify with the Zionist state of Israel, be examined in Hebrew and Zionism, do national service, and pay taxes . . . some of the Arab population (350–400 thousand in Judea, Samaria and Gaza) who hold a refugee passport . . . will have to find for themselves a permanent home . . . Such a home will not be here, and just as we absorbed the Jews of Arab countries, the Arab countries will have to absorb the refugees [residing in the territories].[43]

Another senior Likud figure, Binyamin Netanyahu, Deputy Foreign Minister until June 1992 (subsequently the leader of the Likud Party and currently Prime Minister of Israel), told Bar-Ilan University students on 16 November 1989 that the government had failed to exploit internationally favourable situations, such as the Tianamen Square massacre in June 1989 when world attention and the media were focused on China, to carry out 'large-scale' expulsions at a time when 'the damage [to Israel's public relations] would have been relatively small . . . I still believe that there are opportunities to expel many people'.[44]

On 16 November 1989 the Ministry of the Interior issued a certificate approving the registration of a voluntary organization, 'Amutah, whose single aim was the 'transfer' of the Arabs from Israel and the occupied territories. Avner Ehrlikh (who in the early 1970s was a member of the Executive of the Whole Land of Israel movement, and who had published an article in the daily *Haaretz* of 24 October 1988 calling for the transfer of all 'Muslim Arabs' from the 'Land of Israel' to Arab countries) placed an advertisement and article in the name of the management of this 'transfer' 'Amutah: 'Its principal aim is explicit in the registration certificate: A lobby for explaining the necessity of transferring the Muslim Arabs of the Land of Israel, because this is the most humane and just way to achieve peace in the Middle East'; the only way to prevent the development of a bi-national state in Greater Israel is to 'implement the plan of evacuating the Arabs of the Land of Israel outside the boundaries of the Land of Israel';

we have reached the 12th hour and we should know that this country would be either for us or for the Arabs. And if we want this country [Greater Israel] a decision should be taken immediately to set up a Parliamentary lobby, the aim of which is to bring about that the state of Israel, the whole Jewish people and most peoples understand that peace in the Middle East will be established . . . only if the transfer of the Arabs of the Land of Israel is carried out to Arab countries . . . if the evacuees decide on another destination, it would be the role of the United Nations to provide it for them. I am convinced and certain that the United States could absorb 300–400 thousand of them, France, England,

Italy, Germany and Canada would have to absorb the rest of the evacuees. Only thus the problem of the Arabs of the Land of Israel would be solved in a humane way.

Other Likud activists such as Aharon Pappo – he is also a member of the Israeli Broadcasting Authority Executive – have argued that expulsion would be a humane and practical solution.[45] As many Likud stalwarts, Pappo is not a recent convert to the transfer doctrine. In 1973 he acted as a solicitor for Rabbi Meir Kahane, who was indicted by an Israeli court for his letter writing campaign of late 1972 and early 1973 urging the Arab citizens to emigrate from Israel. Subsequently Pappo, while remaining a Likud figure, has been associated with two movements for Arab expulsion: the 'National Circle' of Ora Shem-Ur and the Moledet Party led by Rehava'am Zeevi. In an article published in the mass-circulation daily *Yedi'ot Aharonot* – shortly after the Zeevi Party joined the Shamir cabinet in January 1991 – Pappo wrote that 'the Moledet movement's joining of the government is important and has a significance because of the latest events which proved . . . that there is no possibility of "living together" with the Arab residents of the Land of Israel [on both sides of the Green Line] . . . the joining of the government by Gandhi [i.e., Zeevi] will give legitimacy to the possibility that indeed, in certain circumstances . . . the solution of their transfer to Arab countries in general, and the desert of Iraq in particular, is possible and legitimate.' He added that Czechoslovakia 'expelled' three and a half million Germans after World War II.[46] Pappo, furthermore, published several articles in *Yedi'ot Aharonot* calling for the imposition of collective punishment on the Palestinians and the expulsion of their leaders.[47] Other Likud activists such as Shim'on Gur – a member of the Herut Centre – and Eli Lopaz – the secretary of the Likud branch in the town of Holon – expressed publicly their support for the Moledet transfer solution.[48]

Moshe Dotan, chairman of the editorial board of the periodical *Haumah* (published by Misdar Jabotinsky), the most important ideological organ of the Herut movement and the Likud Party, is, like Aharon Pappo, another Likud stalwart who is not a recent convert to the transfer doctrine. Dotan's transfer proposal/plan/project

191

appeared for the first time in November 1967[49] in the euphoric period that followed the June war's spectacular conquests. Dotan found it necessary to remind his compatriots that 'the Land of Israel' stretched beyond the newly 'liberated territories'.

> Our claim for a homeland on both banks of the Jordan [River] is a just matter and it has a chance of being realized if it is accompanied by force. The Israel Defence Force is a powerful force and is used for a just matter. The Arabs, perhaps more than other peoples, appreciate force and are bound to take it into consideration.

More immediately, however, Dotan's preoccupation was with the 'demographic time-bomb that is activated non-stop against us' in the newly conquered territories, which overnight quadrupled the Arab population to 1.3 million versus 2.3 million Israeli Jews.[50] Such a large Arab population could not be 'digested' and in order to 'prevent the creation of a bi-national state' and to maintain an exclusive Hebrew state in Greater Israel, 'one must be industrious [ensuring] that it has a decisive Hebrew majority and as tiny a minority as possible'.[51]

In justification of his plan, Dotan cited the transfer campaign of Israel Zangwill – one of the most outspoken and vociferous of early Zionists on the subject – before and after World War I as well as the proposal of Rothschild to transfer Palestinians to Iraq in the 1920s.[52] To ensure that 'the Arab minority within the boundaries of our state would be as small as possible,' Dotan suggested, 'we have to adopt a policy which promotes and speeds up the organized emigration of the Arab minority. Towards the Arabs of Israel [including the Arab citizens], refugees as well as residents, we need to adopt a new approach':

> It is possible to entice and ensure the exodus of individuals and groups to countries overseas, in which the absorption conditions are convenient. Those [departees] who would strike roots in new countries in need of farmers – and the Arabs have acquired in this field no little knowledge from our agriculture – are likely to receive large tracts of land, houses, water and equipment. Every family, whose emigration has brought it

benefit, would attract relatives who remained in villages, or the sons of landless farmers, or the disappointed among their friends. The encouragement of emigration will come from two sides: from the inside and from the outside. We are capable, through the exploitation of our great experience . . . in organizing Jewish immigration, to turn the emigration of [Arab] refugees and youth to an efficient non-profitable humanitarian project.[53]

For Dotan, every Palestinian on either side of the Green Line was a potential candidate for transfer/'emigration'; 'in the emigration of the refugees [residing in the West Bank and Gaza] there is a humane, healthy and just element. This is an act of preventive medicine: we must not leave [this] population . . . in a small plot of land that is poor in natural resources and its ownership controversial.'

Every young worker from the 'Triangle' villages [in Israel proper] who comes to a [Jewish] city in search of work is a potential candidate for emigration. It is known that his purpose in the town, in addition to satisfying his needs, is to collect a respectable sum (6000–8000 Israeli Lira) for paying the dowry for his bride's father. Within a few years he establishes a family with many children in his birthplace village, and because there is not sufficient land in his village also, his children, the number of whom has doubled and tripled, are bound to come to the city. It is worthwhile for our state to ensure the emigration of the young man who comes to the marketplace of our city even at the price of paying his dowry at once and recompensing him for his part in the village land so it would become [Jewish] national property.

Moreover, 'by creating adequate conditions for orderly emigration we would be able to stop the relative growth of the Arab minority and constantly remove the undesirable and dangerous elements . . .'

Dotan argued that this 'emigration/removal policy should be carried out at the initiative and encouragement of the government, but not implemented by it – just as the Jewish Agency deals with [Jewish] immigration. It would not be difficult to work out agreements with those governments absorbing the emigration, and indeed the few initial contacts have certainly proved themselves as having great chances.' Would the Palestinian Arabs accept this mass, organized exodus? Dotan's answer: 'This thing depends, of course, on the conditions and means we would mobilize and on the skill and wisdom we would be able to direct to the success of the emigration project.' As for the sceptics and critics 'who will doubt the practical value of the mass emigration plan of Arabs', he suggests they should simply be ignored.

The destination of the mass, government-initiated, organized Arab exodus should be, according to Dotan, South American countries such as Brazil, Colombia, Paraguay, and Venezuela. 'All these countries as well as Canada and Australia are looking for migrants from the white race, Christians or other monotheists, workers at a certain level who could be absorbed and migrants who would be prepared to work in agriculture . . . Indeed for the refugees in our country these conditions are good'; the Arab emigrants 'would be given the opportunity to start a new life overseas with our guidance and assistance, until they stood on their own feet in the wide open spaces of Australia, Canada, and Latin America which need settlers'.[54]

The 'migration project' of Dotan envisaged an officially-orchestrated, carefully-planned and massively-organized operation:

> In addition to our settlement experience in this country, we have proved that we possess great organizational, planning, technical and economic forces which are successfully operating already for years in Africa and Latin America. If we do harness them for the project of emigration and resettlement we could ensure its success. It is not impossible that other international, national and public bodies would agree to take part in the planning – and perhaps not only planning – of this humanitarian project.

As for the financial cost of this project, Dotan explains:

> The financial problem of putting into effect emigration on a large scale should not deter us in spite of the large sums we would have to allocate. It is possible to imagine that even if the emigration countries would participate (the allocation of land, housing, etc.), we would have to spend a sum estimated at 5000 dollars approximately for the emigration of a

family with 6–7 persons on average. This sum would cover the cost of the flight, and the remainder (not an insignificant sum for an ordinary Arab family) would be handed over to the exclusive control of the emigrating family. The initial reasonable price would be as the following: for the emigration of one hundred thousand families, 500 million dollars would be needed. Let us suppose that the emigration would be implemented over 5–6 years (it must not be executed too slowly otherwise the weight of the natural growth would increase) this means one hundred million dollars annually. If we did not receive foreign aid to finance this plan we would have to be compelled in the worst case to shoulder the entire burden of expenditure. Clearly we would have to care about acquiring long-term loans from financial elements abroad . . . Understandably, it is possible that the sums set are too high, and the allowance per capita will be much lower. However, we must be prepared for every effort to solve once and for all the 'refugee problem' and the Arab 'demographic time-bomb'.[55]

The mass 'emigration'/removal of one hundred thousand Arab families – 600,000–700,000 persons – within a few years, Dotan envisages, 'is likely to change our demographic balance unequivocally and most valuably in many respects . . . We are likely to look forward to the start of 1975, at the end of the five-year plan of programmed emigration, to the following composition in the population of the Land of Israel in its present borders: instead of 1.3 million Arabs (today) [November 1967] there will be about 600–700 thousand Arabs against over 3 million Jews.' With such a decisive Jewish majority of five to one in Greater Israel it would be possible to maintain an exclusive Jewish state.

In conclusion, Dotan argued that the Zionist leaders of Israel should treat his 'emigration plan' as a top priority on their national agenda; the mass Arab 'emigration' is perhaps 'a brutal solution . . . but it is anyway an extreme and efficient [one] for all'. Consequently it is vital that 'our public opinion exercises constant and consistent public pressure on the leaders of our state . . . for the execution of a project which has political, demographic and humanitarian implications and whose results are likely to ensure the future and character' of Greater Israel.

There is no evidence to suggest that Dotan has changed his views on the transfer issue since November 1967. On the contrary, under his chairmanship, the Likud periodical *Haumah* has become a major platform for Likud stalwarts and other advocates of Greater Israel who discuss the transfer solution and advocate it openly. In May 1981 Dotan wrote again in *Haumah*, suggesting that after the 1967 war, 'it would have been preferable to open [the Jordan River] bridges only in the exit direction and to encourage the emigration of [Arab] workers to neighbouring Arab states abundant in petro-dollars. We have lost years, in which dangerous thorns, that have greatly weakened the state, have grown.'[56] Moreover, the editor of *Haumah*, Dr Avraham Heller, has proposed the use of financial and economic incentives to encourage mass Arab 'emigration'.[57]

With the Likud assumption of power in 1977 and the subsequent rise of extreme right-wing forces in Israel, the most far-reaching proposals entered mainstream Zionist thinking and official circles. Such proposals, including Arab population removal, were outlined in an article entitled 'A Strategy for Israel in the 1980s', which appeared in the World Zionist Organization's periodical *Kivunim* in February 1982, a few months before Israel's invasion of Lebanon. The article was authored by 'Oded Yinon, a journalist and analyst of Middle Eastern affairs and former senior Foreign Ministry official. The importance of the article's contents lie in the fact that *Kivunim* is published by the World Zionist Organization's Department of Information. Yinon analyses the weaknesses that characterize the national and social structures of Arab states and concludes that Israel should work to bring about their dissolution and fragmentation into a mosaic of ethnic and confessional groupings. In the short-term, Yinon proposes, Israel should bring about the 'dissolution' of Jordan; 'there is no possibility that Jordan will exist in its present shape and structure in the long-term, and the policy of Israel, whether in war or in peace, must be to bring about the dissolution of Jordan under the present regime' and the consequent 'termination of the problem of the [occupied] territories densely populated with Arabs west of the [River] Jordan, whether in war or under the conditions of peace; emigration from the territories, and economic-demographic freeze in them . . . we have to be active in order to encourage this change speedily, in the nearest time.'

> It is no longer possible to live in this country in the present situation without separating the two peoples, the Arabs [including the Arab citizens of Israel] to Jordan and the Jews to the territories west of the River [Jordan] . . . [The Palestinian Arabs] can only have security and existence in Jordan.

Yinon believes, like many advocates of transfer in Israel, that 'Israel has made a strategic mistake in not taking measures [of mass expulsion] towards the Arab population in the new territories during and shortly after the [1967] war . . . Such a line would have saved us the bitter and dangerous conflict ever since which we could have already then terminated by giving Jordan to the Palestinians.'

The long-term objectives, Yinon suggests, encompass the whole Arab world, including the imposition of a *Pax Israela* on, and the determination of the destiny of, Arab societies: reinvading Sinai and 'breaking Egypt territorially into separate geographical districts'. As for the Arab East,

> there all the events which are only our wish on the Western Front [i.e., Egypt] are happening before our eyes today. The total disintegration of Lebanon into five regional, localized governments as the precedent for the entire Arab world . . . the dissolution of Syria, and later Iraq, into districts of ethnic and religious minorities, following the example of Lebanon is Israel's main long-range objective on the Eastern Front . . . Syria will disintegrate into several states along the lines of its ethnic and sectarian structure . . . As a result there will be a Shi'ite 'Alawi state, the district of Aleppo will be a Sunni state, and the district of Damascus another state which is hostile to the northern one. The Druzes – even those of the Golan – should form a state in Houran and in northern Jordan . . . Oil-rich but very divided land internally strife-ridden Iraq is certainly a candidate to fit Israel's goals . . . Every kind of inter-Arab confrontation will help us to preserve in the short run and will hasten the achievement of the supreme goal, namely breaking up Iraq into elements like Syria and Lebanon. There will be three states or more,

around the three major cities, Basra, Baghdad and Mosul, while Shi'ite areas in the south will separate from the Sunni north, which is mostly Kurdish . . . The entire Arabian Peninsula is a natural candidate for dissolution . . .[58]

Given the auspices under which Yinon's proposals were put forward, this article generated wide echoes in Arab countries[59] giving the impression that the World Zionist Organization was endorsing a detailed plan for Arab population transfer and the destruction of Arab countries. Regardless of whether Yinon's transfer proposal was endorsed by official circles in the Zionist World Organization, the Palestinians, as already demonstrated, fear mass transfer from the occupied territories. To the Palestinians, the massive immigration of Soviet Jews, which was channelled by the Likud government into 'creating facts on the ground' in the form of Jewish settlements, and Prime Minister Shamir's declarations that he wanted a 'big Israel' to accommodate a 'big immigration' from the Soviet Union,[60] aroused the gravest fear of a new 1948 exodus. 'One million newly arrived Jews dropped into the laps of Shamir and Sharon . . . will destroy the (demographic) argument of the Labour Party and strengthen support for transfer,' stated Saeb 'Erakat, professor of politics at al-Najah University in Nablus, and later member of the Palestinian delegation to Middle East peace talks.

The more the Likud became entrenched in power in the 1980s, the more persistent many of its senior government officials and ministers became in their public support for the transfer solution. In 1990 the Likud dissolved its coalition partnership with the Labour Party and formed a coalition government with the far right parties – including the Tehiya, Tzomet, Moledet and the National Religious Party – which lasted until 1992. The leaders of these far right parties were among the most vociferous public advocates of transfer within Israel. In January 1991 Reserve General Rehava'am Zeevi, the leader of the Moledet Party, with its single-minded transfer platform, joined the Shamir government as a minister-without-portfolio and member of the policy-making inner cabinet,[61] thus greatly strengthening the transfer camp within the Likud coalition.

Proposals of the Gush Emunim Settlers and the Political Messianics

The Gush Emunim ('Block of the Faithful') movement, which has played a key role in establishing Jewish settlements on the West Bank, was formally established in February 1974. It had evolved into an organized force of settlers from the youth branch of the Mifdal, the National Religious Party (NRP), which was a coalition partner first with Labour until 1977 and then with the Likud until 1992. Since June 1996 the National Religious Party has been represented in the government of Binyamin Netanyahu by two ministers. It should be pointed out that a National Religious Party (Morasha faction) minister in the Shamir Cabinet, Yosef Shapira, suggested in 1988 that the Palestinians should be paid to leave. The NRP youth, of the Bnei 'Akiva movement, had been imbued with an explosive mixture of Zionist territorial expansionism, fanatic nationalism and religious fundamentalism by their Yeshivot (religious seminaries and high schools), which are funded by the state's Ministry of Education. The Gush Emunim's single most influential ideologue was Rabbi Tzvi Yehuda Kook, who was the head of Merkaz Harav Yeshiva in Jerusalem – and the son of Israel's first Ashkenazi Chief Rabbi – who rushed with his biblical claims toward the West Bank immediately after the 1967 conquests: 'All this land is ours, absolutely, belonging to all of us, non-transferable to others even in part . . . it is clear and absolute that there are no "Arab territories" or "Arab lands" here, but only the lands of Israel, the eternal heritage of our forefathers to which others [the Arabs] have come and upon which they have built without our permission and in our absence.'[62] Before the Israeli general election of 1977, Rabbi Kook spoke explicitly in praise of Meir Kahane and his Kach list which was standing for the Knesset.[63] Kook's politics were described by the Israeli journalist David Shaham as

> consistent, extremist, uncompromising and concentrated on a single issue: the right of the Jewish people to sovereignty over every foot of the Land of Israel. Absolute sovereignty, with no imposed limitations. 'From a perspective of national sovereignty,' he [Kook] says, 'the country

belongs to us' . . . In his judgement, Transjordan, the Golan, the Bashan (the Jebel Druze region in Syria), are all part of the Land of Israel . . .[64]

Immediately after the 1967 victory Rabbi Kook demanded the annexation of the occupied territories, in line with explicit Halacha provisions.[65] At a conference he said:

> I tell you explicitly . . . that there is a prohibition in the Torah against giving up even an inch of our liberated land. There are no conquests here and we are not occupying foreign land; we are returning to our home, to the inheritance of our forefathers. There is no Arab land here, only the inheritance of our God – the more the world gets used to this thought the better it will be for it and for all of us.[66]

Gush Emunim spiritual leaders, as well as the settlers, view the Palestinians as temporary alien residents and as a population living, at best, on sufferance. A Gush Emunim spokesman, Meir Eindor of Kiryat Arba'a, was quoted as saying in 1980: 'The Arabs must know that there is a master here, the Jewish people. It rules over Eretz Yisrael . . . The Arabs are temporary dwellers who happened to live in this country. There are commandments in the Bible concerning such temporary dwellers and we should act accordingly.'[67] According to the Gush spiritual leaders, there is no need to take into consideration the Arab inhabitants since their residence in the country for hundreds of years was prohibited and was based on theft, fraud and distortion; therefore now the time has come for the Arab 'robbers' to depart. As Rabbi Shlomo Aviner explains:

> To what can this be compared[?] It resembles a man entering his neighbour's house without permission and residing there for many years. When the original owner of the house returns, the invader [the Arab] claims: 'It is my [house]. I have been living here for many years.' So what? All of these years he was a robber! Now he should depart and pay housing rent as well. A person might say: there is a difference between a residence of thirty years and a residence of two thousand years. Let us ask him: Is there a law of limitation which gives a robber the right to his plunder? . . . Everyone who settled here knew very well that he was

residing in a land that belonged to the people of Israel. Perhaps an Arab who was born here does not know this, nonetheless the fact that a man settled on land does not make it his. Legally 'possession' serves only as evidence of a claim of ownership, but it does not create ownership. The Arabs' 'possession' of the land is therefore a 'possession that asserts no right'. It is the possession of territory when it is absolutely clear that they are not its legal owners, and this possession has no legal and moral validity.[68]

In a similar disposition Rabbi Kook, who apparently inspired Aviner's apologia, wrote: 'We find ourselves here by virtue of our forefathers' inheritance, the foundation of the Bible and history, and there is no one that can change this fact. What does it resemble? A man left his house and others came and invaded it. This is exactly what happened to us. There are those who claim that these are Arab lands here. It is all a lie and falsehood. There are absolutely no Arab lands here.'[69] This imagery of the homecoming Jew and the Arab invader permeates the writings of the spiritual leaders and ideologues of Gush Emunim, particularly the religious extremists, and implies that the Jew has the right to evict the 'alien' Arab 'invader'. Moreover, these ideologues interpret the Zionist assertion of 'historical rights' to the land as meaning that the very fact of Arab residence on, and possession of, the land is morally flawed and legally, at best, temporary, and therefore the Arabs must evacuate and depart the land for the 'legal owners' of the country.

In 1980 the Gush Emunim movement's Department of Information published an article written by Yisrael Eldad recommending that the best course of action would be to bring about large-scale Arab emigration through the deliberate creation of economic hardship in the West Bank and Gaza.[70] Similar views have been expressed at every level of the Gush Emunim movement by both leaders and rank-and-file members most of whom are religious extremists. Eliakim Ha'etzni, of Kiryat Arba'a, a prominent secular figure in the Whole Land of Israel Movement and the settlers' movement, who later became a Tehiya Party member of the Knesset, spoke at a conference of the settlers attended by fifty leading activists from settlements in the occupied territories held in

Moshav Bnei-Tal in the Gaza Strip in 1980 to discuss the future of Arab-Jewish relations in 'Eretz Yisrael'. According to the account of the conference, published by the official Gush Emunim bulletin *Hamakor*, Ha'etzni stated:

> We must get rid of the real obstacle to peace, which is the Hashemite royal house, and we must not leave Amman [after the IDF has occupied it] except in exchange for an agreement stipulating the elimination of the Hashemite royal house and the elimination of the refugee problem. We must help the Palestinian Arabs to set up their own state on the East Bank of the Jordan . . . The Arabs living on the West Bank, in Judea and Samaria, and in the Galilee and the Negev will then elect the Jordanian Parliament, and the Jews who will settle on the East Bank will elect the Knesset.

Ha'etzni — who like other supporters of the Whole Land of Israel Movement earlier, makes little distinction between the Palestinian citizens of Israel and those of the West Bank and Gaza — added: 'Today there is no plan to make Hebron into a Jewish town . . . but if you ['the Arab neighbour'] think that Kiryat Arba [*sic*] will disappear, you had better remember Jaffa [the Arab town which was largely depopulated in 1948] . . .' Aharon Halamish, another speaker from the Gush Emunim settlement of 'Ofra, was much more straightforward: 'It is not necessary to throw bombs into the casbah or expel the Arabs. There is nothing wrong, however, with making their life difficult in the hope that they will emigrate . . . Perhaps in the end only those will remain who genuinely want to be loyal citizens of Israel, and if they really do, let them convert.'[71] Clearly this settler did not believe that many Arabs would agree to 'convert' and therefore he suggested the encouragement of Arab 'emigration'.

Like early Zionist settlers, who engaged in actual 'redemption' and 'conquest' of land, the Gush Emunim settlers have had a disproportionate impact on the official policies of successive Israeli governments, even when the settlers have acted independently, or in ostensible or real defiance, of the government. For example, during the last few years of the Labour era in the 1970s, settlers established three settlements in heavily populated West Bank areas despite the official disapproval of the Rabin government. Various Labour ministries actually provided material assistance for these three settlements. The Labour government had pioneered settlement policies after 1967 by establishing settlements such as Kiryat Arba'a and the Gush 'Etzion settlements. These early settlements were extremely important not just because land and resources were expropriated from the occupied West Bank, but also because these settlements provided the Gush zealots with a territorial base from which they could grow, mobilize more supporters and exert pressure for further expansion into heavily populated areas. The settlers' disproportionate impact on official policies also stemmed from their dogged religious determination, as well as from further practical pursuit of their objectives.

From May 1977 through the early 1980s it became public knowledge that the Gush Emunim movement enjoyed the personal support of Prime Minister Begin, Agriculture Minister and Chairman of the Ministerial Committee on Settlement and later Defence Minister Sharon, and army Chief of Staff Raphael Eitan.[72] Under the Likud, the settlement activities in areas densely populated with Arabs acquired official authorization and were carried out as government policies. The principal financial supporter of the settlement movement and its activities became the Israeli government and the Jewish Agency.[73] These official bodies provided the settlers with material resources; and the army gave them weapons and explosives and protected them, while ensuring the Arab population remained defenceless. Although Gush Emunim has operated largely among Israel's religious population, it has also drawn support from powerful sources on the largely secular political right, including the Likud, Tzomet, Moledet and Tehiya parties. With the Likud government's encouragement, the militant settlers effectively organized themselves into a private and highly motivated army. Their armed vigilantes, who patrol the streets of Arab towns, were an integral part of the army security system up to 1995.[74] As early as 1981 *Haaretz* correspondent Yehuda Litani warned: 'The West Bank settlers constitute military units . . . They will disrupt any political move towards concessions to the Arabs . . . Their well-stocked ammunition stores in the West Bank will be of great help in this struggle.'[75] Having organized themselves into a militant, well-disciplined, private army, and having always regarded themselves as being subject to divine laws and above the conventional laws of the state as far as Eretz Yisrael is concerned, the Gush Emunim settlers represent the severest challenge to any Israeli government considering ceding West Bank territory to Arab sovereignty.

The ideas of the political messianics current in Israel are not confined to the realm of doctrines and sermons. From the beginning of the occupation and especially since the late 1970s the settlers – whose ideology grants them the divine right to Judaize the territories and who reject the very existence of the Palestinians – were deliberately seeking to foster clashes between Arabs and Jews and to create conditions that would precipitate a gradual Arab depopulation. Attacks against Arab civilians were carried out by Jewish groups, the most famous of which was a secret group of Gush Emunim leaders and members known in the Hebrew press as Hamahteret Hayehudit, The Jewish Underground. A large number of settlers from Kiryat Arba'a and other settlements on the West Bank and the Golan Heights were involved in Jewish Underground activities. Their widely documented activities included the June 1980 attacks on the lives of the mayors of Nablus and Ramallah, in which both mayors were maimed; an attack on the Islamic College in Hebron in July 1983 that killed three students; a plot to blow up the Dome of the Rock Mosque in Jerusalem in January 1984; and an attempt to sabotage Arab buses in Jerusalem in April 1984.[76] The perpetrators of the Jewish Underground, who received assistance from two senior officers in the Civilian Administration, included several army reserve officers and one career officer. Most of the terrorists held key positions in Gush Emunim and the settlers' organizations, including the assistant editor of the settlers' monthly Nekudah, four people who had been members of the Gush Emunim secretariat, committee chairmen in settlers' institutions, a former chairman of the Kiryat Arba'a local council, and his deputy and settlement secretaries.[77]

In fact members of the Jewish Underground were applauded in the top echelon of Israeli society. Individuals who were directly involved in their violent activities such as Uri Maier, Zeev Friedman and Yossi Eindor, were arrested in May 1984. While on trial they were pampered by judges and jailers. Although they were convicted for planting the bombs that maimed the West Bank mayors and for the assault on the Islamic College in Hebron that resulted in the murder of Palestinian students, Israeli Television was forbidden to call the convicted men murderers; it was instructed by the government to call them only prisoners. Moreover the religious parties in the Knesset put forward a motion demanding an amnesty for them. In fact support for an amnesty did not come only from the religious camp. On 19 June 1985, a public opinion poll conducted by *Haaretz* revealed that 52.6 per cent of those interviewed supported an immediate release without trial; 4 per cent supported pardon after the trial; 35.5 per cent opposed a pardon; the remaining 7.9 per cent expressed no opinion. A reputed 'moderate', Rabbi Likhtenstein, voiced his opinion that these Jewish Underground murderers – although they should receive some punishment – should not receive the same penalty meted out to a Jew convicted of murdering another Jew because the soul of a non-Jew had a lesser value than that of a Jew.[78] The former Ashkenazi Chief Rabbi of Israel also expressed sympathy for the Jewish Underground members. Knesset Member Yuval Neeman – Minister of Science in the Shamir government, who supported Arab transfer – defended the Jewish Underground network as acting in self-defence.[79] Later some of the Jewish Underground members were indeed pardoned by President Haim Hertzog.

From Expulsion to the 'Annihilation of the Amalekites of Today'

The spiritual leaders of Gush Emunim – such as the late Rabbi Tzvi Yehuda Kook – are by no means a group on the lunatic fringe. Most of them are influential figures within the mainstream religious population and beyond, and their demand that the Jewish Halacha guide official policies towards the Arab population is widely accepted in religious circles and parties. With the rise of the extreme right and the nationalist political messianic trend in the

1980s, many far-reaching ideas, such as expelling the Palestinians, have entered mainstream Zionist religious thinking. If the very idea that Arab residence in Palestine is based on 'theft', is morally flawed and legally temporary, according to the religious messianics, then Arab removal is the logical conclusion. Rabbi Yisrael Ariel bluntly and explicitly demands expelling the Palestinians as necessitated by Jewish religious commandments:

> On the one hand there is a commandment of settling Eretz Yisrael, which is defined by our sages of blessed memory also as the commandment of 'inheritance and residence' – a commandment mentioned many times in the Torah. Every young student understands that 'inheritance and residence' means conquering and settling the land. The Torah repeats the commandment 'You shall dispossess all the inhabitants of the land' tens of times, and Rashi [Rabbi Shlomo Yitzhaki, a paramount Bible and Talmud commentator in the 11th century] explains that 'You shall dispossess – You shall expel.' The Torah itself uses the term 'expulsion' a number of times such as: 'Since you shall expel the inhabitants of the country with my help.' The substance of this commandment is to expel the inhabitants of the land whoever they may be . . . This is also the opinion of Rashi in defining the commandment. In the same Talmudic passage which mentions the commandment pertaining to the land, Rashi interprets: 'Because [of the commandment] to settle Eretz Yisrael – to expel idolaters and to settle [the people of] Israel there.' Thus according to Rashi the commandment to settle [the land] aims at the expulsion of the non-Jew from Eretz Yisrael and that it be settled with Jews.[80]

In particular, these influential rabbis have demanded that the Muslims and Christians should be removed from, or at least discouraged from living in, Jerusalem. Rabbi Eli'ezer Waldenberg, the Israel Prize winner for 1976, stated: 'I, for example, support the application of the Halacha prohibition on gentiles living in Jerusalem, and if we should apply the Halacha, as it should be, we would have to expel all the gentiles [Arabs] from Jerusalem and purify it absolutely. Also we must not permit the gentiles to be a majority in any of Israel's cities.'[81] In his statement Waldenberg implies not only the expulsion of the Arabs from Jerusalem but also from other towns – such as Nazareth, Nablus, Hebron and Ramallah. Furthermore, the Palestinians should only be given the status of alien resident, and must be reduced to a small minority. Rabbi Shalom Dov Wolpo, who bases his views on discussions with, and on the opinions of, the rabbi from Lyubavich, the Rabbi of the Habad Hasidic religious movement – agrees with Waldenberg: 'According to the Halacha it is prohibited for a gentile to live in Jerusalem, and in the ruling of Maimonides it is forbidden to give a resident alien a place in Jerusalem . . . True, this applies when Israel has a strong hand, but today, too, although it is not possible to expel them by force, this does not mean that they should be encouraged to live there.'[82] Rabbi Wolpo adds:

> if they [the Israeli leaders] had declared at the time of the occupation of Jerusalem and the territories [in June 1967] that they were going to leave alive the residents and give them financial compensation, but they must cross immediately to Transjordan, they [the Arabs] would have been thankful for this until today . . . yet what did the [Israeli] leaders do: they left the Arabs in their location . . . but from the beginning they should have removed them from here.[83]

These extremist religious ideas, which in the past were marginal, became increasingly close to the centre of political thinking in the late 1980s and early 1990s. For instance, 'Ovadia Yosef, the relatively moderate former Chief Rabbi of Israel, and spiritual mentor of the Shas religious party – which had six seats in the Knesset and was represented in the Rabin cabinet until 1993 – ruled that the New Testament should be burned because Christianity is a form of idolatry.[84] The practical effect of this ruling was revealed in the Hebrew daily *Ma'ariv* in June 1985 when New Testament copies found in the library of the base of the army Chief Education Officer were burned by the military rabbi of the base.[85] Three weeks later *Ma'ariv* reported that the influential Knesset Foreign Affairs and Defence Committee had referred to the incident and one of its members (MK and Rabbi Haim Druckman) had justified the New Testament burning.[86] The implication of these ideas and actions is crystal clear: if Christian Arabs are practising a form of 'idol worshipping' and if the Palestinians – Christians and Muslims – are to be discouraged from living in Jerusalem and are to be subjected to the Torah laws of 'resident alien' – a status that is extremely unlikely to be acceptable to the Palestinians – then expulsion becomes a logical conclusion for the political messianics.

Expulsion, however, is not the 'final' solution for this political messianic trend. Frequently these circles identify the Palestinians as the 'Amalekites of today'. According to the Bible, the Amalek were an ancient nomadic people, who dwelled in the Sinai desert and southern Palestine, who were regarded as the Israelites' inveterate foe, whose 'annihilation' became a sacred duty and against whom war should be waged until their 'memory be blotted out' for ever.[87] Although the biblical stories mention that the Amalekites were finally wiped out during the reign of Hezekiah in the eighth century BC, Rabbinical literature dwells on Amalek's role as the Israelites' permanent archenemy, saying that the struggle between the two peoples will continue until the coming of the Messiah, when God will destroy the last remnants of Amalek. Some of the political messianics insist on giving the biblical commandment to 'blot out the memory of Amalek' an actual contemporary relevance in the conflict between Israelis and Palestinians. For example, in February 1980, Rabbi Yisrael Hess, the former Campus Rabbi of Bar-Ilan University, published an article in the student bulletin *Bat Kol* entitled 'The Commandment of Genocide in the Torah'. According to Hess, 'The day is not far when we shall all be called to this holy war, this commandment of the annihilation of Amalek.'[88] Hess quotes the biblical commandment according to which he believes Israel should act: 'Go and strike down Amalek; put him under the ban with all that he possesses. Do not spare him, but kill man and woman, baby and suckling, ox and sheep, camel and donkey.'[89] Hess adds: 'Against this holy war God declares a counter jihad . . . in order to emphasize that this is the background for the annihilation and that it is over this that the war is being waged and that it is not a conflict between two peoples . . . God is not content that we annihilate Amalek – "blot out the memory of Amalek" – he also enlists personally in this war . . . because, as has been said, he has a personal interest in this matter, this is the principal aim.'[90]

Citing Hess's article, Professor Amnon Rubinstein, a Knesset Member representing the centrist Shinui Party and a lecturer in Law at Tel Aviv University, commented: 'Rabbi Hess explains the commandment which instructs the blotting out of the memory of Amalek and says that there is not the slightest mercy in this commandment which also orders the killing and annihilation of children and infants. Amalek is whoever declares war on the people of God.'[91] Professor Rubinstein points out that 'no reservation on behalf of the editorial board, the students or the University were made after publishing this article which was also reprinted in other newspapers'.[92] However, a subsequent issue of *Bat Kol* carried two articles written by Professor Uriel Simon and Dr Tzvi Weinberg severely criticizing the Hess article. Clearly for Hess Amalek is synonymous with the Palestinian Arabs, who have a conflict with Israeli Jews, and they must be 'annihilated', including women, children and infants. His use of the Arabic term *jihad* leaves no doubt against whom such a war of 'annihilation' should be waged.

The concept that the Palestinian Arabs are the 'Amalekites of today' is not confined to Rabbi Hess. In his book, *On the Lord's Side*, Danny Rubinstein has shown that this notion permeates the Gush Emunim movement's bulletins. In 1980, the settlers' magazine *Nekudah* carried an article written by Haim Tzoriyah, entitled 'Right to Hate'. According to Tzoriyah, 'The Amalekism of our generation finds expression in the deep Arab hatred towards our national revival in our forefathers' land.' The same notion propagated by the messianic trend regarding the synonymity of the Palestinians with the Amalekites was discussed widely in the Israeli daily press and even on television. It was also criticized in moderate religious circles.[93] The late Professor Uriel Tal, who was a prominent biblical scholar at Tel Aviv University and who conducted his study in the early 1980s, did more than anyone to expose the 'annihilationist' notions preached by the strident messianic trend in Israel. Tal, who had also done extensive research on anti-Semitism between the two World Wars, concluded that these messianic doctrines were similar to ideas common in Germany during the

Weimar Republic and the Third Reich. The gist of Tal's research was presented to an academic forum at Tel Aviv University in March 1984 and was subsequently publicized widely in the Hebrew press and Israeli journals. Tal pointed out that the totalitarian political messianic stream refers to the Palestinian Arabs in three stages or degrees: 1) the reduction of the Arabs to the Halacha status of 'resident alien'; 2) the promotion of Arab 'transfer' i.e., expulsion; 3) the implementation of the commandment of Amalek, as expressed in Rabbi Hess's article: to 'annihilate' the Palestinian Arabs.[94]

The discovery of the activities of the Jewish Underground organization in the mid-1980s showed that the ideas of the messianic trend were not confined to the realm of sermons. On 2 May 1985, *The Jerusalem Post* published an article by David Richardson which pointed out that at least seven rabbis, among them the prominent spiritual guide of the Gush Emunim movement, were privy to the violent campaign conducted by the Jewish Underground organization. According to the article, a statement confirming this was given to the Jerusalem police by the accused leader of the underground group, Menahem Livni, and his 27-page affidavit was presented to the Jerusalem District Court on 1 May 1985. These rabbis included Tzvi Yehuda Kook, 'Ovadia Yosef, and Shlomo Aviner, as well as Moshe Levinger (a prominent leader of Gush Emunim based in Kiryat Arba'a), Eli'ezer Waldman (then a Tehiya Member of Knesset), Yo'ezer Ariel, and Dov Leor. Waldman, Ariel, Leor, and Levinger all took part in a meeting at which it was discussed and unanimously decided upon to wage a widespread campaign of violence against the inhabitants of the occupied territories. Rabbi Yisrael Ariel – who explicitly demanded the expulsion of the Arabs – justified the campaign of the Jewish Underground organization, implying that the killing of an Arab was not murder:

Any one who searches through the code of Maimonides, which is the pillar of the Halacha in the Jewish world, [and searches for] the concept 'you shall not murder' or the concept 'holy blood' with regard to the killing of a non-Jew – will search in vain, because he will not find [it] . . . It follows from the words of Maimonides that a Jew who kills a non-Jew

. . . is exempt from the prohibition 'you shall not murder'. And so Maimonides writes in the Halachas of murder: 'An Israelite who kills a resident alien is not sentenced to death in the court of law.'[95]

The ideology of the nationalist political messianics, including the theory of the 'Amalekites of today', also found an echo in an article published by the Chief Military Rabbi of the IDF Central Command, Avraham Zemel (Avidan), who, according to Amnon Rubinstein, gave Halacha justification for the 'murder of non-Jewish civilians including women and children, during war'.[96] Another soldier, who was also a Yeshiva student, asked his rabbi about the subject of 'Tohar Haneshik' (the 'purity of arms'). From the answer of the rabbi the soldier concluded: 'During war I am permitted or even obliged to kill every male and female Arab that happens to be in my way . . . I must kill them even if this involves complication with the military law.'[97] Rubinstein cites in his book *From Herzl to Gush Emunim and Back Again* many references made by the spiritual mentors of Gush Emunim to the Arabs as the 'Amalekites of today'. He wrote critically in an article in *Haaretz*:

We are dealing with a political ideology of violence. It is needless to show how this ideology is expressed in the way the Arabs are treated. The Rabbis of Gush Emunim – except for the few brave ones . . . publicly preach incitement to kill Arab civilians, and those who kill civilians, and are caught and brought to court, are later amnestied by the Chief of Staff [General Raphael Eitan], who believes in the use of violence that the Arabs understand. Those who think that it is possible to differentiate between blood and blood are wrong. The verdict on 'Amalek' can easily be extended to the enemies within, the traitors.[98]

Notes to Chapter 5

1. *Ma'ariv*, 16 February 1973, p. 17.
2. Francis Ofner, 'Sketching Rabin Plan for Peace', *The Christian Science Monitor*, 3 June 1974, dispatch from Tel Aviv.
3. Cited in *Yedi'ot Aharonot*, 23 July 1974, p. 2. In 1976, under the Rabin government, Yisrael Koenig, a senior official of the Interior Ministry with responsibility for the northern district, issued the infamous 'Koenig memorandum', recommending that measures be taken to 'thin the concentrations of existing Arab population', of Israel and encourage the emigration of these Arab citizens by covert means. See Chomsky, *The Fateful Triangle*, p. 149.
4. See Amnon Kapeliouk, *Israel: la fin des mythes* (Paris: Albin Michel, 1975), p. 32; Nur Masalha, *Expulsion of the Palestinians: The Concept of 'Transfer' in Zionist Political Thought, 1882–1948* (Washington, DC: Institute for Palestine Studies, 1992).
5. See Chaim Bermant in *The Observer* (London), 21 June 1992, p. 13.
6. Gazit was President of the Ben-Gurion University in the Negev between 1981 and 1985, and subsequently Senior Research Associate at the Jaffee Centre for Strategic Studies, Tel Aviv University, and Director General of the Jewish Agency, 1985–88; formerly Chief of Military Intelligence, 1974–79; and head of Military Government and Co-ordinator of Activities in the Administered Territories, 1967–74, when Moshe Dayan was the 'Caesar of the territories'.
7. The lecture was given on 29 December 1981, cited in *Yedi'ot Aharonot*, 15 January 1982, p. 9.
8. *Haaretz*, 2 March 1988, p. 13.
9. The delegation included Moshe Shamir, Dr Haim Yahil, Tzvi Shiloah, Beni Marshak, Aharon Amir, and Moshe Moscovitch.
10. Cited in Shiloah, *Ashmat Yerushalayim*, pp. 53 and 281. Shiloah remarked that Allon's criticism saying that Hebron and Jerusalem should have been occupied without their Arab inhabitants applied also to Nablus, p. 54.
11. Labour's endeavours to settle the 'Allon plan territories' were indeed considerable. Between June 1967 and May 1977, when Labour was ousted by the Likud, the officially approved settlements established were 25 in the Jordan rift valley, seven elsewhere in the West Bank outside Arab East Jerusalem, and 16 in the Gaza-Rafah regions. See W.W. Harris, *Taking Root: Israeli Settlement in the West Bank, the Golan and Gaza–Sinai 1967–1980* (Chichester: Research Studies Press, 1980).

12. Cited from Yeruham Cohen, *Tochnit Allon* [The Allon Plan] (Tel Aviv: Hakibbutz Hameuhad Press, 1974), p. 13.

13. Bernard Avishai, *The Tragedy of Zionism* (New York: Farrar, Straus & Giroux, 1985), p. 340.

14. In a speech at the session of the Knesset on 28 October 1982 Shim'on Peres, the leader of the Labour party, stated:

> the Arab birthrate, between the Jordan and the Sea, numbers up to 76,000 children a year today, part of them Israeli citizens in every way, compared with 70,000 Jewish children. A majority of 6,000 children . . . Mr Menachem Begin claims that the battle is over Eretz Yisrael. I claim that the battle is over the State of Israel . . . the State of Israel will not be a Jewish state unless a clear Jewish majority is ensured it. Against your claim that we are ready to give up territory, we claim that you are ready to give up the certainty that Israel will remain a Jewish state.

Speech transcribed in *Foreign Broadcast Information Service, Middle East and Africa Daily Report* (FBIS), 28 October 1982.

15. On 5 October 1981 Yitzhak Shamir, then Israel's Foreign Minister, gave a speech at the Foreign Policy Association in New York:

> Public opinion in the West is being exposed to loud clamors in support of the Palestinian cause . . . Arab propaganda is calling for a homeland, as they put it, for the homeless Palestinians . . . It is important to understand the 'Jordan is Palestine' aspect and that the conflict is not, and never was, between Israel and a stateless people. Once this is clearly understood, the emotional dimension that evokes problems of conscience in some minds will be removed. If it is perceived in this light, you have on the one hand a Palestinian-Jordanian Arab state, and Israel on the other, then the problem is reduced to a territorial conflict between these two states. The conflict will then have been reduced to its true and manageable proportions.

See 'Excerpts from Israel Foreign Minister's Speech', in *The New York Times*, 6 October 1981, p. 10.

16. Yitzhak Rabin wrote a hard-line article in *Yedi'ot Aharonot* on 28 February 1992 stating that he would keep at least half of the occupied territories under Israel's control, and would step up the

settlement drive in the Golan Heights. However, he added that he would oppose 'politically motivated' settlements in the West Bank. Cited by Haim Baram, in *Middle East International*, No. 420, 6 March 1992, p. 6.

17. Haim Baram, *Middle East International*, 23 June 1995, p. 4.

18. David Hirst, *The Gun and the Olive Branch* (London: Faber and Faber, second edition, 1984), p. 398.

19. Cited in Elfi Pallis, 'The Likud Party: A Primer', in *Journal of Palestine Studies* 21, no. 2 (Winter 1992), pp. 42–43.

20. Ibid., p. 43.

21. See Danny Rubinstein in *Davar*, 26 January 1979, p. 17; Chomsky, *The Fateful Triangle*, pp. 48–49.

22. See Yossi Melman and Dan Raviv, 'Expelling Palestinians', *The Washington Post*, Outlook, 7 February 1988.

23. Cited in Shiloah, *Ashmat Yerushalayim*, p. 188.

24. See for instance Meron Benvenisti, *The West Bank Data Project: A Survey of Israel's Policies* (Washington, DC: American Enterprise Institute, 1984). Already in 1982 Benvenisti had argued that Israel's policies of settlement, land seizure and resource control had laid the basis for a virtual annexation of the West Bank, which may well be irreversible. See article by David Richardson in *The Jerusalem Post*, 10 September 1982.

25. Matityahu Peled, in *Middle East International*, 14 August 1981.

26. *The Jerusalem Post*, 10 September 1982.

27. Bernard Sabella, 'The Demography of Conflict: A Palestinian Predicament', *New Outlook* (April/May 1991), p. 11.

28. *Ma'ariv*, cited in *International Herald Tribune*, 26 January 1981.

29. *'Al-Hamishmar*, 6 June 1980, p. 3.

30. Avishai, *The Tragedy of Zionism*, p. 298. See also Yossi Melman and Dan Raviv, 'A Final Solution to the Palestinian Problem', *Guardian Weekly*, 21 February 1988.

31. *'Al-Hamishmar*, 16 April 1982.

32. See Amos Wollin in *Middle East International*, 23 April 1982, pp. 3–4.

33. See Yossi Melman and Dan Raviv, 'Expelling Palestinians', *The Washington Post*, Outlook, 7 February 1988.

34. Quoted after Ian Lustick, *Arabs in the Jewish State* (Austin: University of Texas Press, 1980), p. 258.

35. David Bernstein (reporting from Jerusalem), 'Forcible removal of Arabs gaining support in Israel', *The Times* (London), 24 August 1988, p. 7.

36. *Ma'ariv*, 23 June 1989.

37. *Ma'ariv*, 18 September 1979, pp. 1 and 15.

38. Michael Dekel was born in 1926 in Belorussia of today; in his youth he joined Bitar, the youth movement of the Zionist Revisionist movement; he was Administration Secretary of the Herut Movement, 1974–75; Head of the Organization Committee of the Herut Movement, 1975–77; Head of the Likud's election headquarters during the 1977 General Election; and later in the 1980s he became Deputy Defence Minister.

39. See Yair Kotler in *Ma'ariv*, 8 October 1982, p. 19.

40. See *The New York Times*, 31 July 1987, cited in Geoffrey Aronson, *Israel, Palestinians and the Intifada* (London: Kegan Paul International, 1990), p. 321. For the same statement, see also Sh. Z. Abramov, *Haaretz*, 23 July 1988.

41. Cited by Yitzhak Ro'ei, *Davar* supplement, 18 September 1987. Both Ariel Sharon and Yitzhak Shamir held a similar attitude for more than a decade to the effect that Jordan was the 'homeland' of the Palestinians. Shamir, for instance, stated in 1981, while serving as Foreign Minister: 'The Palestinian nation has a homeland and a state where it can find its national, sovereign expression. And if that country is called Jordan today, it doesn't change the fact. And we will repeat it again and again until the world understands.' Cited in Aronson, *Israel, Palestinians and the Intifada*, p. 238; and *Ma'ariv*, 9 August 1981. Jordan is called Eastern Eretz-Yisrael in Zionist Revisionism (the forerunner of the Likud) which emphasized the Jewish claims to both banks of the Jordan River. 'This side is ours, that one will be, too' goes the famous slogan of Zeev Jabotinsky.

42. See Zeev Schiff and Ehud Ya'ari, *Intifada: The Palestinian Uprising – Israel's Third Front* (New York: Simon and Schuster, 1989), p. 95; Benny Morris, *Jerusalem Post International*, 3 October 1987; Arie Haskel (reporting from Jerusalem), *The Observer* (London), 12 June 1988, p. 22; David Bernstein (reporting from Jerusalem), 'Forcible removal of Arabs gaining support in Israel', *The Times* (London), 24 August 1988, p. 7.

43. Yuval Neeman, *Mediniyut Hareeyah Hamefukahat* [The Policy of Sober Vision] (Ramat Gan: Revivim, 1984), pp. 168–69. In fact, shortly after the June 1967 war, Neeman suggested in an article in the mass-circulation daily *Ma'ariv* on 18 June 1967, p. 9, that Israel could 'now' solve the problem of Arab refugees by 'organizing their emigration'. In August 1981, the Israeli journalist Amnon Kapeliouk wrote that

215

Neeman considered the failure of the Israeli army to exploit the 1973 war for 'emptying the Gaza Strip of all its Palestinian inhabitants, once and for all' constituted 'great laxity' in missing a golden opportunity. Amnon Kapeliouk, *Le Monde Diplomatique*, August 1981.

44. *The Jerusalem Post*, 19 November 1989.

45. See Joshua Brilliant, *The Jerusalem Post*, 23 February 1988.

46. See *Yedi'ot Aharonot*, 3 February 1991.

47. See *Yedi'ot Aharonot*, 22 April 1990 and 17 June 1990. *Yedi'ot Aharonot* also published on 15 February 1991 another article in support of transfer written by Eliahu 'Amikam, a well-known journalist, former member of Lehi, and supporter of Greater Israel.

48. See *Moledet*, No. 30, April 1991, pp. 13–14. In 1983 Likud MK Meir Cohen stated that 200,000 to 300,000 Arabs should have been expelled from the West Bank in 1967. *The Jerusalem Post*, 20 March 1983, p. 3.

49. Moshe Dotan, 'Rov 'Ivri Ketzad?' [A Hebrew Majority, How?] *Haumah* no. 2 (November 1967), pp. 242–49. Vladimir Jabotinsky (1880–1940) was the founder of Revisionist Zionism, the forerunner of present-day Likud, whom Prime Minister Menahem Begin considered his spiritual leader.

50. Ibid., p. 244.

51. Ibid., p. 243.

52. Ibid., pp. 245–46.

53. Ibid., pp. 246–47.

54. Ibid., pp. 246, 248.

55. Ibid., pp. 242, 248, 249.

56. Moshe Dotan, 'Ye'udenu Haleumi Bazaman Hahadash' [Our National Mission in the Contemporary Time], *Haumah* no. 1 (May 1981), p. 39.

57. See Avraham Heller, 'Hashed Hademografi' [The Demographic Demon], *Haumah* no. 1 (January 1970), pp. 99–100; and *idem* in *Haumah* nos. 3–4 (September 1976), p. 346. The large number of contributors of articles calling for Arab transfer that appeared in *Haumah* include: Professor Moshe Ater (former economic editor of *The Jerusalem Post*) in no. 76 (Autumn 1984), pp. 289–97; Professor Paul Eidelberg (of Bar-Ilan University), 'Neutralization of the Arab Time-Bomb: The Demographic Problem', no. 90 (Spring 1988), pp. 238–48; Dr Zeev Von Weizel in no. 3 (April 1973), pp. 294–95; Dr Dov Yosefi, 'A Humane Solution to the Demographic Problem', no. 88 (Autumn

1987), pp. 20–26; *idem* in no. 90 (Spring 1988), pp. 362–63; Kalman Katznelson (an intellectual and old timer of the Revisionist and Herut parties) in no. 90 (Spring 1988), pp. 275–76; Dr Yisrael Eldad, 'The Transfer as a Zionist Solution', no. 88 (Autumn 1987), pp. 11–13; Dr Moshe Yegar, 'Zionism, the State of Israel and the Arab Question', no. 2 (May 1979), pp. 175–85; and Dr Mordechai Nisan (a senior lecturer at the Hebrew University school for overseas students) in no. 107 (Spring 1992), p. 272.

58. 'Oded Yinon, 'A Strategy for Israel in the 1980s' [Hebrew], *Kivunim* (Jerusalem), No. 14, February 1982, pp. 53–58.

59. Yehoshafat Harkabi, *Hakhra'ot Goraliyot* [Fateful Decisions], (Tel Aviv: 'Am 'Oved, 1986), pp. 74–75.

60. Cited in Robert I. Friedman, *Zealots for Zion*, p. xxiii.

61. See Ian Black (reporting from Jerusalem), *The Guardian*, 2 February 1991.

62. Quoted in David Schnall, *Beyond the Green Line* (New York: Praeger & Co., 1984), p. 19.

63. Cited in Danny Rubinstein, *Mi La-H' Elai: Gush Emunim* [On the Lord's Side: Gush Emunim] (Tel Aviv: Hakibbutz Hameuhad Publishing House, 1982), p. 91.

64. David Shaham, *Yedi'ot Aharonot* supplement, 13 April 1979.

65. See Kook's article in *Hatzofeh*, 23 June 1967. The article was also printed in a collection entitled *Everything*, edited by A. Ben-'Ami.

66. Quoted in Rabbi Pichnik (ed.), *Shanah Beshanah, 5728* (Hebrew) [Year by Year] (Jerusalem: Hekhal Shlomo Publication, 1968), pp. 108–109.

67. Quoted in *'Al-Hamishmar*, 8 February 1980.

68. Shlomo Aviner, 'Yerushat Haaretz Vehabe'ayah Hamusarit' [The Inheritance of the Land and the Moral Problem], *Artzi* [My Country] (Jerusalem, 1983), p. 10.

69. Tzvi Yehuda Kook, 'Bein 'Am Veartzo' [Between People and Its Land], *Artzi*, p. 10.

70. See also Dr Yisrael Eldad, 'The Transfer as a Zionist Solution', *Haumah* no. 88 (Autumn 1987), pp. 11–13.

71. Cited in *Journal of Palestine Studies* 10, no. 1 (Autumn 1980), p. 150; Rubinstein, *On the Lord's Side: Gush Emunim*, p. 91. The settlers' statements were also published in the Gush Emunim magazine *Nekudah*. See Yehuda Litani in *Haaretz*, 15 May 1984, p. 15. Another settler of 'Ofra, echoing the widely publicized aphorism of the late Prime Minister Golda Meir, said in June 1980: 'after all there are no

Palestinian people. We invented them, but they don't exist.' See *The Jerusalem Post* International edition, 8–14 June 1980.

72. Amnon Kapeliouk in *Le Monde Diplomatique*, June 1980; *Le Monde*, 19 June 1980.

73. Rubinstein, *On the Lord's Side: Gush Emunim*, pp. 157–59.

74. See, for instance, Dedi Zucker, *Report on Human Rights in the Occupied Territories, 1979–83*, International Centre for Peace in the Middle East (Tel Aviv, 1983), pp. 51–52.

75. Quoted in Elfi Pallis in *Middle East International*, 24 April 1981, p. 12.

76. Benvenisti, *The West Bank Handbook*, p. 135.

77. Ibid.

78. See Israel Shahak, 'Israeli apartheid and the intifada', *Race & Class* 30, no. 1 (1988), p. 3.

79. See Pinchas Inbari, 'Underground: Political background and psychological atmosphere', *New Outlook*, June–July 1984, pp. 10–11.

80. Yisrael Ariel, 'Dvarim Kehavayatam' [Things As They Are], *Tzippiyah* [Hebrew], (Jerusalem, 1980).

81. Quoted in Amnon Rubinstein, *Mehertzel 'Ad Gush Emunim Uvehazarah* [From Herzl to Gush Emunim and Back Again] (Tel Aviv: Schocken Press, 1980), p. 123. Rubinstein's reference is *Haaretz*, 9 May 1976.

82. Shalom Dov Wolpo (ed.), *Da'at Torah Be'inyanei Hamatzav Beeretz Hakodesh* [The Opinion of the Torah Regarding the Situation in the Holy Land] (Kiryat Gat, 1979), p. 146, n. 4.

83. Ibid. p. 145.

84. 'Amos Ben-Vered in *Haaretz*, 23 October 1979, p. 8.

85. *Ma'ariv*, 14 June 1985.

86. *Ma'ariv*, 5 July 1985, p. 19.

87. Exodus 17:16; Deuteronomy 25:17–19.

88. *Bat Kol*, 26 February 1980. In fact the association of the Palestinians with the ancient Amalekites was made in a book written in 1974 by Rabbi Moshe Ben-Tzion Ishbezari, the Rabbi of Ramat Gan. See *Yedi'ot Aharonot*, 20 December 1974.

89. *Bat Kol*, 26 February 1980; (1 Samuel, 15:3).

90. Ibid.

91. Rubinstein, *Mehertzel 'Ad Gush Emunim*, p. 125.

92. Ibid., p. 179.

93. See for instance *Torah Ve'avodah* [Torah and Work], no. 6 (Jerusalem, 1984).

94. Uriel Tal in *Haaretz*, 26 September 1984, p. 27; Hanna Kim, 'To Annihilate Amalek', *'Al-Hamishmar*, 12 March 1984; Yoram Peri, 'Expulsion is not the Final Stage', *Davar*, 3 August 1984; Yehoshu'a Rash, 'Uriel Tal's Legacy', *Gesher*, Summer 1986, no. 114, p. 77.

95. Ariel, 'Dvarim Kehavayatam'.

96. Rubinstein, *Mehertzel*, p. 124.

97. Ibid.

98. *Haaretz*, 3 February 1983.

Conclusion

Comprehending the persistence with which official mainstream Zionism, particularly the Labour/Mapai establishment, pursued transfer schemes during the Mandatory period, after the establishment of the state into the 1950s, and in the aftermath of the 1967 conquests is extremely important for understanding and preventing similar transfer plans in the future. At the same time, however, it must be recognized how both in the 1950s and after the June 1967 War the Labour leaders displayed a combination of secrecy, pragmatism and circumspection in the pursuit of transfer schemes, taking into account the difficulty of attempting to carry out an outright mass expulsion and the reactions of Western public opinion as well as Palestinian resistance and criticism from the liberal sector in Israel.

The Palestinians have good reason to fear the threat of mass expulsions. Developments in the 1980s showed that a large section of the Likud establishment and about half of Israeli Jews openly supported the idea of 'transferring' the Palestinians from the occupied territories. Certainly most political groups on the extreme right, including Tehiya, Moledet, Tzomet, the National Religious Party, Gush Emunim and the Whole Land of Israel Movement, would like to expel not just the inhabitants of the West Bank and Gaza, but also the Arab citizens of Israel. One of the justifications for this open, strident advocacy of 'transfer' is the 'logical' conclusion that annexation of the West Bank and Gaza with their Arab population would be detrimental if not disastrous to the whole concept of a Zionist/Jewish state; hence the conclusion that the Arabs should be made, one way or another, to depart. This open advocacy of Arab removal is a clear departure from the past in one sense; traditionally the Labour establishment used to debate, advocate and attempt to promote transfer schemes in closely guarded secrecy.

Moreover, there is good reason to fear that if the Palestinian question remains unresolved, the proportion of Israeli Jews supporting expulsion will rise and more Israeli politicians will come out openly in favour of that solution. The extension of the Zionist structure, through settlement and annexation, over the occupied territories and the drive to 'redeem' the land can only reinforce calls to drive out the Arab inhabitants. The Likud's idea of autonomy, which leaves Israel free to impose its sovereignty over the occupied territories, was unacceptable to the Palestinians prior to 1992. Furthermore, citizenship on any substantial scale is unlikely to be offered in the future by any Israeli government, whether Labour or Likud, and the 'precedent' of the Israeli Arabs after 1949 shows that only a small Arab minority can be tolerated. The secret transfer schemes of the 1950s show that the Labour governments of Ben-Gurion and Sharett were trying secretly to reduce still further the Arab minority in Israel, although forcible means for reaching that objective were avoided.

Throughout the 1980s and until Israel's general election of June 1992, many commentators inside and outside Israel were frequently attempting to answer two major questions: Under what circumstances could mass expulsion take place? What form could it take? Although the answers given to these questions were speculative, commentators pointed to a number of possibilities based on the available evidence. Firstly, the 'transfer', as envisaged by its Israeli advocates, could take a number of forms. It could accompany a war between Israel and an Arab country (or countries), Syria for instance, in which the Palestinians would be seen as taking an active part. Such a possibility could be, in reality, an unprovoked act, embodying a deliberate Israeli government action. Reserve General Aharon Yariv, a former chief of army military intelligence, remarked in 1980 that there was a widely held opinion in favour of exploiting a future war to expel 700,000–800,000 Palestinians. He warned that such a plan already existed and the means for its implementation had been prepared.[1] Secondly, in a non-war situation, a policy of mass expulsion could be attempted 'in retaliation' for escalation of Palestinian 'terrorism' and violent resistance to Israel's policies. If the current peace talks stall, the Palestinians, faced with a settler-colonial regime, which is pressing for 'a land without people', could be left with no option but to resort to violence. On the other hand, the Israeli leaders might be tempted to carry out a partial depopulation by a perception – not necessarily realistic – that the international community was preoccupied with other major crises and events, and that the UN Security Council member states were too distracted and the Arab world too weak and divided to react. Thirdly, the Israeli government could continue with its policy of creating ghetto conditions of daily life for Palestinians – including the creation of economic hardship through the curtailment of employment opportunities in Israel and interfering with the development of an independent Palestinian economy in the West Bank and Gaza. The aim of such policies would be to force the Palestinians to migrate.

Basically, there existed two major trends within the Shamir coalition that held power until June 1992. One trend, which was made up of the extreme Right parties (Moledet, Tzomet, Tehiya and a section of the National Religious Party) and a section of the Likud, was little influenced by pragmatic considerations and believed that Israel was strong enough to do whatever it wanted, including transfer. The second, relatively pragmatic trend, while accepting that settlement and annexationist policies should continue and even be intensified, believed that strategic co-operation or at least a working relationship with the U.S. government – which would oppose mass transfer – must be maintained as a vital Israeli interest. Israel's dependence on the United States for economic and military assistance,[2] particularly while seeking to accommodate the influx of Russian Jews, the pragmatists argued, made the scenario of outright mass expulsion impracticable. The most likely scenario which would have been pursued by the Likud in the short run, therefore, would have been to create unbearable ghetto conditions and economic distress throughout the West Bank and Gaza in the hope ultimately of forcing many of the inhabitants to leave. However the election of a Labour government in the June 1992 election together with the exclusion of the extreme right from power and the acceleration of the peace process made the implementation of mass expulsion a much less likely scenario.

Mass 'transfer' would be difficult to achieve in time of peace and it would be impossible to achieve without much bloodshed. Any attempt to implement mass deportation would encounter physical resistance on the part of the Palestinians, and would therefore require the use of massive and continuous force by the Israeli army. This is in part because the Palestinians are aware of the history of their own two exoduses of 1948 and 1967, and of the fact that what would await them now in exile would be no more favourable. Palestinian resistance certainly would cause the prolongation of an evacuation plan and the mobilization of both liberal opinion in Israel and pressure from the international community to thwart the process of physical removal of the inhabitants. It is very likely, therefore, that if an evacuation plan ever were to be attempted by the army, it would fail to achieve the objective of mass removal.

Moreover, in Israel there is a large section of society that would not remain silent in the face of possible transfer. In the last decade opposition to transfer has been voiced by a large number of liberal and left-wing journalists, academics, writers and politicians, using moral and practical arguments to denounce this solution. Vocal opponents of transfer usually oppose the annexation of the West Bank and Gaza and warn that in a generation Greater Israel may have an Arab majority; that Israel cannot retain the West Bank and Gaza and have peace with the Palestinians and the Arab world; that the Palestinians under Israeli occupation were bound sooner or later to revolt. Amnon Kapeliouk writing for the Mapam-controlled *'Al-Hamishmar* daily on 6 June 1980, denounced this 'horrific' 'final solution' being entertained by people in high official posts: 'The trouble with those who make these satanic plans is that they think that Israel has absolute freedom to do whatever it wishes . . . They do not know that the Palestinians will do all they can in order not to abandon their land, and that from their point of view the most efficient resistance is to stick to their homeland, to the land, no matter how bad the harassment.' Another prominent journalist, Haggai Eshed, writing in the Histadrut daily *Davar* on 17 July 1987, also condemned the idea of 'a final solution': 'to expel the inhabitants of the territories – and perhaps part of the inhabitants of the Galilee [Israeli Arabs] as a "bonus" – as dangerous dreams . . . the expulsion of the Palestinians, totally or partially, would not bring an end to anything. On the contrary. It would be an opening for a war of revenge by the entire Arab and Islamic world against the State of Israel for generations to come.' A similar argument was advanced by the journalist Bo'az 'Evron: if Israel annexes the occupied territories and expels most of their Arab inhabitants a 'more aggressive belt of refugee camps would be created around its borders' and Arab determination 'to take revenge on this foreign body stuck at the heart of the Arab world' would be renewed vigorously. The result would be a permanent war with disastrous consequences for Israel.[3] Another journalist, Hanokh Bartov, writing in *Ma'ariv* on 8 June 1990, denounced the formation of a Likud coalition based on the support of the Transfer Party of Rehava'am Zeevi. Dr Binyamin Neuberger, a political science lecturer at Tel Aviv University, wrote in 1988: 'A democratic state cannot exterminate or expel groups which are not convenient for its establishment. An Israel that would carry out the platform of the Kach movement would stop being a democratic state, and it does not matter if a minority or majority supports the policy of expulsion . . . An Israel that would expel its Arab inhabitants would be a totalitarian–fascist state, even if the government enjoyed the support of a majority which tramples on human rights.'[4]

Several MKs have voiced opposition to transfer. The dovish Labour MK Avraham Burg (currently Chairman of the Jewish Agency), in an interview on Israeli television on 13 November 1988, described the idea of 'transferring' the Palestinians to Arab countries as being like the expulsion of the Jews from Spain by the Spanish inquisitors in the fifteenth century. Former Labour Party MK Aryeh Lova Eliav wrote in an article in *Yedi'ot Aharonot* on 16 November 1988: 'A Jew is someone who is shocked by the concept of transfer regarding the Arabs and relates to it as [to something] defiled.' The leader of the Citizens' Rights Movement, Shulamit Aloni,[5] wrote during the Gulf crisis, which was triggered by the Iraqi invasion of Kuwait, that only negotiations with the PLO would prevent the 'killing, transfer, destruction and loss of humanity' advocated by Israeli pro-transfer parties and groups.[6] Aloni in particular has a record of outspoken support for Palestinian aspirations to statehood, which has earned her death threats from the Israeli extreme right and a constant bodyguard. Though undeniably Zionist, she is regarded by many Palestinians (including many figures in the Palestinian National Authority) as a strategic ally. Likud MK Binyamin-Zeev (Beni) Begin, although dismissing the existence of the Palestinian people,[7] was also reported to have criticized the idea of 'expelling by force 300 thousand' Arab families on moral and practical grounds.[8] Israeli journalist Susan Hattis Rolef warned in *The Jerusalem Post* of 17 August 1992 that those Israelis who were playing around with the 'voluntary' transfer idea as a 'humane solution' to the Arab–Israeli conflict should take a look at what was going on in Bosnia, which has been subjected to ethnic cleansing: 'Every day we see on our TV sets the victims of the "voluntary" transfer and we ask "why isn't the world doing anything?"' According to Rolef, contemporary 'ethnic cleansing' in the former Yugoslavia was similar to what had taken place in Lydda and Ramle in 1948; the only difference was that in 1948 there were no television crews around to shoot the events. The fact that the world was doing very little to stop ethnic cleansing by Serbs in Bosnia did not alter the moral repugnance of their action, Rolef wrote. However, unlike Beni Begin – who is currently Minister of Science and Technology in the cabinet of Binyamin Netanyahu and who adheres to the Likud's hard-line policy of absorbing the occupied territories – the above-mentioned liberal minority is against the annexation of the West Bank and Gaza and if 'transfer' were attempted perhaps would try to stop it. The left of centre politicians of Meretz – led by Shulamit Aloni[9] – and several Labour figures, including Abba Eban, 'Ezer Weizmann, and Avraham Burg might call upon the army, which is still diverse and does not represent a single political grouping, to refuse to obey mass expulsion orders.

One real danger for the Palestinians of the occupied territories is that those forces who wish to expel them comprise an armed element of Israeli society: the settlers of Gush Emunim and their sympathizers in the army, backed by influential Likud and other right-wing leaders. It should also be pointed out that over half a million, or one in seven Israeli Jews, have firearms in their possession. Furthermore, the existence of elements within the army and the Gush Emunim movement that might commit atrocities in order to intimidate people into flight cannot be ruled out. Many questions, however, remain open. For instance, would the army be deeply divided and paralysed in the face of such developments or would it conclude that the only military option was expulsion? In such an event, however, the attempt to isolate the pro-transfer forces from the more moderate sector in the army and in Israeli society would be very important and this, combined with Palestinian physical resistance and pressure from the international community, might thwart any plan to depopulate the occupied territories that might be attempted in the future.

There is no doubt that the Oslo agreements signed between Israel and the PLO in September 1993, which paved the way for other subsequent agreements reached between the two sides since then, have made the implementation of mass expulsion a much less likely scenario. At the same time, however, other ominous developments may still take place. The Labour government that held power until May 1996 was still against the establishment of an independent Palestinian state in the West Bank and Gaza; against Israel's total withdrawal to the pre-1967 borders; against the Palestinian 'right of return'; for the unilateral annexation of East Jerusalem; and for the preservation of most Jewish settlements in the occupied territories. Indeed after the Oslo agreements were signed, Prime Minister Rabin did his utmost to preserve and even strengthen all Jewish settlements in the West Bank. In 1995, the Rabin government allocated 330 million dollars for the completion of bypass roads connecting Jewish settlements to each other and to Israel proper. Moreover, in September 1994 Rabin gave the go-ahead for the construction of about 700 new homes at Giva'at Tal, part of Alfei Menashe settlement, situated three kilometres inside the West Bank.[10] In the spring of 1995 the same government approved the construction of eight thousand new housing units in the town (settlement) of Ma'ale Adumim, located at the centre of the West Bank and half way between Jerusalem and Jericho. A year later, in June 1996, the 4,000 persons of the Jahaleen tribe lost their legal battle in the Israeli High Court to keep land on which they had pitched their tents for decades. They were forced by the Labour government and the Israeli court to make way for 20,000 Jewish settlers who wanted to expand their Ma'ale Adumim settlement by confiscating Arab property.[11] Moreover, the Jerusalem weekly *Kol Ha'ir* revealed on 13 October 1995 that premier Rabin had instructed the Ministry of Housing to expropriate Arab land in order to expand the city limits of Jerusalem to the east, to unite it with Ma'ale Adumim.[12] According to Rabin's plans, various fragments of the West Bank and most of Gaza, which are already administered by the Palestinian National Authority, should eventually be linked to Jordan, forming a Jordan-Palestine state. This was basically the Labour scenario: to partition the West Bank between Israel and Jordan-Palestine, a scenario derived from the traditional Labour formula (or axiom): 'maximum land and minimum Arabs'.

One significant point should be made: when the Labour government recognized the PLO at Oslo, it did so without recognizing its goals of liberating the occupied territories, of bringing an end to the occupation and of decolonizing the West Bank and Gaza. For Labour, the Oslo agreements do not preclude the annexation of one-third of the West Bank and greater Jerusalem. Within this one-third of the West Bank some 300,000 Palestinians reside. Israeli citizenship on any substantial scale is unlikely to be offered in the future by any Labour government to these Palestinians, who, together with the Palestinians of East Jerusalem, face an uncertain future.

Perhaps the long-term hope that somehow the Palestinian refugees in the West Bank and Gaza will move away (discussed in previous chapters) was one factor in the refusal of the Labour government to contemplate an independent Palestinian state in the West Bank and Gaza. A mini state created in 65 per cent of the West Bank and Gaza could not absorb the Palestinian refugees of the occupied territories along with refugees from Lebanon and Jordan and elsewhere. A Jordan-Palestine might absorb the Palestinians of the West Bank and Gaza, along with the refugees from elsewhere, under the guise of settlement in their former homeland, leaving 35 per cent of the West Bank and greater Jerusalem and many Jewish settlements throughout the West Bank under Israeli control.

Moreover, throughout the post-Oslo years, from 1993 to 1996, under the Labour government Palestinian life has got progressively worse. GNP per capita fell from $500 in 1992 to $390 in 1995.[13] There were more Jewish settlers moving into the West Bank, more land seizures to build bypass roads for Jewish settlements, a Palestinian National Authority responding to Israeli demands with more human rights violations, and a brutally effective closure of the occupied territories since February 1996 that has brought 40 to 70 per cent unemployment and left socio-economic devastation in its wake.[14]

But still, it would be wrong to assume that because Palestinian conditions have already become extremely bad, they cannot get any worse. Under the settlement-backing, land-grabbing, new right Likud government of Binyamin Netanyahu, which came to power in June 1996, things will almost certainly get much worse. Confidential Israeli documents leaked to *The Observer* in June 1996 showed that Netanyahu's government has drawn up plans to 'devour Arab east Jerusalem and reduce its Arab community to an insignificant minority'. The godfather of the master plan is Jerusalem's Likud deputy mayor, Shmuel Meir, who believes the Palestinians have no rights in the holy city. His ideas include the demolition of at least 2,000 Arab homes which he claims have been built without planning permission, and the construction of some 7,000 new homes exclusively for Jews in Arab East Jerusalem – which has already 160,000 Jewish settlers in 10 major settlements ringing the Arab sector. 'Every time he [Yassir 'Arafat] says Jerusalem is his, we will respond by building a thousand homes for Jews,' explained one of Netanyahu's advisers.[15]

The Netanyahu government basically adheres to the same hard-line policy – described above – of the Shamir cabinet that held power until June 1992. Prime Minister Netanyahu himself served as deputy Foreign Minister in the Shamir government and most of the current ministers have served in previous Likud administrations. Since his assumption of power Netanyahu has stated that he will continue the peace process. But promises made before and after his election victory, anchored in the political tradition of right-wing Revisionist Zionism and the ideology of Greater Israel, make it clear that Netanyahu will do so only on his own tough terms.

Netanyahu's political positions are more ideological than pragmatic: he says no to a Palestinian state in the West Bank and Gaza; no to withdrawal from the Golan Heights; yes to the expansion of Jewish settlements in the occupied territories: 'we plan to strengthen and cultivate the settlements in Judea and Samaria'. His settlement plans point to the likelihood of a renewal of confrontation and *intifada* in the occupied territories. And if a new *intifada* were to erupt, it would be a far bloodier affair than its previous incarnation of the late 1980s.

Netanyahu's settlement and 'Judaization' policies in and around occupied East Jerusalem also point to the extreme likelihood of a renewal of confrontation and a bloodier *intifada*. In 1948 West Jerusalem was completely 'Judaized' after the Israeli army forced Palestinian civilians to evacuate several large Arab neighbourhoods. Since June 1967 more than 160,000 Jews have been settled in East (Arab) Jerusalem, often on land confiscated from local Arab residents. The recent intensification of these de-Arabization policies is much in evidence. On 10 December 1996 Israeli city planners in Jerusalem approved 132 Jewish housing units being built on Arab land in the centre of the Ras al-'Amud neighbourhood in Arab Jerusalem. This new housing programme, designed exclusively for Jewish settlers, will be partly financed by a Miami-based American Jewish millionaire, Dr Irving Moskowitz, who is also known as a supporter of Arab transfer. (Moskowitz wrote in February 1990: 'the idea of population exchange is . . . the only realistic way for bringing an end to bloodshed [between Arabs and Jews] . . . [and] is the real hope for a durable solution of the Arab-Israeli conflict'.[16]) Israeli Interior Minister Eliyahu Suissa, who announced the government decision to go ahead with the settlement scheme in Ras al-'Amud, justified the decision as part of the government policy to settle Jews in every part of East Jerusalem. 'This is discrimination,' said Palestinian headmistress Nuhu al-Ghul, of Ras al-'Amud. 'On the one hand, they prevent the Arabs from building homes, but on the other they allow Jews to build freely in Arab Jerusalem.'[17] A prominent Palestinian local leader, Faysal al-Husayni, sharply criticising the scheme, said it was part of Israel's unrelenting efforts to Judaize Arab Jerusalem.[18]

Also more recently Israel has been seeking new ways to drive out Jerusalem's 155,000 Palestinian residents: hundreds of families have recently lost the right to remain in the city because, Israel claims, they had chosen to live outside the city's boundaries. Moreover, Palestinian women from Jerusalem married to foreign nationals have been told their residence rights in Jerusalem have been cancelled.[19] Israel has continued to tighten its grip on the Arab sector of Jerusalem, strictly forbidding entry to the residents of the West Bank and Gaza. Israeli practices of denying Palestinians building permits and levying high municipality taxes are also driving thousands of Palestinians out of the city in search of a more affordable place to live. The intensification of Israeli de-Arabization policies in and around East Jerusalem would almost certainly lead to the unleasing of a wave of violence reminiscent of the bloody clashes which followed the opening of the so-called archaeological tunnel near the al-Aqsa Mosque (the third holiest shrine for Islam) in the old city of Jerusalem in September 1996. The opening of the tunnel, which was aimed at tightening Israeli control over the centre of the holy city, particularly around the area of the Muslim shrines, brought Israel to the brink of open war with the Palestinian policemen stationed in West Bank cities and Gaza. Seventy Palestinians and 14 Israeli soldiers were killed in clashes amid scenes reminiscent of the height of the *intifada*, with Israeli troops shooting at Palestinian stone-throwers. As in the first *intifada*, extensive media coverage has brought this mini-*intifada* of September 1996, with the horrors endured by hundreds of unarmed Palestinian civilians killed and injured by the occupation army, into every home.

However, a renewal of the *intifada* will not be sufficient to bring an end to these massive human rights violations by Israel. In the opinion of this author, the international community has an obligation and duty, under international law, to enforce the humanitarian provisions of the Fourth Geneva Convention, with the aim of protecting peoples (such as the Palestinians) under occupation by a foreign power. The international community should and could exert far more pressure on Israel, including consideration of economic sanctions, to protect the Palestinian civilians and force Israel to abandon its plans to de-Arabize East Jerusalem.

Notes to Conclusion

1. Cited in *Haaretz*, 2 May 1980.
2. U.S. economic aid to Israel is $4 billion per year. According to one estimate, American aid to Israel since 1948 has totalled $77 billion. See Avi Shlaim in *The Guardian*, 22 June 1992, p. 27.
3. Bo'az 'Evron, *Hahishbon Haleumi* [A National Reckoning] (Tel Aviv: Dvir, 1988), p. 402. A similar argument was put forward by Dr Meir Pa'il, a former Knesset member, in early 1992:

> Israel will exploit the confusion sowed by [a future] war to expel hundreds of thousands of Palestinians from the areas under its control. Already today, certain nationalist circles in Israel and among the Jewish people, most of them partners and allies of the present ruling [Likud] government coalition, are doing everything in their power to undermine the peace talks and promote this . . . eventuality. This is part of a long-range plan to 'purify' the Land of Israel west of the Jordan River of the Palestinian presence by means of several waves of transfer to be carried out in the course of several future rounds of warfare.
>
> The chances that this perverse, terrifying, and immoral scenario will succeed are quite small. Nevertheless, assuming that this evil and naive dream were put into effect during repeated rounds of warfare over the span of a generation or two, what would be the ensuing fate of the State of Israel? Israel would be doomed to eternal war with the entire Arab world under conditions of severe international isolation and ostracism, an ostracism that could reach such extremes that the Zionist enterprise would be unable to maintain itself socio-economically over the long term.

See *New Outlook*, January/February 1992, p. 36.
4. See Adam Doron (ed.), *Medinat Yisrael Veeretz Yisrael* [The State of Israel and the Land of Israel] (Beit Berl, 1988), p. 331. Professor Natan Rotenstreich of the Hebrew University criticized the idea of 'population exchange' on practical grounds. See *Davar*, 13 July 1987. See also Ihud Ben-Eli'ezer in *1967–1987: Kovshim 'Atzmam Lada'at*, p. 128.
5. Aloni was until recently the leader of the Meretz Party, a dovish Zionist faction in the Knesset whose position has been more

accommodating to the Palestinians than the ruling Labour Party. Aloni was also Minister of Culture and Communications in the Labour-Meretz government which lasted until May 1996.

6. See *Yedi'ot Aharonot*, 27 August 1990.

7. See Zeev B. Begin, 'The Likud Vision for Israel at Peace', *Foreign Affairs* (Fall 1991), pp. 21–35.

8. Cited in *Moledet*, no. 27, January 1990, p. 30.

9. Meretz is a combined force of three parties (Mapam, Shinui and the Citizen Rights Movement) to the left of the Labour Party that had 12 seats between them in the 13th Knesset, from June 1992 to May 1996. Meretz would halt further Jewish settlement, and, unlike the Labour Party, is not adverse to a Palestinian State in the occupied territories.

10. See *MEED* (London), 7 October 1994, p. 16.

11. See Shyam Bhatia in *The Observer*, 9 June 1996, p. 19.

12. See also Haim Baram in *Middle East International*, 23 June 1995, p. 4. See also Sarah Helm, 'West Bank to be snared in a net of highways', *The Independent*, 12 December 1994.

13. Cited in Toby Ash, 'Struggling to survive inside the fence', *The Guardian*, 3 July 1996, p. 16.

14. See Phyllis Bennis in *Third World Emergence*, No. 71 (July 1996), p. 35; Nur Masalha, 'A different peace', *Index on Censorship*, No. 3 (May–June 1996), pp. 18–21; 'Special Report: The Palestinians', *The Guardian*, 3 July 1996, p. 16.

15. Quoted in Shyam Bhatia, 'Israel to squeeze Arabs from holy city', *The Observer*, 9 June 1996, p. 19.

16. See Irving Moskowitz, in *Moledet*, no. 16, February 1990, p. 24.

17. Quoted by Shyam Bhatia, in *The Guardian*, 11 December 1996.

18. Ibid.

19. Ibid.

Select Bibliography

Archival Sources

Central Zionist Archives (CZA), Jerusalem, protocols of the meetings of the
    Jewish Agency Executive, manuscript notebooks of Yosef Weitz diary
Israel State Archives (ISA), Foreign Ministry files, Jerusalem
Institute for Settlement Studies, Rehovot, Yosef Weitz's papers

Published Primary Sources

Ariel, Yisrael, 'Dvarim Kehavayatam' [Things As They Are], *Tzippiyah*
    (Jerusalem, 1980)
Ben-'Ami, Aharon (ed.), *Hakol* [Everything] (Tel Aviv: Madaf Publishing
    House, 1967)
– (ed.), *Sefer Eretz-Yisrael Hashlemah* [The Book of the Whole Land of
    Israel] (Tel Aviv: Friedman Press, 1977)
Ben-Gurion, David, *Yoman Hamilhamah 1948–1949* [War Diary], 3 vols.,
    Gershon Rivlin and Elhanan Orren (eds.) (Tel Aviv: Ministry of
    Defence Press, 1980)
Danin, 'Ezra, *Tzioni Bekhol Tnai* [Zionist in All Conditions], Vol. 1
    (Jerusalem: Kiddum, 1987)
Devrei Haknesset [Knesset Debates] (Jerusalem, May 1976)
Kahane, Meir, *They Must Go* (New York: Grosset & Dunlap, 1981)
– *Lesikim Be'enekhem* [They Shall be Strings in Your
    Eyes] (Jerusalem: Hamakhon Lara'ayon Hayehudi, 1980/81)
Eidelberg, Paul, 'Netrul Ptzatzat Hazman Ha'arvit: Habe'ayah
    Hademografit' [Neutralization of the Arab Time-bomb: The
    Demographic Problem], *Haumah*, No. 90, Spring 1988
Shem-Ur, Ora, *Yisrael: Medinah 'Al Tnai* [Israel: A Conditional State]
    (Tel Aviv: Nogah Press, 1978).
– *Yisrael Rabati* [Greater Israel] (Tel Aviv: Nogah Press, 1985)
– *Te'ud Politi: Hamefarkim* [The Liquidators: A Political Documentation]
    (Tel Aviv: Nogah Press, 1989)
Shiloah, Tzvi, *Eretz Gdolah Le'am Gadol* [A Great Land for a Great People]
    (Tel Aviv: Otpaz, 1970)

– *Ashmat Yerushalayim* [The Guilt of Jerusalem] (Tel Aviv: Karni Press, 1989)

Sharett, Moshe, *Yoman Medini* [Political Diary], Vols. 1–5 (Tel Aviv, 1968–74)

– *Yoman Ishi* [Personal Diary], Vol. 7 (Tel Aviv: Sifriyat Ma'ariv, 1978)

Weitz, Yosef, *Yomani Veigrotai Lebanim* [My Diary and Letters to the Children], Vols. 3–6 (Tel Aviv: Massada, 1965)

– (ed.), *Yosef Nahmani: Ish Hagalil* [Yosef Nahmani: Man of the Galilee] (Ramat Gan: Massada, 1969)

Wolpo, Shlomo Dov (ed.), *Da'at Torah Be'inyanei Hamatzav Beeretz Hakodesh* [The Opinion of the Torah Regarding the Situation in the Holy Land] (Kiryat Gat, 1979)

Secondary Sources

Abu Lughod, Ibrahim (ed.), *The Transformation of Palestine* (Evanston: Northwestern University Press, 1971)

Aronson, Geoffrey, *Israel, Palestinians and the Intifada* (London: Kegan Paul International, 1990)

Avishai, Bernard, *The Tragedy of Zionism* (New York: Farrar Straus Giroux, 1985)

Bachi, Roberto, *The Population of Israel* (Jerusalem: Institute for Contemporary Jewry, 1977)

Benvenisti, Meron, *The West Bank Data Project: A Survey of Israel's Policies* (Washington: American Enterprise Institute, 1984)

Benziman, Uzi, *Sharon: An Israeli Caesar* (London: Robson Books, 1987)

Bernstein, David, 'Forcible removal of Arabs gaining support in Israel', *The Times* (London), 24 August 1988

Cohen, Yeruham, *Tochnit Allon* [The Allon Plan] (Tel Aviv, 1972)

Davis, Uri and Norton Mezvinsky (eds.), *Documents from Israel 1967–1973* (London: Ithaca Press, 1975)

Dumper, Michael, *Islam and Israel: Muslim Religious Endowments and the Jewish State* (Washington, DC: Institute for Palestine Studies, 1994)

Flapan, Simha, *Zionism and the Palestinians 1917–1947* (London: Croom Helm, 1979)

– *The Birth of Israel: Myths and Reality* (London: Croom Helm, 1987)

Friedman, Robert I., *Zealots for Zion: Inside Israel's West Bank Settlement Movement* (New York: Random House, 1992)

Gilmour, David, *Dispossessed: The Ordeal of the Palestinians* (London: Sphere Books, 1982)

Grossman, David, *Sleeping on a Wire* (London: Jonathan Cape, 1993)

Harkabi, Yehoshafat, *Hakhra'ot Goraliyot* [Fateful Decisions] (Tel Aviv: 'Am 'Oved, 1986)

Hirst, David, *The Gun and the Olive Branch* (London: Faber and Faber, 1984)

Jiryis, Sabri, *The Arabs in Israel* (New York: Monthly Review Press, 1976)

Kapeliouk, Amnon, *Israel: la fin des mythes* (Paris: Albin Michel, 1975)

Khalidi, Walid (ed.), *From Haven to Conquest: Readings in Zionism and the Palestine Problem until 1948* (Beirut: Institute for Palestine Studies, 1971)

— (ed.), *All That Remains* (Washington, DC: Institute for Palestine Studies, 1992)

Kim, Hanna, 'To Annihilate Amalek' [Hebrew], *'Al-Hamishmar*, 12 March 1984

Kimmerling, Baruch, and Joel S. Migdal, *Palestinians: The Making of a People* (New York: The Free Press, 1993)

Kotler, Yair, *Heil Kahane* (New York: Adama Books, 1986)

Lehn, Walter and Uri Davis, *The Jewish National Fund* (London: Kegan Paul International, 1988)

Lev-'Ami, Shlomo, *Haim Hatziyonut Nikhshelah* [Did Zionism Fail?] (Tel Aviv: 'Ami Press, 1988)

Lockman, Zachary and Joel Beinin (eds.), *Intifada* (London: I.B. Tauris, 1990)

Masalha, Nur, *Tard al-Filastinyyin: Mafhum al 'Transfer' Fi al-Fikr wa al-Takhtit al-Suhyuniyyan* [Expulsion of the Palestinians: The Concept of Transfer in Zionist Thinking and Planning 1882–1948] (Beirut: Institute for Palestine Studies, January 1992)

— *Expulsion of the Palestinians: The Concept of 'Transfer' in Zionist Political Thought 1882–1948* (Washington, DC: Institute for Palestine Studies, 1992)

— 'Debate on the 1948 Exodus', *Journal of Palestine Studies* 21, no. 1 (Autumn 1991), pp. 90–97

— and F. Vivekananda, 'Israeli Revisionist Historiography of the Birth of Israel and its Palestinian Exodus of 1948', *Scandinavian Journal of Development Alternatives* 9, no. 1 (March 1990), pp. 71–79

— 'On Recent Hebrew and Israeli Sources for the Palestinian Exodus 1948–49', *Journal of Palestine Studies* 18, no. 1 (Autumn 1988), pp. 121–37

— 'Al-Tasawwur al-Suhyuni Le al-Transfer: Nazrah Tarikhiyyah 'Amah' [The Zionist Concept of Transfer: An Historical Overview], *Majalat al-Dirasat al-Filastiniyyah* (Beirut), No. 7, Summer 1991, pp. 19–45

— 'The 1956–57 Occupation of the Gaza Strip: Israeli Proposals to Resettle the Palestinian Refugees', *British Journal of Middle Eastern Studies* 23, no. 1 (1996), pp. 55–68

— *Yosef Weitz and Operation Yohanan, 1949–1953*, Occasional Paper Series (Durham: Centre for Middle Eastern and Islamic Studies, University of Durham, 1996)

– 'Who Rules Jerusalem?', *Index on Censorship*, No. 5 (September–October 1995), pp.163–6

– 'A different peace', *Index on Censorship*, No. 3 (May–June 1996), pp.18–21

– (ed.), *The Palestinians in Israel* (Haifa: Galilee Centre for Social Research, 1993)

McDowall, David, *Palestine and Israel: The Uprising and Beyond* (London: I.B. Tauris, 1989)

– *The Palestinians: The Road to Nationhood* (London: Minority Rights Publications, 1994)

Morris, Benny, *The Birth of the Palestinian Refugee Problem 1947–1949* (Cambridge: Cambridge University Press, 1987)

– *1948 and After: Israel and the Palestinians* (Oxford: Clarendon Press, 1990)

– 'Operation Danny and the Palestinian Exodus from Lydda and Ramle in 1948', *The Middle East Journal* 40, no. 1 (Winter 1986), pp. 82–109

– *Israel's Border Wars, 1949–1956* (Oxford: Clarendon Press, 1993)

Nedava, Yosef, 'Tochniyot Helufei Ochlosin Lepetron Be'ayat Eretz-Yisrael' [Population Exchange Plans for the Solution of the Problem of the Land of Israel], *Gesher* 24, nos.1–2 (Spring–Summer 1978)

Neeman, Yuval, *Mediniyut Hareeyah Hamefukahat* [The Policy of Sober Vision] (Ramat Gan: Revivim, 1984)

Newman, David (ed.), *The Impact of Gush Emunim* (London: Croom Helm, 1985)

Nisan, Mordechai, *Hamedinah Hayehudit Vehabe'ayah Ha'arvit* [The Jewish State and the Arab Problem] (Tel Aviv: Hadar, 1986)

Oz, Amos, 'The Meaning of Homeland', *New Outlook* 31, no. 1 (January 1988)

Palumbo, Michael, *The Palestinian Catastrophe* (London: Faber and Faber, 1987)

– *Imperial Israel* (London: Bloomsbury, revised edition, 1992)

Pappe, Ilan, *The Making of the Arab–Israeli Conflict, 1947–51* (London: I.B. Tauris, 1992)

Peri, Yoram, *Between Battles and Ballots: Israeli Military in Politics* (Cambridge: Cambridge University Press, 1983)

– 'Expulsion is not the Final Stage' [Hebrew], *Davar*, 3 August 1984

Said, Edward, *After the Last Sky* (London: Faber and Faber, 1986)

– *The Politics of Dispossession* (London: Chatto & Windus, 1994)

Said, Edward, and Christopher Hitchens (eds.), *Blaming the Victims* (London: Verso, 1988)

Sanbar, Elias, *Palestine 1948: L'expulsion* (Washington, DC: Institut des études palestiniennes, 1984)

Sayigh, Rosemary, *Palestinians: From Peasants to Revolutionaries* (London: Zed Books, 1979)

Schölch, Alexander (ed.), *Palestinians Over the Green Line* (London: Ithaca Press, 1983)

Schiff, Zeev and Ehud Ya'ari, *Intifada: The Palestinian Uprising – Israel's Third Front* (New York: Simon and Schuster, 1989)

Schnall, David, *Beyond the Green Line* (New York: Praeger & Co., 1984)

Shahak, Israel, 'A History of the Concept of Transfer in Zionism', *Journal of Palestine Studies* 17, no. 3 (Spring 1989), pp. 22–37

– *Jewish History, Jewish Religion* (London: Pluto Press, 1994)

Shindler, Colin, *Israel, Likud and the Zionist Dream* (London: I.B. Tauris, 1995)

Shipler, David K., *Arab and Jew* (London: Bloomsbury, 1987)

Shlaim, Avi, *The Politics of Partition* (Oxford: Oxford University Press, 1990)

Simons, Chaim, *International Proposals to Transfer Arabs from Palestine 1895–1947* (New Jersey: Ktav Publishing House, 1988)

– *Chelm or Israel?* (Australia: Jewish Commentary Publication, 1989[?])

Sprinzak, Ehud, *The Ascendance of Israel's Radical Right* (Oxford: Oxford University Press, 1991)

Teveth, Shabtai, *Ben-Gurion and the Palestinian Arabs* (Oxford: Oxford University Press, 1985)

Yegar, Moshe, 'Hatziyonut, Medinat Yisrael Vehashelah Ha'arvit' [Zionism, the State of Israel and the Arab Question], *Haumah* 2, no. 57 (May 1979), pp. 177–85

Yiftachel, Oren, *Planning a Mixed Region in Israel* (Aldershot, England: Avebury, 1992)

Yinon, 'Oded, 'A Strategy for Israel in the 1980s' [Hebrew], *Kivunim* (Jerusalem), No. 8, February 1982

Zangwill, Israel, *The Voice of Jerusalem* (London: William Heinemann, 1920)

Newspapers and Periodicals

Hebrew

Bat Kol
Davar
Gesher
Haaretz
Hadashot

Ha'ir
'Al-Hamishmar
Haumah
Kol Ha'ir
Koteret Rashit
Lamerhav
Ma'ariv
Moledet
Nekudah
Torah Ve'avodah
Yedi'ot Aharonot
Zot Haaretz

Arabic

Al-Fajr (Jerusalem)
Kol al-'Arab (Haifa)
Majalat al-Dirasat al-Filastiniyyah (Beirut)
Al-Rabitah
Al-Sinnarah (Nazareth)

English

The Christian Science Monitor (Boston)
Forum (Jerusalem)
The Guardian (London)
The Independent (London)
The Jerusalem Post
Journal of Palestine Studies
Middle East International (London)
Midstream (New York)
The New York Times
New Outlook
The Observer (London)
The Times (London)
The Washington Post